The Machinery of Whiteness

Steve Martinot

The Machinery of Whiteness

Studies in the Structure of Racialization

TEMPLE UNIVERSITY PRESS
Philadelphia

TEMPLE UNIVERSITY PRESS
Philadelphia, Pennsylvania 19122
www.temple.edu/tempress

Library of Congress Cataloging-in-Publication Data

Martinot, Steve.
  The machinery of whiteness : studies in the structure of racialization /
Steve Martinot.
    p.   cm.
  Includes bibliographical references and index.
  ISBN 978-1-4399-0051-2 (cloth : alk. paper)
  ISBN 978-1-4399-0052-9 (pbk. : alk. paper)
  1. Whites—Race identity.   2. Racism—United States—History.
3. United States—Race relations—History.   I. Title.

HT1575.M336 2010
305.8—dc22   2009048505

♾ The paper used in this publication meets the requirements of the American
National Standard for Information Sciences—Permanence of Paper for Printed
Library Materials, ANSI Z39.48-1992

Printed in the United States of America

060111-P

Contents

Acknowledgments

M any of the chapters in this book are modified versions of articles that I published previously. Thus, I want to both thank and acknowledge the journals in which they were published. Chapter 1, "Motherhood and the Invention of Race," is a modified version of an article by the same name, which appeared in *Hypatia: A Journal of Feminist Philosophy* 22, no. 2 (Spring 2007): 79–97 (published by Indiana University Press). I am especially grateful to Alison Bailey and Jacquelyn Zita, editors of that issue, for their assistance, insight, and suggestions and for the work they put into the article. Chapter 3, "A Structural Concept of Race," is a modified version of "Race and the Ghosts of Ontology," published in the *American Philosophical Association Newsletter* 6, no. 2 (Spring 2007): 4–10, in the section "Philosophy and the Black Experience." I thank George Yancy, editor of that section, for his assistance and insight into what I was trying to accomplish. Chapter 4, "The Political Culture of Whiteness," contains material from two previously published articles: "Mexico, Iraq, and the Two-Party System: Studies in White Supremacy," *Socialism and Democracy* 19, no. 1 (March 2005): 119–135; and "The Cultural Roots of Interventionism in the U.S.," *Social Justice* 30, no. 1 (2003): 112–137. Great thanks go out to Victor Wallis, editor of *Socialism and Democracy,* for his interest and for his dialogues with me, and to Gregory Shank, editor of *Social Justice,* for his patience with me. Chapter 5, "The Boundaries of the United States and Immigration," is a modified version of an article titled "Immigration and the Boundary of Whiteness," which appeared in *Race/Ethnicity* 1, no. 1 (Spring 2007): 17–36 (published by Indiana University Press). I thank the members of the editorial board of the Kirwin Institute for their vision and questioning of my submission and for the assistance and guidance their questions offered. Chapter 6, "The Dual-State Character of the United States," is a modified version of "The Dual-State Character of US Coloniality: Notes toward Decolonization," *Human Architecture* 5 (Summer 2007): 371–382. My warm thanks go to Behrooz Tamdgidi, the editor of that journal, for his friendship, his social insight, and his ability to organize exceptionally interesting conferences, the kind that permit experimentation with analyses that open new avenues of thought.

In particular, I owe special thanks to Micah Kleit, editor extraordinaire at Temple University Press, without whom this book would not have been possible. He believed in this project, supported it, and consistently offered invaluable encouragement as he ferried it through the long publication process.

Many people participated along the way, as I wrote the articles and then put together this book. I thank Norma Alarcon for never letting me forget the centrality of women to anti-colonial processes; Theodore Allen (unfortunately posthumously; he is greatly missed) and Tommy Lott for their questioning and probing of some of my analyses; Maria Guadalupe Davidson, Emily Lee, and Mario Sáenz for their responses and additions to my general approach; Jared Sexton for his critiques, insight, and editorial assistance; and Stefan Mattesich for being someone to whom I could present my ideas of cultural structure with the knowledge that he would understand and help take them further. I thank Bob Stone, Betsy Bowman, and Cliff DuRand for the many philosophical and political discussions we have had in various parts of the world and for their passion and dedication to the anti-colonialist project. And I thank Sally Sommer, whose own dedication to a pro-democracy ethic, to the power and virtue of community autonomy, has been not only an inspiration but also a source of articulation for many of the ideas herein. I acknowledge Anibal Quijano and Enrique Dussel for the inspiration and new directions both gave to my thinking about the history of colonialism and the structure of coloniality in the United States. I am grateful to Dylan Rodriguez for the strength, passion, and insight contained in his critique of and opposition to that coloniality and to Steven Myers for his belief in my project and his love for the strength of the people. Many others have added their ideas to the mix, enriching my own, including Howard Winant, Ruthie Gilmore, Rick Busacca, Walter Johnson, and Anneka Citrin. And finally, I wish to reach out to and touch Mary Ann Oliveau Brewin, who both stood by me and gave me space in which to work, somehow imagining that something might come out of it.

Introduction

The Shadow of a Machine

When we see a bulldozer knocking down a house, crushing the furniture and belongings of its former inhabitants to rubble, to be scooped into trucks and hauled away, we know what is happening. Large machinery is obliterating an essential part of their lives. Some persons have lost their claim to exist in that place on the orders of someone else with greater power. The bulldozer driver is carrying out that power. We can assume that there were judicial procedures that legitimized this destruction. Or we can inquire what right someone had to destroy the residents' status and habitat, and hope to receive a response commensurate with the damage done.

When, in Jena, Louisiana, in 2006, a different social machinery does the damage during racial hostilities in the high school, things are not so clear. In one incident, a white student pulled a gun on a black student at a convenience store, in response to which the black student knocked him down and disarmed him. Yet it was the black student who was arrested and charged with assault and theft, while no charges were levied against the white student. When something like that occurs, we are not so sure we know what is happening.[1] Racism may be the familiar name for it. But "racism" names the damage, leaving us to ponder the machinery that gives permissibility and legitimacy to such an egregious inversion of basic justice. One can see a bulldozer approaching. But in Jena, when a large piece of social machinery demolishes something essential in a person's life, we do not see it coming until after it hits. By then, after his indictment, this black student's ability to inhabit this world with dignity, which is contingent on his ability to defend himself against assault, has been bulldozed by a cold and distant legal process. His residence in the sanctity of personhood has been judicially damaged, his freedom chained to a bail bond. (Later, when a fight developed between two groups of students, white and black, six black students were indicted for attempted murder.) We can see who signed the order. But the fact that there was an indictment to be signed in the first place marks the operation of this social machinery. It lurks without recourse until it invades the space of certain people's lives. We search for the right of self-defense under the rubble.

In the case of the house, there ostensibly will have been courts, property rights, and deeds involved. Yet neither courts nor deeds have the power to tear down a house; they require the use of real bulldozers. And neither can a court tear down an individual's personhood or dignity without the use of a powerful piece of social machinery. "Racism" is not a big enough term to describe it.

In the case of the bulldozer, irate neighbors may come to the residents' aid, stand in its way, or stop it through appeals to reason, court injunctions, civil disobedience, or even sabotage, in pursuit of the "self-evident truth" that human life is more important, and more sacred, than property rights. This is, of course, risky, and we must pay homage to Rachel Corrie, who was crushed to death in Rafah, Gaza, on March 16, 2003, by an Israeli bulldozer as she stood, clearly visible, between it and a still-inhabited Palestinian house.[2] But how do irate neighbors stand in the way of social machinery that tears apart a black student's life if they cannot see it coming? There may be no surprise when it arrives. Its destructiveness may be totally familiar as the "same old white racism." But to whom can they appeal to stop it before it hits?

People have been responding to the existence of racism for 300 years, attacking its every overt daily expression. Yet after 300 years, it remains, changing form over time, in response to political conditions, while producing more damage. Whenever we have gotten strong enough to interfere with its operations (as the civil rights movements did), it comes back wearing different language, speaking an up-to-date lingo, while creating more of the "same old" effects. These effects, as Leonard Harris tells us, include "polymorphous agent[s] of death, premature births, shortened lives, starving children, debilitating theft, abusive larceny, degrading insults, and insulting stereotypes forcibly imposed" (Harris 1999, 437). These effects, the racial hierarchies and segregations that get taken for granted, are too dire for us to simply watch them occur again and again, responding after the damage is done. Their resurgence, their recurrence, their longevity in the face of centuries of opposition suggest that their source lies deeper in this culture than we had imagined. Something keeps rebuilding that machine, renovating it, something beyond the nefarious individual prejudices and tainted desires by which racism manifests itself.

This book is an attempt to discern the outlines and the nature of that machinery so that we can see it and figure out how to stand in its way.

Oddly, many white people claim that racism is over, a thing of the past. After all, the nation has even elected a black man to the White House. They complain about programs and laws, such as affirmative action, that were designed to overcome the deficits imposed by centuries of segregation and discrimination. These are no longer relevant, many would say. "Today minorities are sucking our blood through government programs," they might claim, without asking what it means to refer to people as a "minority." It would not matter to them that black or brown employment or higher education enrollment did not approach their population proportions for a local area, meaning that whites remained a disproportionate majority in those job categories or on those campuses.[3] Indeed, for many of these white people, the white prosecutor who indicted the black Jena student was himself only "fighting back" against black encroachment. And when 50,000 people (mostly black) showed up in Jena in 2007 to protest the indictments of the black students, the protesters were seen as the "problem."

Many anti-racist thinkers and activists have asked, how can we begin to get white people to resist racism in its institutional form?[4] But this question, though pointing in a good direction, is inadequate if resisting racism means only dealing with effects. Dealing with effects is necessary and not to be skimped. But if the materiality of the history of racism allows it to be taken for granted, its machinery to lurk unseen, then the anti-racist actions of the moment will remain ephemeral. Those who act in a racist manner could then rest secure in the knowledge that what they do as individuals could not be responsible for the devastating social effects, the death, larceny, and insult, that Harris names above.

For the white anti-racist, there is an ethics involved in not seeing below the surface. There is an ethics in ignoring the underlying social machinery, or taking it for granted. If the history of that machinery is part of the history of white people themselves, then their ethics of not seeing becomes part of the ethics of the machine.

To begin an investigation of this machine, let us look briefly at some questions of ethics, of social role models, and of race.

The Ethical and the Judicial

What is an ethics? Simply put, an ethics is what one thinks is the right thing to do or say to others. It is always relational. And it always involves a question of permissibility. One can discover a person's ethics, what they have determined is permissible for themselves, in what they do with respect to others. Sometimes we discover our own ethics in what we find ourselves doing. In these general terms, one can also discover the ethics of an organization or institution in how that institution acts, and in its rules of operation. For instance, we would expect a corporation and a social welfare agency to operate differently, one treating people and land as resources for profit, and the other picking up the pieces, the people thrown away, after a corporation or other social institution has finished using them. These actions reflect different ethics. It is therefore a source of surprise to find a corporation and a social welfare agency acting similarly because both are bureaucracies.

A society can have an ethics. Its ethics consists of what is familiar to its citizens in its social operations. To discover a society's ethics is to discern the foundation of its cultural framework. We know an individual's ethics by what the person does. We know an institution's ethics by how it operates in society with respect to individuals. And we know a society's ethics by what is familiar to its inhabitants.

In the arrest of this black student who had defended himself against attack, we discover an ethics. It is an ethics that contradicts the human dignity preserved by the right of self-defense against wanton assault. We discern it in the fact of the indictment and the arrest, even though (or rather, because) legal procedures were followed. When legality stands in contradiction to an ethics of fairness and human dignity through its criminalization of self-defense, it amounts to an inversion of justice. One could say that legality has become criminal in an ethical sense insofar as it does wanton damage to a person's life. And here we are borrowing the term "criminal" from legal and judicial language, and using it in an ethical rather than a judicial (or legal) sense. That is, not only is it possible for legality to operate in a criminal manner (ethically speaking), but it is precisely that kind of criminality that highlights the operations of the social machine we are trying to discern.

This distinction between the judicial and the ethical is important. The judicial is what punishes acts that violate the law. Murderers are imprisoned for having killed someone. But when the state of Michigan (for instance; other states have similar statutes) condemns juvenile offenders (people under eighteen years of age, and still considered children) to life imprisonment without possibility of parole if they kill someone (and by 2008, 307 young people had been so condemned in that state), it is being criminally unethical.[5] It proclaims a person legally not responsible because under age, and then holds that person responsible to the extent of totally ending his or her life in society. In other words, the state acts in a criminal manner ethically in the way it punishes certain criminality judicially. And it matters that there is a racial component to Michigan's criminal ethics. Although people of color comprise less than 20 percent of Michigan's population, they account for 60 percent of its prisoners and 70 percent of the children it sentences to life without parole.

To make an ethical judgment that the state of Michigan acts "criminally" is to speak metaphorically, of course. There is no tribunal before which to bring the state of Michigan or the city of Jena for their respective criminal inversions of justice. Both have done grievous injury to persons, but it is harm they can ignore because it was committed through authorized legal procedures. Thus, beyond our ethical judgment, we have no recourse. When the U.S. government invaded Iraq in 2003, it violated the U.S. Constitution, international law, and a whole host of treaties to which the United States was signatory (the UN Charter, for one) (Maechling 1990). In what judicial body could that criminality be indicted? When immigrants labeled "illegal" (because undocumented) are held in indefinite detention, the Constitution is again violated. That document states (Article I.9.2) that the right of habeas corpus will not be suspended for any persons (not just citizens). Indefinite detention amounts to kidnapping and false imprisonment. These are felonies committed by the judicial system. In which branch of the government could these felonies be charged?

If "ethics" refers to how one comports oneself toward others, what a person judges to be good, acceptable, and permissible behavior (whether one arrives at that judgment independently or as part of a group to which one belongs), then it has to be considered something very fundamental to human society. Two things follow. One is that one cannot impose an ethics on others. To do so means to tell the other not only how to live but who to be and what to think. To tell someone what to think is to violate their sovereignty as a person. In that sense, the imposition of an ethics is itself unethical, since ethics can pertain only to sovereign individuals and not to puppets. To impose one's ethics on another is to proclaim one's ethics universal, and thus to deny the other's ability or right to do the same thing. All one can do, ethically, is hold another responsible for his or her actions (from the perspective of one's own ethics). But self-universalization is always unethical. When white supremacists present themselves as a social and ethical norm, as the height of human evolution to which all others should aspire, they are not only proclaiming their ethics but universalizing

themselves, and thus acting unethically. When anti-racists tell white supremacists that what they are doing is wrong, they are falling into the same paradigm. The real issue is the criminality of white supremacy, as judged ethically
by the harm it does to people.

Anti-racism may call for an end to the harm racism does, and hold those
who do the harm responsible for it, but that has only limited bearing. It is
the machine that renders white supremacist actions permissible, that makes
racism ethical for the white supremacist, which is our focus here.

The second consideration that follows from the fundamental nature of
ethics is that whatever a person does, at the moment of performing the action
(including speech), he or she must think that it is the right thing to do. As
Hazel Barnes puts it, the ethical is an "inner demand for justification as a
self-imposed necessary relation between actions and judgments by and
within the same individual."[6] Even in the midst of a criminal act, at the
moment of commission, one has to think that what one is doing is the right
thing to do; otherwise one would not do it. What drives an action may not
be thought out; it may simply be a desire of the moment. But it will have
appeared to be the right thing to do in that moment. It is its momentary situ-
atedness as ethical that gives it permissibility and justification. The action's
sense of rightness may change in the next moment. The person may realize
that he or she has done something horrible. But that is a subsequent state
and not the state in which the act was committed. In the moment of commission of a criminal act (in the judicial sense), for the person acting, it is
the victim who is wrong. Even the thief thinks, at the moment of stealing,
that the other's possession of the object taken is wrong in comparison with
his own desired possession of it. Later, perhaps the next second, perhaps a
week later, perhaps only when caught by the authorities, the person may
come to realize that the act was wrong—or maybe not.

If we are to deal with a social machine composed of people who can
invert justice, fairness, democratic procedure, and the ideals of human sanctity, which they rationalize on the basis of a concept of race, we have to be
clear that the people who function in that machine, who speak and act as
parts of its destructive operations, think they are doing the right thing. That
is the big problem with racism and white supremacy.

The Ethical and the Institutional

When we consider governmental actions ethically (as opposed to judicially,
with respect to the law), we find that there can be "legal" crimes (such as
police murders, in which the officers are exonerated)[7] as well as "illegal"
crimes, in which a civilian acts to injure another. In both cases, the person

acting thinks he or she is justified in dominating the situation through an exercise of power over others. Even when a hungry man steals a loaf of bread or a slice of pizza, he is attempting to dominate the situation of his lack of food by imposing that need on someone else. The issue of which forms of domination are valid and which are not involves the question of a social or cultural ethics, as opposed to an individual ethics. What allows some crimes to be considered "legal" is that they are valorized by a cultural ethic. All the anti-democratic forms of racial segregation, discrimination, and disenfranchisement of people of color (even up to the present: in Florida in 2000, well over 100,000 people of color were illegitimately barred from voting)[8] which have been experienced in this country have been ethically criminal (that is, unethical) because they are anti-democratic (an imposition on others of who to be or what to do) but were not seen as judicially criminal because valorized culturally. When a person can injure others in a criminal manner and still feel him- or herself to be honest, or innocent, or civilized, it is society's cultural ethic that legitimizes that feeling.

Under the operation of a cultural ethic, police have been trained to shoot to death anyone who brandishes a weapon in their presence. They even killed sixty-six-year-old Eleanor Bumpurs, an arthritic woman who had a kitchen knife in her hand when officers arrived to evict her from her apartment in the Bronx for being behind in her rent, October 29, 1984. Killing someone who has a weapon in his or her hand neutralizes the threat that such a person presents to other people. But to kill elderly ladies suggests it has an additional meaning. It becomes a mechanical response to that person's transgression of a presumed police monopoly on violence, as if vengeance must be exacted for that person's trespass on police presumption. (When the person is distraught, he or she should receive a humane rather than a mechanical response.)

The absurd extent to which mechanical responses can go is exemplified by instances in which a police officer has shot and killed a man to prevent him from committing suicide. This fact has been euphemized by the expression "suicide by cop." It means a person has acted in a way that brings immediate lethal force to bear on himself, even if his act is only to point a gun at his own head. The cynical nature of this police response needs no elaboration. It signifies that the police officer's job is (in a mechanical sense) to kill a person who does certain things. We now have to recognize that we live in a society patrolled by a police force whose job (in an ethical sense) is to kill people in certain circumstances.

The judicial source of this killing ethic is, of course, capital punishment. Capital punishment means the state can kill a person who kills another, under judicial circumstances. The ethics of capital punishment is an ethics of revenge. The desire to kill the person who has killed someone is a desire for vengeance. A government that practices capital punishment transforms the people of its society into vengeful people, people who can feel good about themselves for having wrought their vengeance (through the state) on those identified as criminal. The existence of capital punishment teaches people that revenge is a good way to be human and sociable. Even sociology gets enmeshed in this ethics. Sociology looks at statistics and asks whether capital punishment is a good way to deal with crime. Most sociological studies suggest capital punishment fails in its purpose to reduce murder rates. But ethically, that is not the point. The ethical question is whether revenge is a good way for people to feel good about themselves, which remains unaddressed. Sociology thus accepts the revenge ethic to the extent that it asks only if the punishment succeeds in its purpose or not.

The essence of a revenge ethic is that it repeats or enlarges the crime it seeks to redress or counteract, by adding the criminality of its act of revenge to the criminality it avenges. The fact that capital punishment fails in its purpose, or that revenge in general fails to diminish crime, is ethically irrelevant to a system that thinks the criminality of revenge is a proper and ethical procedure. To adopt capital punishment as proper is to be vengeful, and to adopt vengefulness as proper is to sanctify the criminality (murder) that one condemns. Under the revenge ethic, one condemns a certain criminality by valorizing it, and valorizes one's own criminality by condemning it in others. That is the problem with capital punishment and with its revenge ethic.

Those who live by the revenge ethic will loudly proclaim, "What about the victim, and the victim's family and friends, who have been harmed by this act of murder?" It is in the name of the living that the murderer is to join the dead. They argue that this would give the families and friends (and the victim, if surviving) some closure on their harm, their injury and pain. Closure for the revenge ethic means murdering the one who murders, or doing the violence of imprisonment to those who dominate others through violence. But this substitution of "closure" for justice is what demonstrates how the revenge ethic makes justice impossible. It dehumanizes people by suggesting they should feel better about committing the same crime as the one for which they condemn the criminal (through vengeance), and it presents this hypocrisy as ethical.

In a society that lives by the revenge ethic, such hypocrisy is all too common. We hear it all the time. "Do what I say, not what I do!" "I am beating you so that you will learn that violence is not a proper way to deal with things!" "We have imposed a trade embargo on Nation X, which we hope will create tremendous problems and hardships for its people, for which we will have been the cause, so that its people will see that they have to remove their present government as the source of their problems and hardships." What saves these "speakers" from seeing themselves as hypocritical is the formal mode in which their views are stated. In the case of capital punishment, the formal procedures the state has to follow to obtain the right to murder individuals who have committed murder separates and sanctifies its own act of murder for it. The law establishes procedures that sanctify its revenge ethic. But in fact, the ethics of revenge only establishes its acts as a role model. When the state valorizes its own right to murder, it valorizes it for the entire society.

The State as Role Model

Let us speculate on the question of role models for a moment. When President Ronald Reagan sent fourteen fighter bombers over Libya in 1986 to try to assassinate Moamar Khaddafi,[9] he was in effect ordering the air force to commit what amounted to a drive-by shooting. One could argue that it is therefore hypocritical for the political institutions of the United States to condemn drive-by shootings when they occur in Los Angeles, for instance. Those who commit drive-by shootings can be seen as simply trying to keep up with the president. If drive-by shootings are to be considered criminal acts, and there is no law that sanctifies Reagan's orders to the air force, then Reagan should have been condemned for it, along with any others who commit drive-by shootings, and jailed.

By extension, if a justice system valorizes victimization by repeating it, it only makes victimization in general more acceptable because committed by the state. Humility on the state's part would dictate that if it reserves the right to commit murder, then any citizen who does likewise should be seen as simply emulating the state. To render murder a truly heinous crime, the state would have to recuse itself from the possibility of providing a role model for murder and repeal the laws that allow for capital punishment. Humility on the citizens' part would require that they not permit their government to commit murder if it is going to condemn murder as a heinous crime.

This line of reasoning runs the risk of appearing wholly irrational or even unintelligible for those imbued with an ethic of revenge. It is not an inconsistency in its logic that would do this but rather its ethics. Ethics is more fundamental than reason. For those readers who are too imbued with a revenge ethic to see that what is being said here is proper, a change of ethics would be required. They would have to live according to a different ethics, and thus live in a different world. To leave a world in which certain acts and thoughts are valorized and sanctified (for instance, revenge), and move to a world in which those same acts would be condemned as criminal, would be an insupportable journey. There is nothing about ethics that is light or superficial.

Now I have to admit that, at present, I have no extant substitute to offer for imprisoning violent criminals or those who engage in anti-social behavior that is injurious to other persons. To have such an alternative, one would have to envision a society in which a revenge ethic had been superseded. An ethics that would abjure revenge would not only seek a different outcome; it would have to have a different concept of crime. "Restorative justice," for instance, sees crime as a break in the fabric of a community, and thus a community concern, rather than simply a matter of the state punishing perpetrators.

In a society that considered crime an unraveling of the social fabric, the social task of justice would become how to mend that fabric, not how to extend the tear through punishment that takes the criminal as its model. Such a different outcome would be possible only in an alternate society, or alternate community, in which the state would become a different kind of role model. It would have to be an unstratified society in which dialogic relations existed uncontaminated by competitiveness or possessiveness (in particular, toward people). It would have to be a society that respected people, so that individuals would not feel the need to return the disrespect and the psychological and emotional harm that accompanies social disrespect. Ultimately, practical alternatives would have to come from people who can in some communal manner see their way to pro-democratically constructing a different ethics for their world.

Of Ethics and Race

Two ideas have been brought together here. The first is that there are many ethics, and they do not necessarily agree with each other. In particular, a revenge ethic and an ethics of pro-democratic justice stand opposed to each other. Second, we need to be able to discern and to describe the machinery of whiteness and white supremacy that stands behind the harm that "racism" commits, and to apprehend its ethics from a knowledge of how it operates. We must describe its origins and its contours, its dynamics and its substance.

"Racialization" is the term I use to refer to the operations of this machine. The term derives from the verb "to racialize." It refers not to the social status of people (of different colors) that produces itself culturally in this society (as Omi and Winant 1994 use the term), but rather to what is done socially and culturally to people, for which personal derogation and alien status are part of the outcome. It is a transitive verb. "Race" is something that one group of people does to others. In the hierarchy of "race," one group racializes another by thrusting them down to subordinate levels in a dehumanizing process. In the "materiality of its history" (as Kincheloe and Steinberg [1998, 5] put it), "race" is something that Europeans, in the course of the colonization of other people, have done to those people. "To racialize" and "to humanize" stand opposite each other, in contradiction (Fanon 1967).

It is the operation of this opposition that testifies to our inability to achieve racial justice in a society that operates on a revenge ethic. The revenge ethic engenders too much criminality in its own name to leave space for the social humanization that, in its profundity, racial justice would require. The task is not only to right the wrongs of this society's past, but to create an ethical structure through which to see how it is that this society could possibly have seen those wrongs as right. It is the wrongs that have been committed in the name of justice and democracy that concern us, and they cannot be addressed through the given (because hypocritical) norms of justice that are based on revenge. Indeed, there is a form of supremacism that lives in a revenge ethic, in the impunity it arrogates to itself, and that further obstructs the possibility of justice. White supremacy, racial injustice, and the revenge ethics are all, as shown below, of a piece.

This book has an ethics—a pro-democracy ethics. Simply stated, democracy means that people participate in making the social and political decisions that will affect them. How people organize to accomplish this, its feasibility or efficiency, for instance, in national decision making or in court procedure, is not the question here. That must be left to those involved. What is at stake is how to articulate certain principles that run against the grain of the given, and to begin the process of opening legal or political operations to participation by those who will be affected by those operations, before they happen. A pro-democratic ethic would require that we make common cause with those barred from social participation in order to bring them into the decision-making process in their own terms. In that sense, all discrimination on the basis of race, gender, or sexuality is part of an anti-democratic ethics. A pro-democratic ethics needs to ask, how are we to understand and respond to an ethics that makes racial or gender discrimination culturally permissible for people?

The focus of this book is a democratizing project.

Of Birth and Race

To understand race, let us begin with the moment of birth. Birth is a social act because there are social meanings that attach to it. It is also a social act because it requires many people: the woman giving birth, a second person at her head to look into her eyes and hold her hands so she knows she is not alone, and a third at her feet to preside over the transformation of the world from one in which this child does not exist into another in which it does. We, the society in which each baby is born, are there in the room with the mother in her labor, receiving and claiming the baby before the mother does.

When the baby is born, the first thing we look at is its sex. In so doing, we bestow something on the baby, something called gender. It is not the mother who does this, but we others, friends and midwives and attendants and doctors, who do it. After all, we know the sex of the baby before the mother does (modern technology aside). We do not ask why the sex of the baby is of primary importance. We take that for granted. It goes without saying. But the gender we bestow represents our knowledge. It represents an expectation, a future and a history, a uniform called tradition that the child will wear in the future. We attach all this to the baby at birth.

Since only two possible sexes appear to our eyes, our bestowal of gender is also binary. In this way, we create limitations. However, the child can surprise us and grow up to choose or become something outside that binary. We are surprised when the grown child lives or picks an alternate sexuality from a broadening spectrum of possibilities. We may even feel troubled by that outcome. We had placed that child in a social category, and given it a role to perform, in a society whose hierarchical binary organization of gender we have accepted. When it lives differently, it is betraying a faith we had placed in it, there in the birth room. The entire social system, of which we were the representatives, will have been discredited and discarded. Our power to define will have been "disrespected." We pass laws to prohibit such an affront, without even seeing the "wrong" in our presumption. The laws we pass only serve to decriminalize the operation of that presumption.

The other category we bring to that birth room is "race." Each time a baby is born, those who attend the birth, as well as the mother, think they know in advance its racial group. Race is not discovered at the moment of birth; the baby is already added to a racial group as if born in the midst of where it had already been. The parents and the community from which they come will be, themselves, the knowledge needed to resolve the issue. Like gender, it is a hierarchical category into which society places this child. And like gender, it enters the birth room from elsewhere, through us, and attaches to the baby. It does not matter who we are, or what we think about race, or racism, or white supremacy; we do this to the baby. It is not thought of in terms of performance, of a role the baby will be given to play or a role we are playing. It is simply another uniform.

If there are surprises, they occur right away. We do not have to wait for the baby to grow up. Yet the sense of betrayal will be the same. The surprises have to do with the father, not the baby—that is, with faulty foreknowledge of who the father is. If the color of the baby is not what is expected (though sometimes it takes a few hours or days to become evident), or if the facial features do not look as expected, there can be consequences. That is the nature of a social hierarchy.

There is something else happening in this scene that is easy to miss, however, and it needs to be seen. What we have done to this baby, we have done knowing that it is something everyone else will also do. While the mother has had her own choices to make, she has had to make them with us and others in mind. For instance, some black women whose skin is fairly light have been known to choose husbands who are lighter in the hopes that perhaps their children will be light enough to pass as white. Other light-skinned black women have chosen husbands who are darker, so that their children will be less ambiguously black, firmly placed within a community that she recognizes needs firmness and extra self-respect to live in its hostile white supremacist environment (X, 1965, 7). Because this environment remains hostile to the birth of a black child (as we see in Chapter 1), it is rare that a white woman will choose a black man as a husband in order that her children will be black. What is not as rare is for a white woman to fall in love with a black man. Their children will be black. *We* are that environment, the one she takes into account, in making her choices. There are no aspects of race, whiteness, or white supremacy that escape this basic relationality between her and ourselves, a relationality in which we impose our ethics as well as our racialized concepts on the child. We do this, not the mother. It is we who commit the unethical act of imposing our ethics, an ethics of racialization, on the child, through our acts of racialization. We do it without seeing the actual color of the child. Color is simply the logo for what we do.

The Individual Discovery of Race

We find ourselves confronting something we thought was an objective condition and discover it to be an active social process in whose unfolding we are all implicated. At the moment of birth, we act with foreknowledge rather than discovery, while it is the child who eventually must discover the *meaning* of race and find it has little or no choice in the matter (unlike the ability to choose gender). When Richard Wright discovers that he is black, he is already six years old. He is shocked to find that his humanness is divided against others he does not know, known as "white people." Toni Morrison and Patricia Williams go through a similar coming to racial awareness.[10] For both, there is dismay and anger. Something has been done to them that was unwarranted. These experiences, it would seem, are typical.

Do white people go through a similar shock of awareness, finding that they are not simply human, but white, and thus different from people known as black? Some do. I remember being unastounded at the discovery. Henry Giroux talks about growing up white and being aware of his whiteness as a non-hidden signifier and condition (Giroux 1998, 127). Thandeka gives an account of white children who, unaware of the difference, find themselves castigated by parents who seek to impress on them the wrongness of befriending black people. These are steps toward their separation into supremacy (Thandeka 1999, 6). For most white people, there is no shock. Instead, there is a sense of honor or prestige. For some, it becomes a conceit; for others, there is a sadness because it marks a separation that was unexpected. When Wright and Morrison make their respective discoveries, something is done to them, suddenly and silently, like an ambush. When a white child is told he is white, something is done to him as well; a new power is given to him to act that is not given the others. That power is not inherent, it is given. One grows up with a responsibility to those others who gave it.

The corollary to this is that whites are not born white. There is no inherency to being white. They are given their whiteness by the white supremacist society into which they are born. One is made white or not according to prior political criteria and prior political decisions. For each white person, others engage in a verification of criteria, of parentage, with respect to the past and the present (however cursorily). If one accepts this whiteness, one accepts a role and stratified position in society.

Likewise, black people are not born black; they are given their blackness by the white supremacist society into which they are born. Many black people born in other lands, such as Belize, or various black (maroon) towns in Mexico or in Ecuador (for instance), when they come to the United States and are told they are black, do not understand what that means. They look at their real color and see themselves and not someone else's social category. Only through an awareness of certain attitudes, when they become the object of a white person's contempt or disdain, does the meaning of color become clear (Yancy 2008, 83). For black people born in the United States, there is a varied process of acceptance of blackness. In response to their relegation by white people to a predefined (black) social category, many black people reconstruct an affirmative black identity for themselves, as a mark of a certain social autonomy (Kelley 2002). It is a means of defending themselves against, and transcending, the derogation contained in the white-imposed identity.

What would white people become if they (we) actually confronted the fact that being white was not inherent in a person, in ourselves and others, but actually a demand that others make on us, a role we must play to fulfill a certain responsibility? Part of what is demanded is that we see others as different, yet attribute that difference to those others and not to ourselves, who are told to see it. Who would white people become if they saw their own eye as an active agent in the production of race through that eye's attribution to others? The so-called colorblindness that has become a prevalent notion these days would be impossible. If the essence of race, for which color is a symbol (of the imposed categorization), exists in the eye itself and not in the object seen by that eye, which has its own qualities, to what could that eye be blinding itself? Who would we become if we saw those others not as different but as living under an imposition of difference? Who would we become if we saw that imposition of difference as something in which we were not only implicated but active agents in producing? Who would we become if we sought to interpose ourselves in that process of imposition, to obstruct it in its primordial moment? Who would white people become if they saw themselves through the eyes of those on whom they impose themselves? Would they see themselves making those attributions? If white people stopped attributing racial difference to others, could they still see themselves as white? Compared to what?

These are deadly serious questions. Many people have died, killed in the name of the sanctity of white supremacy and its system of social categorizations called "race." Many have been tortured and beaten to make them certify that certain attributes are inherent and not socially imposed. The acceptance of a social categorization loses all pretense to being "natural" when it has to be forced—when one is forced to accept, or when one forces others to accept. The problem with "race" is that it is the result of force, the force of imposition that then pretends to an inherency, something to be taken for granted.

George Jackson warned us about this. Speaking about prisons, and semi-metaphorically about race, he says, at the beginning of Soledad Brother, that if you want to understand prisons, look at their administration and not at the prisoners.

> To get to the causes [of racism in prisons], one would be forced to deal with questions at the very center of Amerikan political and economic life, at the core of the Amerikan historical experience. . . . For a real understanding of the failure of prison policies, it is senseless

to continue to study the criminal. . . . The real victim, that poor, uneducated, disorganized man who finds himself a convicted criminal, is simply the end result of a long chain of corruption and mismanagement. (Jackson 1970, 23)

The implication is that if we want to understand race, we must study the "administration" of race. We must look at the political and economic structure (the corruption and dehumanization) of that administration. Is it astonishing that race could be "administered"? It is what happens in the birth room. Over the past decades, from the 1950s to the present, we have seen the nature of racism shift and change its form, while underneath those changes this society somehow manages to reracialize itself, to construct yet another form of white supremacy.

An understanding of the problem of race must begin with how the act of imposition gets transformed into a state of inherency. For something to be taken for granted, those who do the imposing must be able to see themselves as not doing it, in order to see themselves instead as just reaping the benefits of its having been done (elsewhere, by others). Today, in the wake of the civil rights movements, the problem of race is how it is being again imposed, and the meaning of what is being reimposed as the concept of race. These issues occupy Chapters 2 and 3 of this book.

The Administration of Race

Theodore Allen has written a book called *The Invention of the White Race,* in which he describes in careful detail why and how the English colonists in seventeenth-century Virginia developed a concept of a "white race" for themselves (T. Allen 1996, 1997). For Allen, the "white race" is a class concept, an invention used to stabilize and organize colonial society by establishing poor white workers and farmers as a control stratum over the black bond-laborers working the plantations. As he describes it, the colonists' notion of a "white race" signified that the difference between the white workers in the control stratum and the black workers they guarded was actually a cultural and a class difference. It became a cultural difference through its production of a cultural unity, uniformity, and homogeneity among the English in the settlement. And it ultimately became a class difference because it marked a class collaboration between the poor whites of the control stratum and the colony's elite. Not only did the control stratum serve to keep black bond-laborers in their forced labor situation, but it functioned to control and discipline the white workers themselves by giving them the responsibility of policing the black bond-laborers.

It was from the resulting sense of unity and homogeneity that a social concept of white identity first emerged among the colonists. That is, out of the reduction of Africans to other-than-human by the slave codes, the English transformed their own cultural identity from being European to being white.[11] It was this sense of being white that was "biologized" in the eighteenth century by European naturalists to form the modern concept of "race." In other words, it is from the invention of whiteness that the concept of race emerged. (We examine more carefully how all this happened in Chapter 1.)

What is implicit in Allen's title is that whiteness is not a race but rather a story, a fiction written by people in the past. Let us look at a small piece of this story.

According to standard race theory, a white woman can give birth to a black child, but a black woman cannot give birth to a white child. A black person among one's foreparents will make one black, but a white person among one's foreparents will not make one white (Zack 1993, 9). These are conceptual conditions that create different criteria for being white than for being black. There is nothing natural about this disparity between white and black. The disparity in these criteria express a conceptual value system. Value systems exist only for human consciousness, not for nature. Nature does not emphasize one color over others; it simply mixes them in unhierarchical and ecological ways. The necessity for all one's foreparents to be white in order for one to be white is a political decision. It means that there is a condition of purity that attends whiteness and not blackness as a white political invention.

I have discussed elsewhere at greater length the origin of this purity concept in the pragmatics of colonial administration (Martinot 2003b, 22). The early colonial settlements in Latin America and Africa discovered that the children produced by intimacies with or assaults on indigenous women had a color that matched neither the mother nor the father. They were lighter than the indigenous, the colonized, but darker than the settlers. For the settlers, the social status of these children presented a problem. In each colony (Spanish, English, Dutch, Portuguese, and so on), the European administrative group tended to be a minority. Its authority as European would have been diluted should these next-generation children be included according to traditional European patriarchal right, since they would also owe allegiance to their mothers. The indigenous would obtain a claim to participate in the colony's administration, in contradiction to the colonialist ethic of conquest and supremacy. Political pragmatism then dictated that the offspring of mixed parentage would be considered indigenous, or black, but not European, in order not to blur the administrative boundary.

As more children were produced at the borders between these categories, color and bodily variation were found to vary extensively, so much so that the differences escaped clear classification. Ultimately, human coloring (and other characteristics as well) occurs along a continuous spectrum on which there are no natural breaks. "Continuity" means that between any two persons of different shades, a third person can be found whose color will be between those two. The implication was that administration could not rely on mere appearance to ensure the required division of colonial society between colonizer and colonized. Relying on appearance would allow colonialist supremacy to be superseded by a more "natural" organization of society, for instance, by families and clans. To obviate this possibility, a different mode of differentiation was required. An artificial division had to be created in the continuous spectrum of color. The purity concept provided that separation. The purity of European descendancy became the administrative dividing line between the colonizers and all others. Once the Europeans had concocted that first division, they were then able to define other divisions. In other words, Europeanness, and later whiteness, represented the invention of a first differentiation between people that Europeans would later codify as race.[12]

In addition, as a primary instrument for dividing humans into categories, the purity concept, in making essential reference to parentage, linked the political definition of race to biology, providing it with a biological mask. In effect, the purity concept is the essential condition on which the invention of race depends. The Spanish and Portuguese colonialists were satisfied to locate their purity concept in direct European descent. In Virginia it was whiteness that was developed as a first social category. It first appears in the 1690s. And the reason it appeared in Virginia rather than the earlier Spanish colonies is linked to the specific (corporate) form of economic organization of the English colony (as we see in Chapter 1).

In sum, the concept of race, as a politically defined hierarchical system of social categorizations, is only symbolically constructed using color. Once color symbolisms became systemic, however, they were no longer simply descriptive. There is very little that is truly chromatic about these terms. After all, few black people are really black (in the United States), and very few white people are really white. Instead, it was "otherness," as a hierarchical designation, that was defined by the opposition of black to white. To attach a color term as a label to a social category, however, marked a racialization of language itself. It provided a racialized symbol (black, white, and so on) that could then be filled with whatever characteristics or traits might be opportunistically needed by those doing the defining (originally the European colonizers). These might include other physical features, geo-political origin, cultural and intellectual capabilities, and the like. Different traits have been used at different times by white supremacy to fill those symbols.

The important element of this racialization process is the fluidity of its symbolization. Indeed, that fluidity dispenses with the need to refer to anything real once it has served to socially and hierarchically categorize. Symbolization creates what it refers to by its act of categorizing. What is important is the symbolic effect this has on the consciousness of the racialized, as well as on the mind of the racializers. To maintain a colonial system, for instance, the colonizers had to invent a form of consciousness for the colonized that would alienate them in their own minds from their former humanity, their former freedom, and their former claim to their own land. The concept of race, as an "ontological" difference between people, was developed to fulfill this purpose. If the first use of racial categorization was to rationalize European seizure of indigenous people's land and their imprisonment in forced labor, its current forms of symbolization (which include assumed "criminality," the "illegality" of some immigrants, "terrorism" as applied to local resistance movements) serve to rationalize a massive prison industry, a hyper-exploitative agricultural economy, and global interventionism (which we examine more closely in Chapter 4).

In sum, "race" names a system of socio-political relations in which whites define themselves with respect to others they define as "non-white" for that purpose. Because whites are the definers, "race" is inseparable from white supremacy. That is, "race" as a concept is inseparable from the white hierarchical domination that constructs it. Whiteness marks the primary symbology of race, in terms of which other symbols, and the divisions they name, become definable, again by whites. It is by exercising this power to define that whites render themselves the "transcendental norm" (as George Yancy puts it [2008, xvi]). In the matrix of that process, whites see themselves as virtuous, civilized, law-abiding, secure, and superior.

Historically, the primary defining relation of race is that of whiteness to black people, since it was through the oppression of black people that Europeans invented themselves as white in the first place. By extending this originary white/black binary,[13] whites have defined "other" races at will, through the generalizations, derogations, and symbolizations they have created and defined for those others.

It is important to understand that whiteness, and the system of racialization it has produced for itself, have nothing to do with blood. "Blood" is simply a metaphor for the fact that ancestry becomes a factor of account through the purity principle.[14] It is the "motherhood disparity" that is both the source and the demystification of the so-called one-drop rule. In the birth room, when the child is categorized, it is we who are "there" in the room who do it, and not the "blood" of the child. Nor does the categorization process have anything to do with the complex process of conceiving and giving birth to a child. We do it, not the mother.

On White Self-Decriminalization

Having its origin in coloniality, "racialization" emerges from a history of criminality, including kidnapping, false imprisonment, forced labor, murder, contempt for personhood, assault, torture, and theft of land. In all this, whiteness signified dominance, or the production of dominance, and as Ruth Frankenberg argues, still does (Frankenberg 1993, 231). "Race" and whiteness remain a power hierarchy that takes that criminality as its tradition. Today, in its daily relationship to black people, for instance, it models itself on that colonialism through its violation of the (social) contract (disenfranchisement), stalking (in department stores and police profiling), social exclusion (school tracking and neighborhood segregation), consistent terrorism (police brutality), fraud (redlining and disparate mortgage rates), extortion (felonization of misdemeanors), and blackmail (plea bargaining). All of these constitute elements of the process of racialization. Insofar as the primary symbology of race has become the criminalization of the racialized, the sociopolitical function of that criminalization is precisely to decriminalize whites in their acts of racialization. It is the relation between the criminalization of others and white self-decriminalization that marks the history of race and whiteness in the United States.

Let us mention a few moments in the trajectory of this relation. In 1800 a group of free African-Americans from Pennsylvania petitioned Congress to end the slave trade and begin the abolition of slavery altogether. A mere twenty-four years had passed since the Declaration of Independence had proclaimed all to have the right to liberty. Though the petition was mild in its terms and correct in its utilization of respectable channels of political expression, it was rejected outright by Congress, and resulted in a move to deny (that is, to criminalize) the right to petition for African-Americans (Litwack 1961, 34).

In an 1806 congressional debate on how to deal with smugglers of slaves into the United States after the slave trade was banned, some suggested that the smuggled slaves should be freed and released, thinking that would dissuade the smugglers. Southern Congressmen argued that free black people "threatened to become 'instruments of murder, theft, and conflagration,'" and that while slavery might be cruel it was the only way to ensure "the safety of the white community." Both sides then agreed that Africans, if freed, would perish quickly with no one to give them assistance (Robinson

1971, 325–326). In other words, at the highest levels of government, pro-slavery and anti-slavery advocates united in affirming this white supremacist "realism" that no one would provide these victims of criminality (e.g., kidnapping, enslavement, abandonment to the elements) a helping hand. Where white criminality toward black people was acceptable, a pro-democratic ethic of political or social inclusion of people wronged by their capture remained undiscussable.

When black people were disenfranchised under Jim Crow, it meant that they could not testify in court against a white person. Thus, white decriminalization with respect to black people was even written into the law and into court procedures. When police barriers and electoral malfeasance prevented more than 100,000 black people from voting in Florida in 2000 (see note 8), the issue that was permitted to emerge as a political concern was not the criminality of the police or electoral personnel who had deprived people of the vote, but rather that people themselves had voted in an inept manner (hanging chads, for instance). Those prevented from voting were given no voice.

In contradistinction, a myriad of socio-political institutions (corporations, unions, political parties, electoral systems, etc.) have constructed themselves in a manner to maintain white dominance over the social categories into which whites have placed all others (hiring bias, segregationism, etc.). Individual racism has relied on that institutional integument to preserve the culture of domination that makes individual racism both possible and permissible.

Today, during the first decade of the twenty-first century, the same ethic persists. In Jena, black self-defense is criminalized and white aggression is decriminalized. Immigrants from Latin America, without proper papers, are detained indefinitely when not immediately deported, even though indefinite detention is a violation of the Constitution. The Constitution holds that habeas corpus shall not be withheld from anyone except for extreme (military) threats to public safety. The mere fact that these immigrants do not have the proper papers is used to decriminalize the violation of its own Constitution by an entire branch of the Justice Department (Immigration and Customs Enforcement [ICE]). Yet only marginal organizations, such as the ACLU or immigrant rights movements, seem to recognize the criminality of this. (We look more closely at the connection between slavery and being an "illegal" immigrant in Chapter 5.)

This sense of legitimate violation of the Constitution is not unconnected to the white purity concept. White self-decriminalization, central to the ethic of whiteness, provides it with its sense of cultural purity. This "cultural" purity is not the same as the original white purity condition by which

whites defined themselves and race in the first place. What it marks, however, is an extension of that originary purity concept to the domain of social
identity, insofar as both define themselves through what they have defined
as "other."

But the ethical inversion contained in white self-decriminalization works
against itself. To construct whiteness out of a purity concept implies imposing a non-purity, an impurity or corruption, on others through that "white"
perspective. They become less than human. But to associate the purity condition with an anti-democratic dehumanization of other people means to
depend on the criminality of exclusionism, and on the necessity to decriminalize the whiteness produced. The originary purity concept thus corrupts
itself. Whiteness cannot escape the corruption of basing a sense of humanity
(and of its humanity) on an exclusionism.

One reason many white people wish to think of themselves as simply
human is to evade the inherent corruption that whiteness imposes on them.
The exclusionary ancestry that has produced one as white stands in contradiction to being "just human." But to shift identification in that way means
to submerge oneself in a corrupted concept of the human because it emerges
from white society, already imprisoned in a supremacism and its artificial
division of humanity. To seek to see oneself as simply human without dismantling the purity/corruption binary by which whiteness has defined itself
is to accept the white supremacist corruption of the human. The idea of
being "simply human" might allow white people to think of races as existing
in some kind of parity, on a horizontal plane. But this horizontality is then
only another form of decriminalization of the criminality of having imposed
a vertical hierarchy on people in the first place. Many white people claim
that whiteness and white supremacy are not the same thing, and they seek
a sense of whiteness that is not supremacist. We examine whether this is a
possible position to take, or whether one's non-acceptance of white exclusionism implies a non-acceptance of whiteness itself, in Chapter 7.

But as Frankenberg warns us, white people simply assume a natural or
universal significance for what they do or say. For them, the assumption of
individuality seems assured, since they can "dys-consciously" (to use Frances
Rains's term [1998, 87]) ignore their participation in what is done to other
people socially. The white individualist, for instance, is one who thinks he
or she can escape what the system does because individual acts are by nature
not systemic. But such "innocence" is a luxury provided the hegemonic,
which allows them to ignore the fact that the meaning of their acts is precisely systemic. That is what "hegemony" means. Indeed, "hegemony" is itself
one of the meanings that individualism is given. To seek dys-conscious comfort in one's individualism ignores the fact that the meanings individual acts

obtain are social meanings, given by others, and that the acts of those of a hegemonic group are thereby given hegemonic meanings. It is a reflection of the white self-decriminalization ethic that for the hegemonic mind, a white person's acts represent only themselves while a black person's acts (for instance) represent "their race" (McIntosh 1997).

The Structure of Racialization

This description of the originary structure of whiteness has been based on three facts: the "motherhood disparity" of the "white race" story, the undivided continuity of biological variation, and the fact of colonialist origins (leaving for later the actual story of how those colonial origins unfolded). These factors are sufficient to produce an outline and initial analysis of the structure of whiteness and race.[15] The implication is that whiteness is actively produced historically as a system of social practices. It does not simply emerge in the world, out of nothing. Social practices are things that people do. As Marilyn Frye puts it, "If one is white, one is a member of a continuously and politically constituted group that holds itself together by rituals of unity and exclusion" (Frye 1995, 115). White people "do" race in the sense of "committing" certain practices, actions, and attitudes (see note 13). What white people do to others through those practices, however, tends to remain unseen by their white perpetrators once the practices become elements of a cultural structure in which they simply "go without saying." Because these practices necessarily produce harm in others, through the force of thrusting them into social categories, of disparaging them and making them other than who they are, they are ethically criminal practices. Though they may be "legal" in the terms of the culture that whites have constructed for themselves (using derogatory terms, for instance), ethically they remain criminal practices (derogatory terms are really forms of assault— weapons using words but weapons nevertheless).

For racialization to be an active process done to others, there must be an interest in doing it. Because whites invented themselves as a race through their racialization of others, it follows that whites are the only group that has had, and still has, an interest in it.[16] This is not "interest" in the sense that a student may be interested in mathematics, but in the way a stockholder has an interest in a corporation. That is, there are both material and cultural benefits to be gained.[17] While the original "interest" was to consolidate a colonialist regime, today that interest expresses itself through other forms of power. To understand the major contours of that power, we have to understand how racialization and racial domination are, for white people, a dependency relation.

Whiteness is a dependency of whites on those they racialize in the same sense that all domination is dependent on those it dominates to maintain its identity as dominant. As Peter McLaren puts it, "The excluded . . . establish the condition of existence of the included" (1998, 68). White interest in racism and racialization emerges from the necessity to defend and protect white racialized identity from that dependency, that is, to maintain the system's hierarchical character. If whites were to cease to dominate, or cease to exercise a determining white power over any situation, they would lose their identity because they would lose control over the source of that identity in others. (Many white people might disagree with this; we examine it politically and philosophically in the chapters that follow.) Whiteness, insofar as it produces "race" for itself through its racialization of others, can persist only to the extent it can maintain its sense of supremacy by keeping those others in place. This is what Toni Morrison calls the "metaphysical necessity for Africanism" on the part of whites in the United States (1992, 64). That is, even in their absence, there is for the white consciousness a "presence of black people" in all aspects of white society and identity. The white interest in race and racism is thus a need to render those on whom it depends dependent on itself. Those on whom it depends have to be kept in "place." For this reason, social power has to be exercised to subordinate, and all attempts by the subordinated to establish autonomy must be expunged. This control does not have to occur in racial terms; the rhetoric of "color-blindness" will serve the purpose as long as the one color the colorblind can see is "white" (Goldberg 2002, 222). For race to exist, however, white power must remain at its center, and thus white racism must remain at the center of white power.

But power is never absolute. Against it, many in the Black community have constructed an autonomous black identity as a form of self-defense and a survival strategy against the hostilities of white supremacy, and in that sense they have a different interest in "race." Though whiteness depends on defining black people as black for the purposes of self-definition, white people do not define Blackness. It is black people who have defined Blackness for themselves as an aspect of resistance, the creation of a rehumanizing social identity, a communal sense of dignity and self-respect.[18] Blackness is a black appropriation of what had been imposed on black people (by whites) in order to transform it into something of their own. In various ways, and under a multiplicity of guises, it produces a structure of cultural and social identity arrayed against white imposition of subjugation and inferiorization.[19] A Black culture specific to the United States has formed out of this need for resistance, and it has produced a history and a social tradition with global influence during the twentieth century, from the alliance of the civil rights movements with African liberation struggles to jazz and hip-hop. Black power, which emerged from the civil rights movements, was a call for social and cultural autonomy. It was for that reason that it was ultimately seen as a threat by whites and targeted for intense repression during the 1970s by both the white mainstream and the government (e.g., Cointelpro [Churchill 2002]).

In sum, to the elements of a structure of racialization already enumerated (which include a purity concept, a coloniality, a process of political defini-tion, the creation of a white racialized identity, and a paradigm of white decriminalization through the criminalization and denigration of those whom whites racialize), we must now add the element of repressive power, deployed against the autonomy of the racialized.

Race as a Socially Active Process

The system of racialized social categories that constitute the existence of "race" can now be seen to be essentially a binary relation of racializers and the racialized, of the supremacist and the inferiorized (originally invented in terms of white and black). This division is its fundamental character, upon which it attaches a variety of visible traits.

Insofar as whites, as a society of racializers, produce "race," there are meanings which accrue to their everyday actions as whites, simply because their whiteness symbolizes the racialization of this society, and which do not accrue to black or brown people's actions (and vice versa). For instance, because racializing practices are extant as socially instituted, every white face then appears to the racialized as a member of that institutedness. A person with a white face cannot not act white. That is, within the overarch-ing milieu of white racializing society, each white face becomes a racializing action toward those others who are racialized by white society. Because they had been made not-white by that whole society, they are again made not-white by that face. Each white face ceases to be a thing and becomes a white action. And this occurs only because it is embedded in a matrix of past and present oppressions (discrimination, segregation, hyper-exploitation, gratuitous hate and hostility, torture and murder), whose persistence it recalls. In other words, there is always a dimension of unacknowledged racism (in the form of existential racialization) that accompanies each white person by dint of the symbolism given his or her whiteness by white racial-ized society.

These are meanings that accrue to the social interactions between indi-viduals despite their desire to think they can act individually without taking those social meanings into account. If white people wish to rehumanize their faces, it is not their appearance that they must change but the structure of racialization that gives that appearance its symbolic meaning.

In the United States, black people grow up in a different world than whites do. Having to deal continually with white supremacy is not something white people face. But it leaps out at black people with hostility at the most unexpected moments.[20] One should not be surprised that some black people see each white person as a potentially hostile encounter. This is not prejudice; it is simply the fact that a black person cannot tell from the outside if a white person is aggressively supremacist or not. The possibility that he or she might be is established by the persistence of white supremacy as a social fact and mode of organization in the United States.

It is difficult for many white people to understand the difference between being a racializer and being the racialized because it is hard for them see that the racialized live in a different world, made different by the hostilities and ambushes of white people. Having an interest in maintaining social categorization, on the one hand, and wishing that white people would just leave one alone, on the other, are incommensurable social attitudes. Many white people may not like this, but they (we) have not yet figured out how to dismantle the institutedness of whiteness or the structures of racialization. The two worlds cannot be just wished into coincidence. The structures of whiteness and of racialization that make them different would have to be dismantled. Yet most anti-racist white people continue to speak in terms of "race" as if it were biologically real, thus hiding from themselves the fact that it is something that white people and white society "do," through a system of social practices for which they are to be held responsible. This is not a guilt trip; it is the existential dilemma that white people face (hooks 1992, 342).

Not all white people are supremacist, though very few non-supremacists will actually contest the actions of supremacism. After all, whites do not grow up having to deal with white supremacy as an assault on their own persons. Some do encounter such assaults, however, when they attempt to contest supremacist or racist actions or situations. In general, most will at one time or another have to deal with white supremacy as a demand on their own behavior. To the extent they accede to that demand, they gain the respect of some (supremacist) white people, and to the extent they do not, they gain the respect of others (anti-supremacists). Each white person makes a separate decision somewhere along the line from which part of the spectrum of white groups (from supremacists to anti-supremacists) each wants respect. Subsequent comportment toward black people is then conditioned by that decision. But that comportment is enacted in order to gain the respect they desire from certain whites. It is a question of membership, not of freedom (of choice). What most white people remain blind to is that their comportment toward black or brown people is in reality a performance for other whites. White people's comportment enacts how they live their white membership in white society, for which black or brown people are the means. Even radical anti-racists fall into this paradigm. And of course, it goes without saying that most black people do not generally enjoy being the means by which white people make decisions concerning their particular political identities.

Frantz Fanon (1967) recognized that "race" was something done to others, and he counterposed the term "to humanize" to the verb "to racialize." Insofar as "to racialize" means to separate others from their humanity by rendering them a category of persons to be dominated, for Fanon, white society is to be indicted as the source of that dehumanization. That is, whites dehumanize others and dehumanize themselves through their racialization of others. He warned the many peoples who were in the process of liberating themselves from colonialism that to rehumanize themselves they needed to abandon their idealization of, or their desire to emulate, white or European culture. They would be looking in the wrong place. He was not the first. The list goes back to Frederick Douglass, David Walker, Nat Turner, W.E.B. DuBois, William Wilberforce, Robert Owens, and others. Theodore Allen (1969), a contemporary of Fanon, coined the term "white skin privilege" to refer to a bargain that had been made between the white working classes in the United States and the white capitalist elite to keep people of color suppressed and dependent. It meant that exploited white people had not only dehumanized themselves by participating in the processes of racialization, but also traded away their ability to rehumanize themselves through their own struggles against their own exploitation. It is a form of double dehumanization that persists to the present.

It is because "race" (the generation of racial differences) is an active white-oriented process (a process in which whites have a primary interest) that the idea of society suddenly becoming "colorblind" is a sham. Color is not a spectacle or landscape one can just turn away from; it is a system of symbols for social categorizations constructed by racializers. That system continues to exist whether one looks at it or not. As David Goldberg points out, white supremacy gains three major benefits from the colorblindness rhetoric (2002, 217). First, it silences the public critique or analysis of everyday racism, and of the social structures of that racism. Second, it obstructs the ability to tie contemporary racism to its historical past because it pretends that past has been transcended. And third, it relegates any attention to racism to the private domain and away from consideration in the public sphere. The "colorblindness" slogan thus names a covert relation between the ongoing process of racialization and white racialized identity. It has been used as a shorthand by many white people for preserving white domains (jobs and institutions) in as "pure" a condition as possible.

In summary, the concept of "race" for white people in general names active practices of categorizing other people as "non-white" in order to render "color" symbolic of an imposed social condition, through which white people can continue to see themselves as white. When black people adopt "Blackness" as the name of their own autonomous social practices, they are engaging in acts of resistance that turn what had been imposed on them to their own account. Race, then, is never abstract. It is always constituted by a real systemic conflict of socializing acts (imposition against resistance, resistance against imposition) in which an entire group (whites) participates in contextualizing the performance of a social identity that white racializing practices produce for them.

There is a difficult corollary to this. If it is white people who "do" race, who have the power to racially categorize people, as the essential operation of racializing themselves as white, then there is no difference between whiteness and white supremacy. If to be white means to think or to operate (consciously or unconsciously) in terms of the power implicit in the exclusionist purity principle through which others are defined and excluded as "nonwhite," or other, then it is supremacist. White supremacy brought itself into existence by inventing the modern concept of race for itself as a hierarchy in which whites occupied the highest level by definition (that is, by assuming the power to define). It has disguised this power under a "naturalized" (horizontal) conception that humanity is divided into comparable races, among which the white race simply fought its way to the top, in order to dominate. The ethics of white supremacy revolves around the self-proclaimed sense that white people are the social norm and can dominate because of that.

The Relationship of Anti-racism to Structure

Racialization persists, under the disguises white supremacy gives it, as something that white people carry on endlessly with respect to others. It is constituted by practices guided and conditioned by an underlying cultural structure. Yet this remains a difficult idea to grasp, even for white anti-racist thinkers and activists. One reason for this is their insulation in the present from the historicity of that cultural structure.

Monica Patterson, for instance, suggests that "whiteness" is a pseudonym for Westernization and Eurocentrism as an ideology (Patterson 1998, 118). That is, one learns it. But that does not explain its need for violence, or for prisons, or its dependency on inferiorization procedures by which it decriminalizes that violence. To see whiteness as an ideology embedded in the matrix of EuroAmerican culture means it inherits its exclusionist value (its purity concept) from that culture. But the logic of that value is that if the system of social categorizations ever broke down, a true multiculturalism would take over. Whiteness would no longer be what there was to learn. That would mean that whiteness was not a facet of EuroAmerican culture, but its very envelope. That is, whiteness is the historical context in which modern EuroAmerican culture is embedded.

Howard Winant points this out in his critique of the new abolitionist project. The new abolitionists propose that white people should abandon their whiteness and the supremacism that comes with it, as the solution to the problem of racism and racial oppression. By throwing off whiteness as a social construct, whites would rejoin humanity. After all, if whiteness is given to white people at birth, then surely it should be possible to give it back. Winant suggests, however, that simply advocating the repudiation of whiteness "fails to consider the complexities and rootedness of its social construction" (or "racial formation") (Winant 1997, 48). For him, the appearance of similar racial practices from era to era on the foundation of those complexities suggests that white identity is more than a cloak (or ideology) to be discarded. Its tenacity suggests it has roots in a cultural structure beyond the individual. Insofar as a cultural framework is a coalescence of people within a sense of common belonging, individuals cannot repudiate that belonging without answering to others in that cultural framework.

For Frankenberg, whiteness "generates norms, ways of understanding history, ways of thinking about self and other, and even ways of thinking about the notion of culture itself" (1993, 231). This self-normativity is what leaves whiteness an "unmarked marker" for race. It simply constitutes the assumed point of view, the "universal" condition, the perspective that is taken for granted (Frankenberg 1993, 239). But if others are socially marginalized, pushed outside that universal, or excluded from it, then it cannot be a universal except for those dominating. In other words, the white presumption to universality only universalizes whites themselves. The content of the normative, its history and its consequences, which call on dimensions of the force and power of racializing activity, can only be an imposition of universality, driven by the presumption to impose. That the imposition is ongoing, unceasing, and not just "once and for all" means that its historicity is central to it.

The centrality of that normativity has also to be recognized as a matter of life and death. John Edgar Wideman presents an instance concerning his brother. A close friend has died because of shoddy and inadequate diagnosis and care at a hospital in Pittsburgh. Four friends, all young black street guys, sit around talking after the funeral. They are angry at "whites in general who had the whole world in their hands and didn't have the slightest idea what to do with it." It is a veiled indictment of the crime committed by the doctors who just let their companion sicken and die (Wideman 1984, 63). From this view outside white society, whites had wasted all their power and knowledge just to play with the world, forgetting or ignoring the fact that other people existed. Those who held the world in their hands could have been doing better things all along, such as establishing justice and a sense of humanity. "The man owned everything worth owning and all you'd ever get is what he didn't want any more." This is a view of whiteness not as ideology but as historical wastefulness.

In effect, the exclusionist purity condition for whiteness, its sense of supremacy, and its production of impurity and inferiorization through a self-supremacization imposed on others constitute a direct structural connection between white racialized identity and the entire spectrum of banal and murderous racist actions that manifest racism on a daily level.

To better understand this relation, let us look at an instructive example. In California, the three-strikes law was a ballot initiative that provided a mandatory life sentence for criminals who committed three crimes, two of which were felonies. The campaign to pass this initiative involved writing the law, collecting signatures, raising money, buying media time, and getting out the vote. The purpose for those who worked on it was to create longer prison sentences for people they did not know but who they were proclaiming, before the fact, in a generalized, decontextualized way, to be incorrigible criminals. The idea of the law was to impose a generalized otherness (categorized as "hard core" or "unredeemable") on those people, for which they would be imprisoned for life. Insofar as the law has succeeded in sentencing masses of non-violent offenders to life imprisonment, it expresses a campaign to hold many responsible for the few who actually commit violent crimes, for which the campaigners are the instruments or weapons. In adopting the generalized revenge paradigm represented by this law, people allowed themselves to be weaponized by the campaign to pass it.

The people who worked on the campaign came to comprise a vast alliance and association unified by their common purpose. As they worked together in this effort, the campaign defined an identity for them. For some, that "identity" provided the opportunity to feel "heroic," to be seen as defenders of the sanctity and purity of society against despoliation by a criminal "element." For others, it provided a sense of social tranquillity, or a defense of private property, or family values. Some later regretted having been involved, once they realized that the law tended to corrupt justice through its autocracy, rather than foster it. (We do not have to rehearse the excesses inherent in mandated life imprisonment—for instance, for a person caught stealing a slice of pizza—for such stories have become endless in three-strikes states.)

Though many eventually understood that campaign to have perpetrated a tremendous injustice, they continue to live that identity. It was an identity that people constructed for each other in concert through the process of defining others they did not know on the basis of an a priori concept, without looking carefully at what that actually meant. Neither did they look at who it made them be through their imposition of an identity on those subjected to life imprisonment. In their relation to the campaign, they linked their identity to an institutionality (life imprisonment) that constituted that identity through identification with it.

As long as one refuses to think of its injustices, the punishment that buries those caught and exiled by the law can be considered an act of purification, an exorcism of corruption producing social virtue and respectability. As long as the excesses do not have to be accounted for, one need not ask what might be askew or dehumanizing in the law's very conception. Similarly, in racialization, white people purify themselves by creating an otherness in others so they can in concert think of themselves as white, as a common purpose, whether they look at how it was done or not. They can think of themselves as virtuous and respectable as long as the anti-democratic processes set in motion by whiteness (as exclusionary and dehumanizing) do not have to be accounted for.

The Task: To Examine the Structure of How "Race" Is "Done"

Before we can figure out how to create a society in which no one in the United States has to see his or her world dominated by white coloniality, and in which the racialized do not have to continually face their racialization at the hands of racializers, and in which black and brown people do not have to see white people as white, and in which the white purity concept has been replaced by structures of pro-democracy and justice, we have to fully understand the structures of racialization as they exist today. To decolonize the color-coded social categorization we call "race" will require decolonizing white people along with the elimination of the many forms of social colonization.

So far, this discussion has outlined two originary principles, the purity condition as an anti-democratic exclusionary principle, and a structure of activity by which white people racialize others (do "race") in a socially instituted manner. These principles are the foundation on which white people construct their white racialized identity. For each individual white person, to want or to accept that purity condition is to want or accept that coloniality as well as the normativity of white exclusionism. Whites generally take these principles for granted, without concern for their role in building that identity or for what they become in doing so. The criminality contained in those principles remains typically ignorable for them. Aside from the acts of violence that maintain coloniality by suppressing the autonomy of the racialized, the fundamental criminality of these principles lies in their being imposed on others. The power to impose (through terror and imprisonment), and the power to define that constitutes its content, drive the operations that racialize.

In truth, the colonialism that brought race, racism, and white hegemony into existence was only a technological opportunism from the beginning. It succeeded because the Europeans had the military technology and the moral turpitude to act barbarically enough toward others (killing, kidnapping, and terrorizing) to both conquer and enslave them, instead of simply respecting the people they found on other shores. To the extent white people are still capable of violence in order to avoid facing their dependency, their contemporary violence and that of the origin of race participate in the same coloniality.

To understand "race," we have to understand this cultural identity, the political relations between the individual and the social in their racializing operations, the structure of racialization that guides those operations, and the forms of power these take. They are all evident in the indictment of the black student in Jena, in the machine that could simply bulldoze his life.

Today most people provisionally accept the idea that "race" is a social construct. The conditionality of their acceptance, however, emerges from an inability to abandon the notion that race is a biological fact, or inherent in some sense because inherited. The motherhood disparity with which we started should dispel this hesitancy, of course. To continue to think that a biological feature symbolizes race is to have already forgotten that symbolization is a cultural activity that exists only for those who define or accept it. The fact of symbolism is a confluence of social activity and a historical construction of meaning.

Nevertheless, it is insufficient to say that race is a social construct. That statement defines not a fact but a task. The task is to describe the structure that has been constructed socially. If "race" is a structure of social activities, practices, and meanings, we have to describe how that structure conducts or directs those activities, as well as how it gives them the meanings they take. Our task is to describe the contours of this structure, beyond the well-known and well-worn ideological notions of "racism," so we can see it.

The historical question that gives urgency to this investigation is the fact that over the course of 300 years, masses of people have said "Stop!" to racialization and it has not stopped. What are the weapons the racializers have used to offset such a demand? Why do those who wish to stop this bulldozing machine not have weapons as powerful? What would white people become if they found that they themselves were weaponized in what they did—that thinking themselves free as white, they were actually swords in a hidden hand that directs them at others who are targeted? Would they wrench themselves out of that grasp in order to be free, or would they call on it to get busy so they could taste blood again? What is it about the history of whiteness that this choice can actually be articulated and not seem wholly unintelligible?

Since the late 1980s much work has been done toward accomplishing this task. There have been extensive critiques of whiteness, what it is, and what it means, in attempts to add to the struggle against racism. They have been from the sociological (Ignatiev, Kincheloe, Delgado), literary (Morrison), historical (T. Allen), philosophical (Yancy, Martinot), and political (Roediger) perspectives. The present work is not designed or intended to compete with any of these critiques. And these works of the past few decades need not be seen as competing with one another. The work is too important not to see each effort fitting somehow into an eventual totality. In some cases, there have been polemics, but for the most part, researchers have understood that the topic is so profoundly embedded in the cultural framework of the United States that no particular work stands a chance of being definitive or all-encompassing. We are far from dispensing with the problem. The struggle to free the world from the criminality of white supremacy will be long and hard.

This book focuses on the following topics. First, it addresses the instrumentalization of women as a necessary step in the formation of a concept of race. This is related to the way the state continues to instrumentalize women for the purpose of ongoing racialization. How the state functions to continue the racialization of U.S. society through the prison industry, police impunity, and the two-party system extends that analysis. But there is a philosophical question with which such a discussion of the state confronts us. We live in the wake of the civil rights movements, when the structures of racialization were pushed back. It is unnerving to realize that they have come forward again in new form, but with the same content. It poses the question, what is it about white racism and white supremacy that this society cannot just let go? Will the many attempts people have made to re-conceptualize race allow us to apprehend its inordinate tenacity? Even those attempts at philosophization can be shown to be racialized. In other words, the structure of racialization even reaches deep into our very attempts to understand it. What this philosophical knot represents cannot be ignored.

The book next examines the politics of racialization and analyzes the culture of interventionism—why and how U.S. government interventions in other nations obtain general (and generally white) support; how an anti-immigrant populism has threaded its way through U.S. history; and how white supremacy takes a populist political form.

If the bulldozing machine of racialization can be seen, we can become pro-active toward stopping and dismantling it. This book is dedicated to expunging white supremacy from the earth. It is first necessary to analyze the structures of whiteness and its racialization of other people. These are complex issues. By presenting them in their complexity, I attempt to reveal the difficulty of the task. I do not want to sugarcoat anything. I do not want to create false hopes—for instance, that if only white people did such-and-such, then the problem of racism would be resolved. There is an entire cultural structure that must be transformed before white supremacy and its racisms are eliminated from U.S. social practices.

Motherhood and the Invention of Race

The Regina McKnight Case

An article in *The Nation* from December 3, 2003, titled "Criminalizing Motherhood," tells an old story (Talvi 2003, 4). It is the well-rehearsed tale of a familiar prosecution, though one that the state nevertheless offers as a precedent. Yet it uses a social logic that has long inhabited U.S. jurisprudence. In the cold clang of its historically practiced procedure, it pretends to forget, while recalling by reenacting, a principle that has governed the United States culturally since its inception.

> Regina McKnight is doing twelve years in prison for a stillbirth, carving out a dangerous intersection between the drug war and the anti-choice movement. In the eyes of the South Carolina Attorney General's office, McKnight committed murder.
>
> Her crime? Giving birth to a five-pound, stillborn baby. As McKnight grieved and held her third daughter Mercedes's lifeless body, she could never have imagined that she was about to become the first woman in America convicted of murder by using cocaine while pregnant.
>
> The absence of any scientific research linking cocaine use to stillbirth didn't matter. Nor did it matter that the state couldn't conclusively prove that McKnight's cocaine use actually caused Mercedes's stillbirth. What mattered was that South Carolina prosecutors were hell-bent on using McKnight as an example.

Thanks largely to the efforts of the former Republican Attorney General, Charlie Condon, now running for U.S. Senate, South Carolina is the only state in the nation with a child-abuse law that can be applied to "viable fetuses." . . . McKnight, now 26, was the first to be imprisoned on a murder conviction under the "viable fetuses" law. In October McKnight lost her best shot at release when the Supreme Court decided not to review the case, allowing the conviction to stand by default. (Talvi 2003, 4)

What the article only allusively notes is the fact that McKnight is black. It does, however, note that she is a seasonal tobacco farmworker, living homeless, and at the time of her pregnancy, grieving the death of her own mother, who had been run over by a truck at an agricultural site.

Clearly, the state has no concern with McKnight's health as a mother; the provision of better labor conditions and protections would have directly enhanced the baby's biological well-being. And neither is McKnight's misery a concern; that is precisely what the state uses against her by prosecuting her for drug use rather than providing her with prenatal medical care. McKnight's health and her humanity are irrelevant. Whatever defense she might have wished to offer concerning her homelessness, her bereavement, or the duress of her daily toil was discounted in advance. For South Carolina jurisprudence, it was not her homeless exposure to the elements, nor the malnutrition attendant on underpaid agricultural labor, nor the exhaustion of long work hours that took her baby's life. The state's only interest was in an unseen toke at an unguarded moment. Its true concern, in making an example of McKnight, was a structure of law beneath which a mother must labor to produce a social product (a presumed "viable fetus") for the state.

For the state, the concept of "viable fetus" is simply a rhetorical device for delivering this black woman into its control. Since the plausibility of the drug indictment, the absence of data, causality, or reason grounding its argument, did not matter to the state, only the nature of the person indicted could be its concern. The real content of its indictment is the fact that McKnight is a black woman. In other words, South Carolina jurisprudence is not unracialized. Black women's bodies became a form of instrumentality for the control of all women because the state knows that whatever argument it wishes to make, or whatever power position it wishes to take, it has but to do so with respect to a black body, a person whose personhood can be abrogated with impunity, and that will sufficiently establish its case. In other words, it is the state's identity as a white state that is being constructed through its demonstration of supremacy over a black body.

In *Killing the Black Body,* Dorothy Roberts offers a meticulously developed history of how the state has used legal machinery to control black childbearing. She gives statistical evidence that in South Carolina, when pregnant black women go to the hospital for prenatal care, they get drug-tested and, with few exceptions, when testing positive, are reported to the district attorney by the hospital, whereas pregnant white women do not (D. Roberts 1997, 158). At the time of her writing, Roberts noted that black women constituted 90 percent of the cases of drug use reported by hospitals in South Carolina, and that black women were reported by the hospitals ten times as often as white women. The arrests that come through the hospitals are of women who are poor, generally on Medicaid, with no resources to see private doctors. That is, their poverty is also used to turn them against themselves. These are the women who need care the most and get it the least.[1]

But there is a long history of the control of black women's bodies and their childbearing in the United States, going back 300 years, which Roberts rehearses. During slavery, black women were positioned as the producers of children who, for plantation enterprises, represented the production of human capital—bond-laborers who could be used as both exploitable workers and commodities for sale. The law both allowed and encouraged the violation of black women in order to impregnate them, as a mechanism for the increase of plantation wealth.

Whereas under slavery African women were punished for not producing children, recent policies toward women of color have reversed this, punishing them for getting pregnant. Roberts cites the campaign of forced sterilization attached to prenatal care for women of color. Medical care for black welfare cases is withheld in the case of pregnancy unless the woman consents to be sterilized (D. Roberts 1997, 40). In addition, when the state discovers a pregnant black woman's drug use, it becomes an excuse to demand abortion by threatening the mother with a jail sentence on a drug charge (rather than offer counseling against drug use during pregnancy).[2] In these many ways, through institutionalized judicial and medical procedures, and under various threats of prosecution, the judicial system forces black women not to bear children (D. Roberts 1997, 150–180).

In other words, in both historical eras, the state has functioned to turn mother and fetus against each other. In using the judicial mechanism of drug prosecutions, the state essentially repeats its own history of control over black women through their maternal capacities. Under slavery, the fetus became the material representation of her violation and her servitude. In the present, the state uses the fetus to materially involve the mother in the criminal justice system, and thus to symbolically criminalize her as a mother. It becomes the instrumentality of her judicial dehumanization. Both violate the woman by engendering a contradiction between her womanness and her humanity.

Roberts argues that liberty is based on the idea that the government has no right to intervene in an individual's life. Totalitarianism is the name of a governance that reserves that right to intervene for itself. As human beings, the poor have need of resources that only the state can provide. To the extent the state uses these human needs to intervene in an individual's life, it is totalitarian. Indeed, forced sterilization, mutilation of the body, and kidnapping (into prison) on the pretext of medical care are all crimes against the humanity of these black women.

Social justice would insist that women have the right to bear children as much as they have the right not to, and that these rights be located in a woman's relation to herself: in her body and her social and economic well-being. Where and when the law seeks to control motherhood, it doubly abrogates those rights. In McKnight's case, social justice is withheld twice, in the state's abrogation of responsibility for her health as a person and a pregnant woman, and in her prosecution as a black woman for a lost pregnancy in the face of the state's failure to protect her.

Not only is poverty a problem for poor women; it symbolizes the very existence of social problems as such. Insofar as poverty makes it more difficult to obtain decent health care, prenatal care, drug therapy, or decent living conditions in which to bear and raise children, it points to health, maternity, and personal misery as aspects of social conditions that remain socially unaddressed. Instead, state procedure first criminalizes the poor and then penalizes them, before dealing with them as people (D. Roberts 1997, 308). In using black women as its instrumentality, the state constructs itself as both totalitarian and white supremacist. In other words, the state is not white by definition; it constitutes its identity and sanctity as white through its derogation of black people.

All this occurs under a long and insidious historical shadow. The Dred Scott decision was famous for its key line, that no black person has any rights that a white man is bound to respect. The Thirteenth and Fourteenth Amendments were passed in 1866 to overturn and dismantle the meaning of the Dred Scott decision (A. Allen 2006, 166). But it apparently did not work. Roberts has painted a portrait of its contemporary form in which it could be said that black women have no rights to motherhood that the state is bound to respect. In other words, the Dred Scott decision was never actually repealed.

At the end of the state's performance in South Carolina, a black woman sits in prison, a white prosecutor self-righteously proclaims an important precedent to have been set, and a committee in New York loses an attempt to rectify this miscarriage of justice. An entire history of segregation and wanton racialized violence is retold in this small legal event. In considering McKnight's prosecution as a precedent, the state commits an act of historical amnesia. The scene it reenacts is in fact 300 years old, a series of acts that decriminalize brutality and the harshness of labor and living conditions by criminalizing their victims. It threads its way through U.S. culture and history, appearing in different guises, with different names and places, repeating the torture and legal murder of thousands of men and women, most of whom remain unnamed, the "strange fruit" of a "manifest destiny," sacrificed to state sanctity.

The Matrilineal Servitude Statute

The McKnight case and the Dred Scott decision, though 150 years apart, both make implicit reference to a single cultural principle, a common antecedent that established the instrumentality of black women (and women in general) in the middle of the seventeenth century. The year is 1662, a moment prior to the birth of slavery as well as of the concept of "race" itself. A strange statute, stating the principle of "matrilineal servitude," was passed by the Virginia Colonial Council. It marked a singular moment, a significant step toward the future invention of the concept of "race." "Matrilineal servitude" means that a child takes the servitude status of its mother rather than its father. In 1662, the women who were wrenched out of Africa and brought to Virginia had not yet become "black women," and the English had not yet arrived at seeing themselves as white. Racialization had not yet occurred.[3] What the matrilineal servitude statute did was send the colony careening seemingly irreversibly toward both the codification of slavery and the invention of a social process of racialization.

The title of the act in 1662 was "Negro Women's Children to Serve According to the Condition of the Mother," and it read:

> WHEREAS some doubts have arisen whether children got by any Englishman upon a negro woman should be bond or free, Be it therefore enacted and declared by this present grand assembly, that all children born in this country shall be held bond or free only according to the condition of the mother. And that if any christian shall commit fornication with a negro man or woman, he or she so offending shall pay double the fines imposed by the former act. (Hening 1809, 2:170)

Notice the binary designations: in the first sentence, "English" is set opposite "negro" within the more traditional reference to people by geo-political origin, while in the second sentence, "christian" is set opposite "negro" as a small cultural shift that would eventually (in three decades) replace "christian" with "white" (Martinot 2003b, 65).

The stipulation that children of bond-laborers, whether English or African, would take their mother's status (including release to freedom should the mother complete the terms of the contract, if that existed) reflected the Colonial Council's decision, made during the 1650s, to shift its plantation labor force to Africans. Previously, English indentured bond-laborers constituted the bulk of the work force. The statute's focus was clear. It was designed to enhance plantation wealth through the transformation of a woman's childbearing capacity into the production of bond-laborers, with primary attention paid to the children of African women. Responding to the pragmatic administrative problem of the children of African mothers by English fathers, it reflected an intention by the elite to reduce the social status of the Africans below that of the English. It projects a future for Africans that required curtailing the existence of African-descended people who were free. And the child of a free English man and a bond-labor African woman would have been free under ordinary patriarchal inheritance standards.

In the mid-seventeenth century, bond-laborers in general, whether English or African, were held as "chattel." That meant they were considered property and could be traded or sold during the term of their servitude. What the matrilineal servitude statute implies is that the elite intended to reduce Africans to perpetual servitude. Its focus on African women served to incorporate their sexuality and maternal capacities into their chattel status as a form of production, producing laborers who would also be considered commodities. African women were thus to be transformed into a special domain of sexuality, while their sexuality was reduced to a mode of wealth production at the same time. Under such conditions, any sexual violation of an African woman was then implicitly recharacterized (decriminalized) as "wealth production." Ultimately, this ability to use African and African-American motherhood for the purposes of wealth enhancement was institutionalized in the form of breeding farms (Stampp 1956, 245).

The overall effect of the statute was not, however, restricted to African women. Sexuality was devalued in English women in the process of relocating it in the bodies of African women. That is, by validating the violation of African women as the cultural site of sexuality itself, in the name of and in the interest of plantation wealth, sexual being was in the same gesture withheld from English women. English women became instead the desexualized site of validated motherhood as the concomitant of the commodification of African motherhood as capital. Motherhood was functionalized for English women in the process of appropriating motherhood as production in the African.

Thus, the statute marked the beginning of a process of social differentiation between the English and the Africans. The Africans were implicitly inferiorized through the special degradation of African motherhood, while English women were given iconic value as propriety itself in requiring that they not be sexual beings, while still bearing children that the colony could certify as wholly "English."[4] The act of defining African motherhood as economic production renarrativized English motherhood in turn to be a form of "cultural production." This relation constitutes the form of Regina McKnight's fate, 300 years later. Her condition as a woman is of no concern to a white politico-cultural structure focused on her functionality as a bearer of children, yet her children are of no concern to this structure except as instruments for the cultural control of all women.

For both English and African women, cultural identity and personhood were transformed. African women were more directly placed in thrall to profitability by the transformation of their labor and their childbearing capacity into property (D. Roberts 1997, 24). And English women were placed in thrall to the production of the unblemished heirs to that property. They were both robbed of their womanness as persons and robbed of their personhood as women, dismembered by sexuality turned against motherhood and motherhood turned against sexuality. That differentiation, imposed through motherhood, was the first step toward defining a social as well as juridical separation between bond-labor and free labor that eventually divided "African" and "English" into separate social categories.

It did not, however, have an immediate effect on class relations. At the time, English and African bond-laborers made common cause in escaping, as well as in their relation to landowners. Because labor organization was considered sedition and suppressed with extreme brutality, escape constituted the safest avenue of resistance. That aspect of class solidarity lasted long after 1662. But the statute did begin to divide those women who were able to form a family of their own from those who were not because they were trapped in the category of property, which increasingly placed their children out of reach. This differential affected the men, dividing them between those who could live a family life and those who could not insofar as their children by the women they loved were condemned to become ledger entries. Nevertheless, if the matrilinearity statute's ultimate effects were to drive the English toward each other socially, leaving the Africans excluded and outside, it was a process that did not happen quickly. During Bacon's Rebellion of 1676, the solidarity between the two groups was still strong. But the stage was set.

The Question of Structure and Identity

We can see parallels of logic, instrumentality, and purpose between the seventeenth-century capitalization of black motherhood and the present state's criminalization of it. The logic is that by which the control of sociality and community is to be gained through the control of women (Federici 2004). The instrumentality for the process was the control of motherhood. And the purpose was the social cohesion of the controlling society—European settlers in the former instance and white society in the latter. These parallels may hide behind a historical amnesia (which allows proclaiming certain events "precedents"), but they never completely disappear. They lurk as an underlying structure of cultural thought, which the present state obeys as its cultural logic, its way of thinking about and valorizing what it is doing. What we seek to do is use these historical parallels as a lens through which to perceive the contours of that underlying cultural structure.

The early legislated act concerning the use of motherhood takes on a special meaning when seen through McKnight's prosecution. And conversely, McKnight's fate takes on a strange historical aura when seen through the lens of that earlier moment of colonial history. McKnight lost her baby because her entire life situation, beginning with her daily labor to keep herself alive, was conditioned by that history. From matrilinearity and the codification of slavery to the debt servitude of Jim Crow, and finally to the contemporary impoverishments of migratory labor, there is a sequence of forms of exploitation which all depend on an instrumentalization of women that recalls that earlier moment. The changes in that sequence of forms all remain coded with the same hierarchical categorization of people that, in the early eighteenth century, was eventually called "race."

Within this entire racialized framework, a sense of justice or humanity toward McKnight as a black woman (for instance, guaranteeing humane work conditions and health care, or seeing homelessness as a violation of human rights) would be unrecognizable, and perhaps even an unforgivable act, insofar as it would violate the sanctity of white society and its coloniality. Instead, the devaluation of black people is what has always been forgivable. Whether that devaluation occurs through an unhampered discrimination by individuals or bureaucrats or through institutional policy or at the hands of mob violence, there is a permissibility and impunity internal to an identification with whiteness that constitutes itself through that devaluation. The confluence of the two, of permissibility and impunity, forms the basis of a social ethic that inhabits whiteness and identifies it as a cultural structure, because it is through its being a structure that individual acts of impunity are rendered permissible, that is, through which individual acts are granted impunity in the first place.

A cultural structure expresses itself through the familiarity of certain actions. But it also expresses itself through a cultural logic. In McKnight's case, that cultural logic grinds away, discounting her arguments, her condition, her very being, condemning her to a zone beyond any possible moral persuasion of her captors. It is that cultural logic that renders the injustices of state medical and social institutions against black women unquestionable. It had defined itself in its overturning of patriarchal right in the seventeenth century, and in its special dehumanization of women through the instrumentalization of black women. It flaunts the acceptability of women being its instrument precisely by its ability to criminalize them without needing data or evidence.

Familiarity is a matter not simply of repetition but of a presupposed permissibility applied to social actions. The meanings of those actions constitute elements of a cultural commonality. Consciousness of that commonality is a consciousness of a center congealed and guarded against an excluded periphery, a periphery produced as "marginal as a consequence of the authority invested in the center," as Isaacs and Mercer (1996, 455) remind us. The logic of that commonality produces meanings that constitute the insularity of its social customs and institutions. This cultural insularity becomes the matrix in which institutional operations (such as segregation) and daily individual racist actions become the source of familiarity for each other. As a white person, one centers whiteness as a social norm by thinking and speaking it, and one thinks and speaks whiteness as an identity by identifying with the familiarity of its institutional operations (Rodriguez 1998, 43).

In other words, the construction of whiteness is the meaning of the parallelism and familiarity between these two moments of U.S. history. It is the meaning of their cultural relation to each other, insofar as they reflect an underlying structure that constitutes the way they present themselves as sufficiently familiar social actions to be taken for granted. It is within that structural matrix of familiarity that white people constitute their white racialized identity. Personal identification with institutional practices in their familiarity is what constitutes one's individual familiarity to the others of that social framework, one's sense of belonging to it.

White racialized identity is not a psychological identity. To see one's acts of hostility or contempt or patronizing objectification toward black people as having a certain social sanctity goes beyond psychology. It does not answer the question, "Who am I?" Instead, it concerns *what* one is in a social framework or system of social categorizations. It encompasses one's ethical possibilities, that is, what is permissible socially as structured by the underlying cultural logic that produces that racialized identity.

In sum, white racialized identity is a system of cultural activities that expresses the relation between the individual and the institutional. The individual constitutes his or her identity through identification with a social institution and through enactments of its ethics. And conversely, white racialized identity is what white institutionality takes for granted in the sanctity of its hegemony. That is its cultural logic.

A cultural logic is not a cultural tradition. A cultural tradition occurs in the open air, as that by which people articulate for each other what they are doing. An elected official who wishes to institute new policies must combine a view of the future with an invocation of the past by which his or her constituency (and other officials) will examine his proposals (Skrentny 1996, 146). And a use of the past varies as social conditions change. In contradistinction, the process of racialization that has occurred in recent decades (the repeal of affirmative action, the development of a prison industry, the economic and cultural famine imposed on black communities) does not take Jim Crow as its tradition. Nevertheless, it obeys the same structure that Jim Crow obeyed, albeit in terms transformed by the civil rights movements (as we see below). It is the ability to see the operations of a cultural structure underneath the changes in cultural tradition that we are addressing here.

The Political Economy of Virginia

Two kinds of structure need to be distinguished. The first is the pragmatic, composed of social and political operations. These include the corporate organization of businesses, political parties, the elections of officials, the organization of cities and counties, arrest and court procedures, imprisonment and law enforcement operations, and the legality of behavior between individuals. This level of structure constitutes the social order. The second level is the source of legitimacy for what occurs in that social order. It is what needs a historical lens to be discerned. The permissibility of extreme labor exploitation, of massive imprisonment for non-violent drug use, of imprisoning McKnight for a stillbirth, is given by an underlying cultural structure. The assumption that elected representatives really represent the people who elect them (when experience teaches that they do not), the idea that politics is more properly run by men than women and by whites than people of color (though some women will be let into the process—by men; and some black, Latino, Native American and Asian people will be let into the process—by whites) are other aspects of cultural structure. Cultural structure comprises a linking of actions and meanings rather than a chain of command and responsibility (as in corporations). It does not reveal itself in totem structures of kinship, like those that Franz Boas or Claude Lévi-Strauss describe for a clan or tribal society. Instead, it reveals itself in the way historical moments reflect each other across periods of time, a kinship of historical events.

To understand the structure of racialization as it exists today, we therefore have to start with its history and historical origins. In particular, to understand the role that the matrilineal servitude statute played in the historical origins of the concept of "race," we have to look at what led up to it and what followed from it. It is to those histories that we now turn.

Because a structure of racialization could not have existed when race was first invented, in returning to its origins we must dispense with the aid of familiarity or an assumed cultural logic.[5] We must look at the unfolding of colonial events with eyes denuded (if possible) of their own racialization.

When the English first arrived in Jamestown in 1606, they did not think of themselves as white, nor did they consider slavery a part of English law. Though Winthrop Jordan contends that the English came to the Americas with a racial prejudice against black people firmly entrenched (Jordan 1977, 4), whatever prejudice some of the English might have felt could not have been a racial prejudice. In the early seventeenth century, the English had not yet racialized the Africans, as evidenced by the fact that they had not yet racialized themselves. They did not begin to refer to themselves as white until the 1690s, after almost a century in the New World (Hening 1809, 3:86).

It was the process of evolving a system of slavery that formed the substance for racialization. That system responded to a greed and a settler clash with the land that was satisfied and resolved only through a specific form of labor control. It differed from the slavery instituted by the Iberian colonization of Mexico and South America insofar as it took a corporate form rather than one of conquest and caste hierarchy. The corporate form transformed laborers' bodies into forms of capital, which provided the economic ground for a different form of commodification than in the Iberian colonies (see note 8 below). In the latter, labor was often worked to death and replaced, more so than in the English colonies, where a socio-economic niche was created by the process of capitalization of the black bond-laborers' bodies (T. Allen 1997, 38–45, 223–228).

The North American English colonies began as corporate organizations whose purpose was to generate profit for investors back in London (Martinot 2003b, 109). The Colonial Council served as an on-site board of directors, and the settlers, from the aristocratic landowners to the bond-laborers, were all corporate employees. An individual's social status was contingent on position in the corporate stratification, which in turn was determined by wealth in goods (including the marketability of bond-laborers) and land. The Colonial Council's functions were to ensure a stable supply of labor for the plantations, to arrange access to foreign and domestic markets, to guarantee internal social order, and to provide for the general enrichment of the colony.[6] Its first cash crop was tobacco (a drug for which an international market rapidly developed), requiring large landholdings for mass production. Labor supply for its tobacco plantations was thus its most pressing problem.

Prior to its discovery of tobacco production, the colony had faced severe starvation. It had settled land it did not understand. It remained ignorant for years of how to grow the food crops appropriate to that land, holding adamantly to its stratified corporate organizational structure rather than engaging in cooperative agriculture, as did the indigenous. Finding survival difficult, it demanded absolute allegiance to the colony and to Englishness from its member settlers, to the point where those who left the colony to live with indigenous communities (a number of different Algonquin societies) were recaptured by the colonial militia and publicly tortured, often to death (Zinn 1980, 24). This insistence on political allegiance, the colony's primary response to crisis, has lasted until the present—for instance, in loyalty oaths and pledges of allegiance in its schools, a requirement peculiar to the United States among all industrial nations.

Organizationally, what characterizes a corporate structure is its stratification of administrative control. Each stratum directs those below it and takes direction from those above. In the colony, social mobility was minimal; attempts to change one's condition without elite consent were considered subversion. On the other hand, potential class conflicts, such as those between elite plantation owners and small farmers, tended to be attentuated by that strict stratification (Martinot 2003b, 135). The effect was to prioritize managerial status over economic interest. One's responsibility was to those above, with effectively none toward those below.

This corporate ethos has cultural reverberations even in the field of labor organization. In nineteenth-century craft unions, skilled workmen gave precedence to their control of unskilled laborers over class solidarity with them, typically excluding those laborers from their organizations. In general, labor unions in the United States have tended to adopt a corporate structure, with an executive board playing the role of board of directors, a middle management of business agents, and a membership among whom autonomous organizing is seen as anti-union behavior (subversion) and repressed. For such a form of organization, allegiance remains a primary consideration. In U.S. labor history, for many union struggles, organizational solidarity has taken precedence over class solidarity. Indeed, all major strikes in the United States (the San Francisco and Oakland general strikes being exceptions), such as the railroad strike of 1877, have found themselves undermined by other unions who retreated from solidarity for reasons of jurisdictional sanctity or organizational allegiance.

In the Virginia colony, the first laborers employed for the production of tobacco were English subjects brought to the colony under "indenture" contracts. These contracts required the laborer to work for fourteen years, after which he or she would receive a small plot of land, some money, and full citizenship. As news of the hardships in the colony reached England, enlistment diminished. The Virginia Company compensated for the deficit by using English convict labor or paupers kidnapped off English streets. Before their release, indentured laborers were regarded as "chattel," which meant they could be considered property, to be traded, sold, or used to pay debts (T. Allen 1996, 98).

When the first Africans arrived in 1619, they were conscripted under comparable conditions of servitude: fourteen years of labor with a land grant on release. What socially differentiated them from the English bond-laborers was not their appearance or origin but the fact that they were not English, and thus were not deemed eligible for a contract under English law. Only a few dozen were brought to the colony until after 1650, when the colonial elite decided to shift the work force to African labor. The shortage of English labor contributed to this decision. But also, as towns and settlements developed along the Atlantic seaboard, there were greater opportunities for the English to escape. Escape was less of an option for Africans because of their color and because they found themselves in a wholly alien social environment.[7]

When the question of perpetual servitude for Africans was first raised, it was essentially an artifact of the different political economy under which they were held. Whereas English bond-laborers could be transferred through sale of their contracts, the transfer of Africans required presenting their actual bodies in the market (Martinot 2003b, 50). As a proxy for the contract, the African body became a legal instrument. As trading of laborers increased, routine auction facilities for Africans were developed.

These auction markets functioned to standardize the bond-laborer's exchange value (much as the value of corporate stock is determined on the stock market). On the basis of current auction prices, landowners could take the market value of their laborers into account in computing their estate wealth. Thus, it became a factor in the political status of the landowner, which depended on wealth. In contradistinction, the value of English bond-laborers was fixed by how many years they had left to work under their contracts. They lost transferable value as their release date approached. Insofar as the specifics of exchange gradually shifted the Africans over to a category

of capital, their servitude was extended even against the most solemn prom-
ises. The landowners then sought to have those extensions legalized. Though
perpetual servitude for Africans was a contested issue for several decades,
the colony gradually invented means of legitimizing it (extended servitude
as punishment for misdeeds or escape attempts, for instance) (Boskin 1979,
43). In effect, the condition of perpetual servitude evolved out of the contingent capitalization of the African body under English jurisprudence, and
a desire for political influence and upward mobility in the colony's corporate
structure.[8]

It was in the midst of those decades of contestation over the issues of
perpetual servitude that the matrilineal servitude statute was enacted. Thus,
a period of transformation of a cultural and linguistic character, which would
eventually produce the concept of race, was initiated.

How the Colony Produced Whiteness

Bacon's Rebellion of 1676 provided the impetus for the massive reorganization of the colony in which the cultural process set in motion by the matrilineal servitude statute was brought to fruition. Bacon's Rebellion is today
widely recognized as the historical threshold across which the colony stepped
to evolve its form of slavery and its concept of race (T. Allen 1996, 242).
Most commentators on the rebellion see it as the impetus for dividing the
colonial labor force. Howard Zinn, for instance, credits the fact that African
and English bond-laborers were fighting together in Bacon's ranks for the
panic that seized the colonial elite and drove them to extreme solutions (Zinn
1980, 55). What they succeeded in creating was not simply an ideological
division between the English and the African bond-laborers, however (which
is how many people think of racism). If it were simply ideological in its origins, it would not still work today, 300 years later. Ideology does not have
that much staying power; history always succeeds in undermining it. Racialization was more profound than that. Its real focus was not simply to turn
white workers against black but to create a different sense of unity among
the English, to weld them into a coherent cultural structure through a social
and juridical exteriorization of the Africans.

Nathaniel Bacon was a newly arrived young plantation owner, a scion of
the aristocracy, who set about organizing the small farmers at the periphery
of the colony. These small farmers were mostly former indentured bond-
laborers who had received land from the Colonial Council on reaching their
release date. They were given land on the colony's periphery to serve as a
buffer between the colony and the Algonquin. Since political status depended
on wealth, and land expansion was prohibited by the Council in the interest

of trade relations with the Algonquin, these farmers were condemned to an inferior economic condition. Bacon first led them on unprovoked raids against the Algonquin and then attacked the Colonial Council for insufficiently protecting them from the Algonquin counterattacks (Breen 1976, 200). The ensuing war between Bacon and the council almost destroyed the colony.

The elite's response was to restructure the colony in order to obviate further upheaval (T. Allen 1996, 242). Its first step amounted to a fear campaign, warning the English against a projected threat of "Negro insur- rection" (as it was termed in the statutes; Hening 1809, 3:492) while recall- ing the hardships endured during Bacon's war. The focus on the Africans as the threat, though Bacon's Rebellion had been English-led, effectively "Afri- canized" the concept of rebellion itself and created a gratuitous English social anxiety about it. The second step was to augment that anxiety by bringing more Africans into the colony and increasing the hardships of their labor conditions. In other words, rather than alleviate their condition or give them liberty as laborers, the elite chose to give the Africans exigent cause to contemplate revolt.

The purpose for intensifying the instability of the colony was to engender a social paranoia among the English, a psychological need for a security state, and a general dependence on social solidarity and allegiance against the Afri- cans as an "enemy within" (Martinot 2003b, 64–68). A siege mentality was created that prepared the colony to accept the codification of permanent servitude for all Africans, against the juridical tradition brought from England. The codification of slavery in 1682 established a form of totalitarian control, of forced labor and debased social conditions for the Africans, reducing them to a form of subhumanity in the eyes of the English (Breen 1976, 36).

The profound social alterity thus imposed on the Africans and Afro- Americans culturally extended the division initiated by the matrilinearity condition, which had provided the soil on which a hierarchical difference signified by "black" and "white" could germinate and gave it greater material social reality. The primary goal of this process was not to use race to name a social division, but to name an insularity generated among the English with an exclusionary term (whiteness, defined through a purity condition) that would impart a sense of settlement consensus and cohesion. Thus, a coher- ent social community was constructed by a most forceful mode of political and economic oppression of the Africans.

The final stage in creating the social identity of whiteness (added to the paranoia and its instigation of an anxious social solidarity) was the organiza- tion of a system of violence: the slave patrols.[9] The patrols, constituted dur- ing the early decades of the eighteenth century, were conscripted from poor whites, farmers and laborers, under elite control. Their purpose was to stop runaway slaves and disrupt any sign of organization or autonomy among them. The patrollers rapidly discovered that violence against the Africans was greeted with approval and gratitude by the settlers (who had begun to identify themselves as white) because it represented for them the suppression of incipient slave resistance or rebellion and thus soothed their white paranoia. Even the most gratuitous violence against the now-racialized-as-black bond-laborers, if presented as a stifling of rebellion and a repression of slave autonomy, was welcomed by colonial society. The patrollers, traditionally marginalized as poor, found that their violence brought them acceptance, inclusion, and demarginalization in colonial society. Their violence not only generated a sense of overall white solidarity and cohesion but signified that the paranoia had been justified. Finally, it responded to that paranoia's demand for action as the expression of the social solidarity it generated.

Of course, the patrollers' violence only reflected that previous social violence of rendering people property in the first place, a violence that became a property of the property owners (whites). The violence served to increase the sense of threat, and with it the demand for white solidarity, which necessitated greater violence in turn. This cycle of paranoia (a sense of threat), solidarity, and violence endlessly concretized the colony's insularity and generated its sense of white racialized identity. That cyclicity is the structure of white racialized identity as such. It is from this cyclicity that the concept of whiteness, and thus race, was born. It manifests the shape or contour of the invention of whiteness and race in its essential self-referentiality, by which it imposed itself on others. An integration and collaboration of classes, a cohesion around a new cultural identity, a communal consensus on the properness of the violence, a coherence in the face of the sense of threat, and a sense of the validity of enslavement itself were the broad cultural effects of this cycle. With the birth of slavery, the English felt secure; with the birth of racialization, they could to feel "civilized" and genteel even about having barbarically imposed themselves on the Africans. Contemporary instances of this sense of virtue and civility accompanying the imposition of barbaric violence on other people have occurred in the carpet bombing of rural Vietnam, the unprovoked U.S. invasion of Iraq in 2003, and the growth of the prison industry.

The emergence of whiteness represented a new consciousness, a new social identity for the colony. This new social identity added itself to the sense of being "English," creating the ground of a superseding future national identity, and formed the cultural basis for the independence movement (Zinn 1980, 68). The colonists did not reject their English origins by becoming white, but they shifted their allegiance to a different socio-cultural identification. They became, as they say in the Declaration of Independence, a different people. Its opening sentence begins, "When, in the course of human events, it becomes necessary for one people to dissolve the political bands which have connected them with another . . ." In other words, their own white identity, while linked to the English by "political bands," was necessarily different. And in calling for independence, they projected a concept of a "white nation," a motif that threaded its way through the fabric of the independence movement, from Benjamin Franklin's musings on the subject in 1755 (*Observations Concerning the Increase in Mankind*) to the Immigration Act of 1790, which provided citizenship only for white immigrants. The project for independence did not seek social or political change; the capitalist structure of plantation agribusiness and slavery was satisfactory. What the independence movement sought, for both cultural and economic reasons, was to take control of the slave system, through which their white identity had been constructed, and to lay autonomous claim to the vast continent that stretched to the west. White identity and the control of that wealth were two sides of the same thought (Martinot 2003b, 25).

This same cycle of whiteness is discernible in the McKnight case. The state, the prosecutor, the jury, and the Supreme Court were all in consensus that this black woman was a threat to society, a criminal who had wantonly killed her child, to which the violence of incarceration was a proper and valid response.[10] The injustice she suffers is not simply racial prejudice or the estrangement of personhood and motherhood from each other in her. Her blackness was there to be used as a social "threat" and to open an avenue of legal violence. Indeed, the absence of evidence or causal relation in her prosecution testifies expressly to the state's desperate need for a sense of menace (D. Roberts 1997, 158). It is the recurrence of this structure that marks its purpose to reaffirm white social cohesion. The routine drug testing of black pregnant women but not of white that Roberts reports forms part of this unifying function, an offer of inclusion in the state's consensus to white women. In short, the state produced McKnight as a threat without substance by charging her with ultimate criminality without evidence, in order to respond to her with a violence designed to sanctify the conjunction of the state and its citizens as white. Thus, it served to vindicate white society in the wake of the civil rights movements just as the invention of race and a slave system vindicated the colony in the wake of Bacon's Rebellion. W.E.B. DuBois notes a similar process promulgated in the wake of Reconstruction: Jim Crow, chain gangs, debt servitude, and mob rule were all instituted to reconstitute white identity in the wake of the shocks it suffered from the abolition of slavery (DuBois 1935, 700).

The Redefinition of Society through Gender

Now that we have seen the cultural direction the colony took in its reorganization after 1676, let us look back more carefully at the inner workings of what guided the direction of that reorganization.

Two separate laws are contained in the one 1662 enactment. The first was the matrilineal servitude statute. The second was a prohibition of sexual relations between English and African persons. Recall the wording: "If any christian shall commit fornication with a negro man or woman, he or she so offending shall pay double the fines imposed by the former act."

The two laws clearly work in tandem. Because the children of free English women by African men would be free, the sexuality of those English women had to be carefully regulated. The existence of such children would conflict with the elite desire to hold all Africans and African-descended persons (African-Americans) in bondage. Thus, English women were to be constrained to ensure against this possibility. The penalty was only a fine, but an inability to pay the fine would result in indentured servitude. Of course, women were only nominally free under English patriarchy anyway, except for the purposes of its legal rhetoric.

The ban that the enactment establishes on what we now call "miscegenation" clearly failed in its purpose. It became the first of a long series of ever more severe such statutes, the last of which went out of existence in the United States only in 1965 (*Loving vs. Arizona*). Before 1662, there had been a religious ban on such intimacies or unions, but no secular restrictions on marriage (Godbeer 1999, 92). Longer servitude was imposed on both men and women bond-laborers who married, but there had been no stipulation as to the geographic origin or appearance of either partner. What the passage of this first anti-miscegenation statute signifies is that intimate relations between Africans and English were all too common, and undesirable, at least for elite interests. Otherwise, why bother banning them? After all, the colony was not a democracy; law was not responsive to a "will of the people." It was used by the elite to create social norms rather than express or represent them. If a statute was enacted, it signified that the elite confronted an extant practice it felt compelled for some reason to curtail. By passing such a law, the elite weaponized real human attraction and affection, transforming them into instruments to drive a wedge between those they could consider Christian (soon to be racialized as "white") and those they had decided to capitalize as bond-laborers (soon to be racialized as "black"). Thus, the statute implies that the elite already envisioned reducing the Africans to perpetual servitude, against which any intimacy that might lead an English man to take a protective if not patriarchal stance toward an African woman would be obstructive.

Though Jordan (1977) has argued that the English brought an antipathy to people of color with them when they crossed the ocean, the implication of common attraction suggested by the need to prohibit mixed marriage would tend to contradict his hypothesis. Had there been the kind of cultural antipathy he suggests, instances of mixed marriage would have been minimal, rendering official prohibition unnecessary. But in fact, neither this 1662 law nor subsequent laws succeeded in curtailing the practice. Each new law was broader in scope and more emphatic in its punishments. Indeed, in 1681 (the year before slavery was codified), the punishment was shifted to the plantation owner who allowed a mixed marriage, intensifying the social prohibition by aiming higher on the social scale. Rather than express a racism, as Jordan surmises, the chain of intensified bans on mixed relationships constituted one of the mechanisms for the invention of "race," and thus for the production of racism.

While matrilinearity legitimized the sexual violation of some, anti-miscegenation laws violated the legitimacy of sexuality for all (D. Roberts 1997, 41). The two conjoined to make normative the juridical violation of the humanity of women through their instrumentalization, and the violation of patriarchal tradition for the purposes of augmented wealth. Though its ultimate purpose may have concerned wealth, its effect was the reconstruction of social identity.

Though focused on reducing women to different forms of productive resource (African women as the producers of laborers, and English women as the producers of heirs to the wealth that labor produced), the matrilineal servitude statute also transformed the gender identity of men. Gender, like race, is a relational form of social categorization. If masculinity's definition of itself is contingent on its own definition of femininity, then any attempt to redefine female identity will transform male self-definition and identity at the same time. In the case of the English, the reduction of English women to the chaste breeders of a pure race transformed English men by trapping them in the role of policing the women's sexual purity and propriety on a cultural plane (beyond the surveillance that may have attended their personal feelings). Thus, the sexuality of English men was not only reduced but severed from their emotional life. Even when married, an English man would find himself essentially celibate, wedded to the desexed signifier for propriety and the cold purity of ancestry rather than to a warm woman.

In effect, men left themselves with only themselves to relate to, resulting in the conflation of the hyper-masculinism and homo(non)erotics that

W. J. Cash describes for the southern frontiersman and planter in the first section of his book, *The Mind of the South* (1941). In short, the statute changed not only the form of masculinity but the substance of male hegemony.

For women (both the violated and the inviolable), escape from these boundaries required doors of resistance. As each African woman watched this trap fold down on her, pinning her in its own darkness, where could she turn to reject her imposed status? White women were being led to imprisonment in the attic or prepared for the marble pedestal that would then be guarded by all white men. The African woman's refusal to bear children only violated her own selfhood. But whether motherhood occurred within family or outside it, the children she bore remained not hers. Family in either case was rendered impossible (Spillers 1987). And in the process, African men were reduced along with African women to a form of capital to be deployed as productive resources for profit. Neither could white women turn to African women for assistance; the African women already symbolized the stripping of white women's physicality as women, leaving them the mere germinators of generations. The overall effect was to render sexuality an extension of the market, and the bond-labor market an extension of sexuality. This "color coding" of sexuality and the resulting sexualization of color augmented the emerging "color coding" of labor.

Africans and African-Americans were transformed into mediations of the property relations between English men, while all women (English and African) were conscripted to mediate the relation between English men and their property. Property relations were rendered inseparable from gender relations, not simply with respect to inheritance or a division of labor, but as a proprietary categorization of people that would later be canonized as "race" and nation. In effect, women and womanly being were deployed to shift prior juridical distinctions between laborers to a different bio-cultural (racialized) plane.

"Race" brought about a separation between English and African peoples that was not ethnic, not cultural, not sensual, not based on bodily characteristics (though it used them to symbolize itself)—and it was an economic separation only insofar as it was politically defined to be economic (the decision that African bond-labor replace English). "Race" amounted to an artificial cultural separation based on the instrumentalization of women. It arose from a double objectification of sexuality and motherhood that turned them against each other, and concretized itself as an invented white racialized identity grounded in a purity concept essential for the very derivation of all future racial divisions.

On the Role of Anti-miscegenation Laws

At the time the matrilinearity statute was enacted, the colonists could not know what they were heading toward. They did know, however, that everything they did was to an extent conceptual because they wrote that into their laws. The social status of a child is conceptual, imposed politically. The difference between English and African women was conceptual, imposed to construct a social distinction out of a bodily difference. The idea pursuant to their artificial purity principle that men and women of different color should not be intimate was nothing but conceptual, a socially distorting anxiety that eventually became obsessive (and still is). As an example of that obsessiveness, the Maryland colony published in 1664 a denunciation of "freeborn English women [who] forgetful of their free condition and to the disgrace of our nation do intermarry with Negro slaves" (Alpert 1970, 195). To tacitly admit that a "freeborn" condition could be "forgotten" means it is something other than innate, granted instead as a privilege by male governance as a "national" resource.

But miscegenation generated more than a conceptual difference to which psychological antipathy could attach. Eva Saks argues that anti-miscegenation law represents the "power of legal language to construct, criminalize, and appropriate the human body itself" (1988, 39). In that sense, anti-miscegenation law is a necessary prologue to slavery, one consistent with an ethos of slavery (a cultural admission that the form of slavery the English were evolving was ethically permissible to them). The principle that heritage is definable by statute means that it forms part of the system of entitlements characteristic of property (which also only comes into existence through juridical enactment). And if it was primarily the elite that had an interest in preventing miscegenist practice, it signified a political purpose beyond the economics of matrilinearity.

Anti-miscegenation laws established a norm of socio-political control over bodies beyond the economic relation of labor or enslavement itself. In codifying sexuality, these laws provided the social ground for the eventual links between the totalitarian control of bodies condemned to forced labor and the ethics of the cultural identity that could assume and valorize that function of control for itself. They extended the appropriation of women as producers to the human body in general as property. In other words, before property in persons could be racialized, it had first to be transformed through a sexual division of labor. That is, before the properties of a person could become "race," they had first to become a property of property (Saks 1988, 50). In both respects, matters of property trumped matters of personal relationship.

When something is raised to the level of a cultural norm, it is given a power that transcends mere law. Though the colony had for decades sought in vain to break the natural tendency toward solidarity between English and African bond-laborers, it was only the profound cultural difference produced by a structure of racialization that offered success. After the division of women along color lines formed a border between an English cultural cohesion (desexualized propriety) and an African-American stratified productivity (forced labor and sexualized property), it constituted a boundary behind which English society could insulate and consolidate itself, producing a self-identification as "white." In short, in cyclic fashion, the state's redefinition of sexuality conditioned the evolution of forms of property; its redefinition of forms of property (as body) conditioned the evolution of racialization; and its evolving definition of race conditioned forms of sexuality. Cheryl Harris (1993) has argued that whiteness itself has become a form of property, a property that white people can cash in on (which Theodore Allen [1969] called "white skin privilege"). This genealogy of race shows, however, that whiteness itself, as an identity, was an extension of property, a cultural identity generated to be the ethical basis for the enslavement of labor.

Matrilineal servitude might appear to be a natural adjunct of anti-miscegenation standards (after all, we look back from a social moment in which mixed [white/non-white] couples are still extraordinary). But the division of women against themselves in the interests of wealth, property, and a racialized social identity was not adjunct to anything but colonial greed. Nevertheless, it ultimately gave rise to a cultural structure that is more profound in its conditioning of social relations than greed could ever be.

Structurally, these categories engender a second cyclic process. Sexuality, seized as property in Africans and desexualized as propriety among the English, extended the body-as-production to commodified personhood. Commodified personhood formed the grounds for the codification of slavery and the transformation of colonial allegiance (through paranoia and enforced social solidarity) into a structure of racialization whose ultimate product was a white social identity. Slavery, the ultimate extension of the body as property, imposed on all interpersonal relations (both English and African) a commodified character. Through racialization, it rendered all forms of personhood a matter of property. The control of sexuality, commodified personhood, and person as property by which sexuality is controlled turn round and round, building, reconstructing, and contextualizing each other endlessly as a cultural structure.[11]

Insofar as the foundation of slavery, matrilineal servitude, and anti-miscegenation worked together toward the invention of race, we find ourselves at the originary point of intersection of class, race, and gender. Let us dispense with the notion of "intersection." In that originary moment they are inseparable, and it is the structure of that inseparability that establishes the scene of colonialist assault on humanity that emerges as whiteness and the replacement of the human with racialization. The control of sexuality occurs within the use of property to separate social classes. And sexuality has historically been a primary focus of white supremacy. It is the unending white panic over the concept of mixed couples that drives the still compulsive white refusal to abandon neighborhood segregation.[12]

The Colony's Identity Crisis

I have been using the term "paranoia" to signify a social or communal attitude of fear, which functions as an essential element in the cultural structure I am calling "white racialized identity." My use of the term has clearly been metaphoric, since "officially" or technically it refers to an aberrant activity of an individual psyche. For an individual, however, the psychological content of what is diagnosed as paranoia is itself metaphoric, insofar as it names an ephemeral condition of threat that can only be described circumstantially. The term as diagnostic, then, is doubly metaphoric, since an observer's description of another person's consciousness can only trope the impossibility of direct perception or experience with that other's consciousness.

"Social" paranoia refers to a conjunction or consensus of people in a social domain who have a common presentiment of threat. There is an essential difference between something experienced by an individual as a source of fear and something that induces a collective fear in a social group. The first is a threat to one's identity in the sense that one's psychic survival is in question. The second becomes a source of identity built on the ability to partake in a communal response. Many forms of nationalism feed on the fear of imminent threat of aggression from another nation, producing a solidarity that then forms a significant aspect of national identity. A communal paranoia can arise from a group's oppression of others, out of a fear of rebellion, retribution, or the revelation that one's justification of oppressive conduct is in actuality the valorization of injustice. When that paranoia produces communally accepted forms of discrimination or hostility against the oppressed, the resulting system of hierarchical social relations then provides the content for the identity collectively constructed through identification with that social condition or system. The paranoia characteristic of white racialized identity (as an essential element of its initial historical construction) is peculiar insofar as it allows white people to feel comfortable about themselves in their white solidarist consensus at the same time as they feel threatened.

The ephemeral nature of white identity's social paranoia can be demon-strated by a counter-example. In the midst of the civil rights movements, the threat level experienced by white people diminished because they could see the justice of the movements' goals, as well as the brutality of the police. The presence or image of thousands of black people marching and demon-strating for equality and participation was not something contained in the prior white narratives of who black people were—narratives through which white identity had previously constructed itself. Silently, no longer able to explain the reality perceived, those narratives ceased to work in the world, and the identity they buttressed eroded. As George Yancy puts it, "Black resistance calls into question the philosophical anthropological assumptions of white racism, assumptions that deny the reality and complexity of Black self-determination" (2008, 112). Where white identity depended on seeing black people as a certain preconceived kind of threat, these demonstrations undermined that stance. When the white narratives of threat ceased to work, it allowed a new ethos of equality to emerge, at the same time producing an identity crisis in white society as a whole.

Similarly, when the Virginia colony overturned English patriarchal com-mon law by establishing matrilinearity (Godbeer 1999, 115), it was in response to a profound identity crisis. That reversal had its origins in the insularity the colony had established for itself (against the indigenous, who not only refused forced labor but counter-attacked). Dissociating itself from the world of the indigenous as alien nations, the colony retreated into her-meticism and an internal homogeneity in which it could pride itself on its sense of propriety and civility. That is, it balanced its corporate greed with that sense of law and propriety. It was for this homogenous hermeticism that the eventual presence of Africans posed a problem. They were both alien and internal to the colony, and brought that greed and civility into collision with each other at the level of social identity.

This identity conflict had early roots, not only in the colony's response to the land and the indigenous, but in ambiguities in its own sense of gov-ernance. This can be seen in a small incident recorded very briefly in the colonial records of 1630. An Englishman named Hugh Davis was whipped for having sexual relations with a "Negro" (Hening 1809, 1:146). At the time, his act violated no prohibitory law, and the absence of statute was consistent with the small number of African bond-laborers in the colony. The record states that Davis was whipped "before an assembly of Negroes and others," for the offense of "defiling his body" by "lying with a Negro woman." One might wonder at the psychological disorder that would see sensual practices as "defilement" while not seeing the pain and damage to the body being whipped as itself "defiling"—but that is another matter.

What is odd about the incident as reported (a single, very terse line in the colonial records) is that "bodily self-defilement" was a religious notion, and violated only religious doctrine, whereas Davis's punishment occurred under secular authority. The case thus resides at the interface between institutional identities of governance.

The fact that the report prioritized the "Negro" contingent of the audience is puzzling. The traditional purpose of punishment is deterrence. The report's focus on the Africans would suggest they were the target of this deterrence. If the purpose of the punishment was to dissuade the Africans from sleeping with the English, why whip the English partner? Were the Africans being instructed in the Christian concept of bodily defilement by witnessing the damaging of a Christian body? Perhaps the Africans were using sexuality as a way of transforming or alleviating their own condition, as an extension of the settlers' own advice to them to use baptism and conversion to Christianity for that same purpose—that is, as an avenue toward freedom. Perhaps Davis had raped the woman and her compatriots filled the audience to see him punished. But nothing suggests this. On the contrary, if that had been the case, it would have been the woman who was punished since, in the seventeenth century, an assaulted woman was presumed to have misused her sexuality. Indeed, nothing was reported about what happened to the woman. Given the colony's subsequent failure to write an anti-miscegenation statute that worked, it is possible to construe the encounter between this English man and the unnamed African woman as one of mutual attraction.

We are left to conclude that the punishment was primarily designed to create fear among English men about sleeping with African women. In light of the elite's apparent intention to disassociate English and Africans (Boskin 1979), the report's terseness must have been strategic. Though the Africans were to be proscribed as a site of sexual desire (Davis's presumed actual offense), that focus was disguised by emphasizing the African component of the audience in punishing the Englishman, making it look as if the problem (or the formal target) was really the Africans. The punishment's goal, then, was an instrumentalization of Africans for the purpose of keeping the English in line, reaffirming an insular English social identity as a form of social control. Occurring between institutional identities of governance, the incident can be seen to represent a shift from religious to secular authority, for which the creation of a hierarchical social differentiation between English and Africans was the means.

David Goldberg writes, in his treatise *The Racial State,* that the state emerges to stem the danger of heterogeneity in favor of homogeneity and uniformity, or what he calls the "inherently homogenizing logic of institutions"

(Goldberg 2002, 30, 33). Institutions buttress their authority (and their authoritarianism) by suppressing hybridity and "otherness." For Goldberg, the concept of race represents the ambiguity between the state's goal and a heterogeneous social reality over which it presides. As a response to the unavoidable meaning of this ambiguity for the state, race marks the conflation or confusion of fact and value, nature and norm, description and prescription (Goldberg 2002, 93). In the concrete terms of the Virginia colony, that ambiguity would mark the interface between the secular and the religious, which later became a zone of transition from Christian supremacy to white supremacy.

Goldberg's treatment of the state is a little too abstract because it leaves out the process of the historical evolution of race as a concept within the political and economic developments in the colonial situation. He posits that race directly reflected a need for homogeneity without describing where that need came from. Thus, he also leaves out the colony's ethical need to rationalize slavery, requiring a cultural transformation of social identity to whiteness and white supremacy that was already a conflation of fact and value. To impose an inferiority on others, and then to claim that it is natural, is a primal confusion of fact and value, with value given priority. This is a Christian operation; it reasons from a value to a naturalized fact, principally because for Christianity the world itself is a fact that is produced through the operation of certain (religious) values.

In effect, the arcane politics of Davis's punishment, occurring without authorization of law, revealed a political crisis, the elite's inability to rule in a traditional way in the face of the social heterogeneity that the African presence posed. Its ad hoc differentiation between the English and the Africans represented the elite's primary response to that political crisis.

If the matrilineal servitude statute represented a further development of the colony's identity crisis, its explicit focus on African women was its attempt to stem that problem. The differentiation of African from English women transferred the patriarchal ethos of domination from the domain of the family to the more complex control of labor and production, by rendering motherhood both economic production and capital enhancement. By reclassifying servitude through the redefinition of sexuality and gender, the colony reestablished a mode of English homogeneity as hierarchy itself, generated through an extension of the purity concept. That is, whiteness constituted the new homogeneity. In short, patriarchal crisis and the drive toward wealth enhancement had the effect of engendering a new social identity. Because a sense of a threat is central to this process, the conclusion is unavoidable that whiteness and social paranoia, whiteness and the need for a threat, are inseparable.

The inherency of paranoia to the cultural structure of whiteness in the United States is still extant. It was the presumptive logic that informed the invasion of Iraq in 2003. The government had but to invoke weapons of mass destruction (though non-existent), an Iraqi nuclear threat (that proved to be forged), an Iraqi connection to Al Qaeda (also non-existent), and both official and populist support for a highly illegal invasion against a sovereign nation was justified almost automatically. The extent to which the critical faculties of a society lapsed into torpor in the face of this flimsy fabric of menace suggests that feeling threatened was somehow an indispensable comfort to people.[13] After six years of war, which has killed well over a million Iraqis without gaining either their acquiescence or their gratitude, the U.S. populace seems reconciled to considering the war's criminality just a big mistake.

A paradigmatic example of this ethic of paranoia is evident in the following dialogue between an anti-war activist and a man whose son was in Vietnam in 1965. The activist explained that the Vietnamese were fighting for the same kind of independence from colonialism that had been the goal of the American Revolution. The Vietnamese were trying to throw off foreign domination and establish national sovereignty for themselves, and the United States had invaded to suppress their ability to do that. The father got angry and responded, "I have to support this war. My son is over there. He could be killed." For the father, it was more important to valorize the potential threat to his son than to withdraw his son from any possibility of threat by bringing him (and all the GIs) home and ending the war that way.

This historical notion of cultural paranoia does not exclude Richard Hofstadter's thesis of a "paranoid style" in U.S. politics; it goes beyond it. For Hofstadter (1966), the paranoid political style consists of the invention of specific "dangers" to the "American way of life," against which a national defense can be developed. As cases in point, the anti-immigrant campaign of the 1830s and the anti-communist campaign of the 1950s expressed themselves in the same rhetorical form, namely, the need to defend against a foreign power and foreign ideology intent on subverting the American way of life (in the 1950s it was Russia and communism, and in the 1830s it was Austria and Catholicism). But the cultural paranoia of the "white nation" and of white racialized identity is a question not of "style" but rather of the coherence of identity, both national and individual. In effect, it is white paranoia that makes Hofstadter's political paranoia work. A sense of threat is essential for white racialized identity to recognize itself, both as U.S. citizen and as white. It is the preservation of the purity concept that is at stake; and conversely, the purity concept rationalizes the indispensability of a paranoia. Without both, the idea of whiteness would not be possible.

The Forms of Purity

Two forms of purity have played significant roles in the development of the United States as a racialized society, a society of white racialized identity. The first is the social purity (homogeneity) of the colony, designed to preserve the autocracy of its colonial administration. The second is the ancestral purity of whiteness at the core of the socio-juridical generation of the meaning of race itself. Both are used to govern sexuality. Ultimately, these two purity concepts (of colonial administration and whiteness) extended themselves to a third form, the self-sanctification of white supremacy as the cultural purity of the "white race." Where the first sense of purity is a social exclusionism and the second is an ancestral exclusionism, the third is both cultural and ideological.[14] It is with respect to the third that the idea that racism is an "ideology" is relevant.

In both an analogical and a historical sense, these three forms of purity link themselves to the three components of white racialized identity. The first, the insularity of the colonial settlement, links to the decision to construct it by locking out heterogeneity as a threat, by making those who are different into a threat in order to treat with them across a social boundary defined by nothing but a fear of their potential trespass. The second, the ancestral, links to the valorization of a social solidarity, a social uniformity, a purity of existential being. And the third reifies the binary between purity and corruption through gratuitous violence that makes its victims other than who they are, inventing them as impure and barbaric in order to render the barbarism of white supremacy a virtue. From the mutilation and rape and branding of slaves to the lynching of emancipated African-Americans to the torture and murder of black people in U.S. streets by the police (beating people in the street constitutes state-sanctioned torture) to the renditions and torture of people picked up in the streets of Afghani and Iraqi towns during U.S. invasions, the violence has been considered an act of social accomplishment, and goes unpunished and even uncensured for that reason.

This is recognizable as a form of messianism. The messianic adjunct to the purity concept is the claim that white (European) civilization is a gift to the world. As a "gift," it must see the world as other, against which it demands of its own citizens (the white members of the white nation) that they stand in allegiance and solidarity, and that the other on whom the "gift" is bestowed (imposed) be grateful (Hartman 1997). Its logical extension is that the other's failure to demonstrate gratitude renders that other both alien and enemy. Should the other insist on autonomy, it implies a rejection of the "gift" and thus a criminal intention on the other's part, since the bringing of the gift is already the provision of justice and the decriminalization of the giver. Rejection of the gift is thus a metaphoric aggression to be countered by actual violence disguised as self-defense. When "enemy combatants" are arrested in their own streets in Baghdad, they are charged with the crime of attacking the United States, though the United States stands in those streets as a foreign invader.

The Nature of Racism and Prejudice

In this analysis of the structure of racialization, we can see the underpinnings of white racism as it has come to be understood. Many now see racism as a socially programmed response to other people rather than a symptom of personal feelings, something taught rather than experienced. Indeed, it can be shown that personal feelings toward certain other people are produced by the fact that one's responses to those people are socially programmed. The social programming is produced both by the social and political inferiorizations forced on the other and by the cultural structure that makes that inferiorization and oppression permissible. What is not often comprehended is how obedience to that programmed response (prejudice) implies that one is not free—dys-consciously so. White identity loses its freedom through its identity-dependency on the other. But this dependence is then disguised by means of a standard inversion. The ethic of whiteness and white supremacy determines that it is the other (a black person, for instance) who is perceived as the source of one's felt unfreedom. And prejudice against the other person becomes the name for the need, at the behest of one's programming, to hold against that other its being the source of one's felt unfreedom.

We can no longer discuss racism as something that is simply based on prejudice. Its structural determination and its identity-involvement must be taken into account. Prejudice must be understood as having a social rather than an individual character and foundation. All prejudice begins with a generalization about another person. To prejudge means to judge prior to experience, based on something other than the individual. One prejudges based on "what" the individual is (group membership) rather than "who." That "what" is a generalization whose real focus is the group. Generalizations claim to be derived from experience with the group. This, however, is a patent impossibility. All people present themselves as individuals. And they can be experienced only as individuals. To experience a person through the generalization of a group cannot be derived from direct experience with that individual or any others. To generalize them means to obtain that generalization from elsewhere, and from others, since one cannot arrive at a generalization from experience of individuals by oneself. Whoever those others are from whom one receives the generalization, and whatever reason one might have to accept it, one then imposes it on an individual one meets in order to encounter that individual as already generalized. In the absence of a generalization, one must confront an individual in his or her individuality, and relate to him or her directly, without prejudging. The point of the generalization is to obviate that direct encounter.

Nevertheless, one must choose to accept the terms by which one generalizes people because they come from elsewhere than one's encounter with those whom one prejudges. In accepting the generalization, one shows that one respects its source. Those others could be the media, or politicians, or community leaders, or parents, or close neighbors. Whoever they are, the prejudice one receives from them is not a relationship of antipathy between oneself and a person prejudged, but a relationship of respect between oneself and those who provide the generalization. The hostility one may express toward the generalized other is only an element of the generalization itself. Prejudice is thus a form of chosen commonality and solidarity with those people who provide the generalizations.

The inverse of this commonality is that a generalization renders the person generalized unknowable. Since a person can be known only as an individual, to pretend to know him or her through an imposed generalization received from others means to know the generalization and not the person. In that sense, the antipathy expressed as prejudice has to be a faked antipathy, a performance for the persons one has chosen to respect, since one cannot have real feelings (aside from paranoia) toward someone one has generalized and thus rendered unknowable. Indeed, it is a characteristic of generalizations that they contain instructions concerning the kind of antipathy one is expected to feel toward the generalized individual. Generalizations provide a form of script to be followed in order to gain the respect of others. In that sense, the antipathy that accompanies prejudice is a form of unfreedom that one accepts as membership in and solidarity with the people who provide the generalization.[15] In effect, prejudice is a component of racism only insofar as racism is the name for the system of generalizations about a racialized group, in which prejudice names the system of scripts for performing or acting out that racism.

In Summary

The instrumentalization of women is central to the concept of "race," for obvious reasons. Women give birth to men as well as to other women. Women give birth to all the people who will be criminally forced to labor for others without pay. Women give birth to those who will be trained as the soldiers who will seize other people's land for its resources and settlements. Women give birth to the sources of all elite wealth.

If race is the result of one group racializing others, those who deploy their power of racialization for the production of wealth, social coherence, and their own social identity must take control of women. Women have to be instrumentalized if the race of a child is to appear natural rather than simply the result of political definition. Giving race a biological character and controlling women are two sides of the same coin.

The quirk of the Virginia colony was that, in insisting on English insularity, it centered itself culturally on a purity concept that could be concretized only through the control of motherhood. In the Spanish colonies, women were not guarded sexually in the same way and were thus instrumentalized differently. It was the English sense of colonial insularity, coupled with the corporate structure of the colony, that determined that a racialized concept of whiteness would emerge there, and not in the Spanish colonies. In the latter, mixed relationships were not prohibited, and hierarchical dominance never separated itself from the geo-politics of direct European descent. European purity rather than whiteness remained the controlling identity.

"Gender" and "race" remain hierarchical social structures that have never been independent of each other. They name forms of power. Whatever redefinitions race and gender have passed through at the hands of the state were and are mutually conditioning. The social categorization of persons as "races" by white supremacy derives directly from the anti-miscegenation statutes that appropriated gender and sexuality as property. The formal instrumentalization of black women, and thus of black people in general, remains as essential today for the social coherence of white society as it was in the seventeenth-century colony.

2

The Racialized State

Impunity and the White State

Three principal concepts emerge here. The first is the centrality of the instrumentalization of women for the construction of a structure of racialization, that is, for the development of the concept of race as a social structure (a social construct). Second, the primary purpose of the operations of white racism and white supremacy is the consolidation of an internal coherence and consensus for white society, white culture, and whiteness itself as a social structure. That is, whiteness and white society can constitute themselves only by racializing, by dehumanizing and dominating other people they define as non-white for that purpose. The third is the possibility of discerning and describing the underlying cultural structure of racialization in the United States, that is, the cultural structure that guides as a template the reconstitution of whiteness and white supremacy in different historical periods, by finding parallels in the forms of institutional racializing operations at different historical moments, though they be applied to very different socio-economic environments. We have looked at the ways white racialized identity was constructed in the wake of an identity crisis in the seventeenth-century colonies, and some of the ways it has reconstituted itself in the wake of the crisis to white supremacy engendered by the civil rights movements. In this chapter we examine the extension of the structure of racialization to the operations of the state, with a description of the three major historical moments wherein white supremacy was attacked by pro-democracy movements and what it used in each case to reconstitute itself against those movements.

If women embody the generative power of the human being, they should reside at the core of non-hierarchical community instead of being subjected to the domination of those who cannot embody that generative power but only objectify it. Domination is always a social relation whose existence requires a state to guarantee its continuance. Without a state, the subjugated walk away and find autonomous modes of existence for themselves.[1] Those who go after them, who attempt to resubjugate or suppress them, who seek to undermine their autonomous existence or bring them back into obedience—whether to organizational allegiance, military directive, law, myth, or administrative order—constitute the state. If property can be used to exploit labor (as capital), then it does not matter how democratic the state claims to be; it will never allow enough democracy for laborers to vote about the ability of property to exploit labor, let alone vote it out of existence. The state's job remains to keep laborers from walking away and constructing an autonomous existence for themselves. In a society in which there is domination, there can be democracy only for the dominant. The institutions that serve as the state are always designed to guarantee that domination will have a form of impunity (and sometimes naked force) available to it for the maintenance of obedience and obeisance to the cultural organization that they govern.

For instance, the structure of impunity (slavery and white hegemony) played a role in the writing of the U.S. Constitution, and thus in the formation of the political system of the United States itself. Donald Robinson has described how the existence of slavery, and the refusal of the southern states to consider liberation of the slaves, conditioned the debates in the constitutional convention and produced specific aspects of the governmental structure of the United States. The bicameral legislature (a second house based on proportional representation), for instance, was demanded by the southern states not because they had greater populations than New York or Massachusetts, but because they estimated that, as slave states, their population (including the slaves) was going to grow faster and the second house would ensure their hegemony in the federal government (Robinson 1971, 177–181). The separation of federal and state powers with strict limitations and boundaries was demanded by the southern states to prevent the federal government from making the existence of slavery an issue for itself, to either regulate or abolish it (Robinson 1971, 210–233). Ironically, the anti-slavery delegates agreed to leave mention of slavery out of the Constitution because they were convinced that the slave system was dying and would soon disappear anyway. After the invention of the cotton gin, however, the plantations became the nation's primary source of economic earnings, trade revenue, and capital through the volume of cotton produced.

The role that impunity played in the construction of the constitutional state continued in a different form after the abolition of slavery. After the Civil War, Reconstruction brought white and black people together in the southern states for the political task of representing the people. The story of its overthrow has been extensively researched.[2] Not only were the Reconstruction governments demolished, but any vestiges of racial conjunction created by them were rapidly disassembled by laws of segregation and disenfranchisement. The exclusion of black people from politics and social participation was enforced by murderous populist violence, led by paramilitary gangs (e.g., the Ku Klux Klan). And a political economy to replace slavery was developed which again chained black agricultural labor to the land through debt servitude, a crop lien system (Goodwyn 1976) upheld by a system of generalized white impunity toward black people (French 1969).

For instance, under the Jim Crow economy, black tenant farmers or sharecroppers were tied to white landowners or commercial establishments through usurious debt. The farmer would mortgage his crop in advance to a lender to get the money to buy seed, farm tools, and equipment, as well as food for subsistence during the growing season. When the crop was harvested, the lender would seize and sell it and keep what the farmer owed for formerly advanced retailed goods from the proceeds—usually pushing the farmer deeper into debt (DuBois 1903, 88–118; Goodwyn 1976, 26–32). Any attempt to escape this vicious cycle by running away or by secretly saving part of the crop for personal purposes would lead to arrest and incarceration, typically under forced labor for the state on chain gangs. Black imprisonment was often indefinite, at the whim of the prison administration. Just as slavery, which amounted to indefinite imprisonment on a plantation at forced labor, was the center of the pre–Civil War economy, so the prison and the chain gang, as a site of forced labor, functioned at the core of the Jim Crow economy.

Enforcement of this system was expected of the entire white population, which was granted impunity, both legally and personally. Enforcement involved unending hostility or paternalism, gratuitous demands for obeisance from black people, campaigns of terror (beatings, mob murder, entertainment violence), all conjoined in a universal form of surveillance in which the white population watched a black person's every move. Whites were empowered to control when a black person had to smile or when to seem grateful for the cruelty or hate heaped on them (Smith 1949). The violence of Jim Crow enforcement was also applied to those whites who showed insufficient allegiance to the system; the primary purpose of its racism, after all, was to generate a unity and solidarity among whites. In short, the rules of segregation of public facilities and private interactions constituted a huge fractal boundary, guarded by all white people, whose purpose was to maintain the coherence and cohesion of white society.

It is the form that white racialized identity took under Jim Crow in the South that has become the traditional archetype of the white supremacist mind in the United States. The axis of its paranoia was the fear that black people intended and desired to enter white society in order to corrupt its social and cultural purity (symbolized by the white obsession with black sexuality). White solidarity appeared in the form of a demand for white allegiance. And its violence was ubiquitous, a generalized impunity toward black people. Disenfranchisement and the denial of a black person's legal right to testify against a white person were simply guarantors of that impunity. While every white person may have benefited materially, psychologically, or culturally from this system, most paid for that benefit with a loss of freedom, a need to constantly assure other whites that they were indeed on duty, guarding the sanctity of white society and white racialized identity.

The problem with that archetype is that it clouds one's vision toward the form that racialization and white supremacy have taken since the civil rights movements. When the civil rights movements put an end to Jim Crow, they swept away the 90 years in which U.S. society lived and accepted the criminality and unconstitutionality of Jim Crow laws and social norms, replacing them with voting rights acts, unignorable demands for equality, and affirmative action programs to bring black and brown people into full participation in the social domains from which they had been excluded. Though much of it may have been begrudged, it nevertheless represented ethical progress made by white society, even if only a pragmatic mode of crisis management in the face of black rage at white reticence to obey its own laws and ideals. White society found itself without its impunity, without its control over its white/black border, and without its unity or consensus as white (Skrentny 1996, ch. 4). When it began to rebuild itself, it could not do so in Jim Crow (traditional white supremacist) terms, and did not.

It is important to understand the difference. To do so, we have to apply what we know about the structure of racialization, on which whites could call to reconstitute the coherence of white culture and society. In order for whites to reracialize themselves as white through their racialization of others as non-white, those others had to be fixed in place again. Let us look at how this was done during the last quarter of the twentieth century.

The Reconstitution of White Impunity

The first step in this reconstitution was the production of a threat. Affirmative action was decried as "reverse discrimination," to create the sense among white people that they had become victims. Many proclaimed affirmative action as a sign that black people wanted "to take over everything." A second threat was located in the political consciousness of African-American, Native American, Chicano/Chicana, Asian, and other communities. The communal autonomy that gave people of color a sense of social and personal dignity and self-respect was attacked as separatist. Organizations such as AIM, La Raza, the Black Panthers, and other black power organizations were assaulted and destabilized by the police and by FBI Cointelpro operations (Churchill 2002).

The sense of white solidarity that emerged in the face of what whites had decided were threats to themselves (regardless of the pro-democratic character of what they sought to suppress) was a civilian white populism (as opposed to its former para-military form). It fought to beat back affirmative action using organizational networking, media campaigns, and court cases, beginning with the Bakke case in 1973. Racist or reactionary radio and television talk shows were organized to galvanize white nationalist opinion— Rush Limbaugh and the shock jocks, for instance. And ballot initiatives were organized in many states to prohibit affirmative action policies (for instance, California's Proposition 209 in 1994). An anti-abortion movement was organized during the early 1980s, and given much publicity, to roll back the autonomy of women. Gradually, social programs (e.g., affirmative action, job training, day care centers) were defunded (throughout the 1980s and 1990s) and then canceled. Commercial or productive investment in communities of color by local residents was subject to usurious interest rates. Credit was denied to black business ventures (redlining), and employment opportunities in or for communities of color were closed, undermining their autonomy (Wilson 1997). Those people who could escape and integrate themselves into the system (e.g., athletes, politicians, army officers, entertainers, corporate executives) eventually constituted a brain drain on those communities.

Two other social factors were required to complete the reconstitution of white racialized identity and the coherence of white culture: an institutionalization of impunity and a rhetoric of racialization. In the wake of the civil rights movements, a white para-military populism was no longer socially acceptable as a location for white impunity, as it had been under Jim Crow. And a rhetoric of racialization had to accord with the language of equal rights, though with the same effects as Jim Crow. Both aspects were resolved during the 1970s.

To replace the rhetoric of Jim Crow, a language of "minorities" was developed. Before the civil rights era and the Voting Rights Act, the populations now referred to as "minorities" were lumped together in white parlance as the "colored races." The razing of barriers to voting in the 1960s, and the access that African-Americans, Chicanos, Native Americans, and others obtained to the electoral process, changed that.

In democratic procedure, the concepts of "majority" and "minority" refer to the outcome of a vote. The term "minority" refers to the group that has been outvoted. Reference to a group of people as a "minority," however, assigns them to being outvoted before any vote is taken. To be a "minority" is to be outvoted in advance and a priori. It ceases to refer to procedure and becomes the name for a state of being. As a state of being, it is relegated to a political exterior, outside the white majority and unintegrated into the political arena in which the white majority has hegemony. "Minority" designation constitutes a form of exclusion. No group makes itself a minority. It is thrust into minority status by a majoritarian group that thereby preserves and guarantees its own majoritarian status.

In short, a group becomes a "minority" by being minoritized by a majoritarian group. There is no such thing as "a minority"; there are only minoritized groups. Thus, minoritization repeats the same relationality to whiteness as racialization, in which white people racialize themselves by racializing those they define as non-white, to be excluded in "otherness." "Minority" remains a term within the vocabulary of democratic procedure, while in its white supremacist usage it signifies exteriority and exclusion from the mainstream political arena. As a term of exclusion, it ceases to have democratic content and becomes a term of social difference. In effect, "minority" is a euphemism for racialization.

To understand the form that the re-institutionalization of impunity has taken, let us begin with the power of the state and, in particular, the prisons and the police. Today the United States has the largest prison system in the world (in numbers and per capita), housing 2.3 million people, 75 percent of whom are people of color. People of color, comprising roughly a quarter of the U.S. population, do not commit 75 percent of the crime in the United States. That means the prison industry signifies something other than law enforcement.[3]

One procedure indispensable to producing this prison population is the routine and generalized use, throughout the United States, of police racial profiling. And here, we are reminded of George Jackson's (1970) counsel, to focus on the source and administration of an institutionality (like the police or prisons) rather than on those subjected to it. Profiling means that a police officer can stop a person on the street if he or she fits the "profile" of a criminal suspect or someone the police can say they are looking for. Racial profiling means that if the police can claim their suspect is of a particular race, then anyone of that race can be stopped as fitting the profile.

When Charles Stuart, a white man, shot his white pregnant wife in Boston in 1991, and claimed a black man had done it, hundreds of black men throughout that city were stopped, harassed, and interrogated by the police in the next forty-eight hours, to the point where it was extremely dangerous for a black man to be out on the street (Sharkey 1991).

Racial profiling presumes that all people of color are or potentially are criminals, and that police procedure can be seen as preemption. Such police procedures, along with a media focus on black or brown crime, have imposed an atmosphere of general criminalization on people of color. The excessive degree to which black motorists are stopped and searched (the designation "Driving While Black" has long since ceased to be jocular) is an expression of the permissibility granted to the police by this general criminalization of black or brown people.[4] On the whole, profiling implies a gratuitousness and extra-legality in police procedure.

The police authorize their routine racial profiling by referring to a database they have compiled from their own statistics and prior arrest records. These, they claim, provide patterns, which they then use to profile possible suspects. But both database and arrest patterns were constituted through racial profiling in the first place (Martinot 2003a, 207; C. Parenti 1999, 48). What this omits is the difference—indeed, the opposition—between suspect apprehension, which is part of law enforcement, and profiling, which is not. Racial profiling cannot be based on law enforcement statistics because it is the inverse of law enforcement. In law enforcement, a criminal act is committed and the police look for a suspect. In profiling, the police commit an act of suspicion and then look for a crime for the supposed suspect to have committed.

The legal domain that endows racial profiling with special power is the category of "victimless crime laws" (of which drug possession laws are the most frequently used). Victimless crime laws permit the police to accuse and apprehend people without recourse to a complainant. Obviating the complainant allows an officer to suspect or determine criminality autonomously and to extend "probable cause" to a spectrum of arbitrary or gratuitous decisions concerning search or control.[5] This extension of "probable cause" reduces police accountability and due process, rendering their operation increasingly autocratic.

Victimless crime laws were also central to Jim Crow police operations during the first half of the twentieth century. Loitering, malingering, vagrancy, drunk and disorderly, and the like were modes of behavior used to arrest people on police raids into black communities and villages, principally in the South. The police would arrest people to gain the bail money or to provide free labor to agricultural establishments while the victim of the arrest worked off his sentence.[6]

The autonomy the police obtain through the victimless crime laws is enhanced by augmented obedience regulations. An officer's arbitrary ability to demand obedience and to charge disobedience has been deregulated, investing each officer with the power to require whatever level of obedience to himself that he desires. This gives an officer the ability to criminalize any person at will. He has simply to issue a command or handle a person in a way that will be disrespectful or humiliating to that person. Should the individual defend his or her dignity or self-respect, it can be interpreted as disobedience and charged as resisting. By provoking resistance to humiliation, the officer has the power to criminalize dignity or self-respect as "resisting arrest" and to "respond" to it with force (Rabb 2006). Though police manuals may describe the proper uses of force, it is left to the officer to determine the level of obedience desired from a detainee, for which force is then authorized.[7] In other words, the standards of obedience have been strengthened to the point of police impunity. A police department that sanctions profiling and impunity is arrogating a form of despotic governance to itself (D. Roberts 1997, 297). And since the criminalization of persons is the domain of the judiciary, police officers become judicial powers in and of themselves. That is, each officer becomes a law unto himself. This is, in effect, what impunity means.

All impunity is criminal because it makes people or police a law unto themselves, and thus outside and beyond constitutional law. It marks a lawlessness that has always been the ethos of white supremacy. Police impunity has constructed a despotic system of control over the racialized, at the same time imposing a security ideology on white society which produces the necessary solidarity with police violence and impunity in the name of defense against the "threat" posed by the criminalized. Forgotten is the fact that the original "threat" from which this emerged was that of racial equality, affirmative action, communal autonomy, and the like.

The substitution of police presumption before the fact (profiling) for a responsiveness to actual evidence of criminal activity after the fact (law enforcement) constitutes the contemporary structure of decriminalization of police harassment and routine brutality toward people of color. The victims of police profiling get redefined as "aggressors" through police impunity, in terms of which the police can then present themselves to white society as its social defense against a "problem." It is the same paradigm by which the slave patrols served to consolidate colonial society as white. This self-decriminalization through the criminalization of target individuals at will, and of entire communities through general harassment, has served to excuse and exonerate a long list of police officers who have killed black and brown persons. (See the Introduction, note 7.) It is a procedure that remains in routine operation in all U.S. cities, despite some protest, because the mythology of the police as honest and non-criminal legitimizes their criminalization of people of color in the public eye.

Judicial officialdom has ratified and legitimized police racial profiling through biased prosecutorial procedures. Black and brown people are routinely charged with felonies and plea bargained into prison (Taylor 2006) where white people would be charged with misdemeanors.[8] Black men are incarcerated at 6.5 times the rate of white men (Sabol, Minton, and Harrison 2007). People of color also get longer sentences for identical convictions— 49 percent higher for federal drug offenses (Meierhoefer 1992). The cocaine laws are the most overt example of this judicial bias. The sentence for possession of 100 grams of powder cocaine (used mostly in white communities) is five years; that for 5 grams of crack cocaine (used mainly in black and brown communities) is 20 years (Taylor 2006).[9]

The social effects of this judicial abuse are catastrophic yet familiar. Not only does felonization of a population ensure massive unemployment (a general tendency not to hire people with a record), but routine felony charges amount to systematic disenfranchisement (14 percent of black people by 1998, according to Fellner and Mauer 1998; see also Street 2003). Over the last 30 years, one out of every three black men under the age of 30 has been through the judicial system, according to Mauer and Young (1995), a rate that has not changed significantly since then, according to the Sentencing Project.[10] To continually remove a sizable number of people from a community in this way constitutes a massive disruption of its social coherence.[11] The aura of criminalization that police (with media collaboration) have overlaid on communities of color only serves to rationalize a disinvestment of capital. As a community gets the reputation for criminality, businesses close and leave, decreasing the possibilities for a communal economic life. A general financial obstruction of community asset accumulation ensues, leading to further impoverishment and misery. The "collateral damage" of this process is that crime itself actually becomes a major (if not the only) means of survival for those growing up under such forms of induced economic famine.

In addition, the criminalization of women has become a critical aspect of this repression of community. Women are the mortar that holds a community together. They are the conduits of cultural continuity, the base on which manhood, family, patriarchy, masculinism, artistic creativity, and class consciousness all build themselves as a superstructure (Federici 2004). Since 1990, the fastest-growing sector of the prison population in the United States has been women of color (Hazley 2001).

One could say that these target communities of color have essentially been embargoed. Two of the first institutions that decay under such an embargo are education and health care. In their absence, the community itself becomes a prison, its people disabled from escaping or organizing themselves to fight for self-determination and autonomy. That embargo, maintained by complex civil processes that do not have clearly overt manifestation (such as redlining), has the same effect as an international embargo, which is by treaty a crime against humanity. And of course, when a community is embargoed, so that the means of survival are curtailed, such a community, rife with poverty and unemployment, will become crime ridden and drug infested, with gang violence and petty crime. Against the petty crime, violence, and drug trafficking that emanates from such a situation, the police, continuing their assault on their victims under the cover of a defense of social "order," take on the role of an occupying army. Instead of lifting the embargo, society has instituted police rule.

This structure of police authority, against which civilians have little recourse, coupled with racial profiling, has effectively criminalized race (color). In effect, the police have substituted themselves for the color line. Through their autonomous operations, the police divide civil society into two groups, those racially profiled (racialized) and those not racially profiled (whites); that is, those whose humanity will be discounted and criminalized and those whose humanity will be respected. It amounts to a process of segregation, different in form from that of Jim Crow but with the same content and ethos. And it has funneled masses of people of color into the ultimate segregation of prison.

In sum, all the dimensions of white racialized identity under Jim Crow have been reconstructed in the wake of the civil rights movements, and the sanctity and coherence of white society have been reconstituted. This does not mean that many black and brown people have not climbed into positions of leadership or managerial status. Just as black politicians were able to function and represent the black communities of the northern cities during the Jim Crow era, so today white society is sufficiently reconsolidated to allow black politicians and media personalities to function at the national level, even to that of president.

The New Structure of Segregation

A history of the threats by which white society in the United States has constituted its cultural coherence needs to be written. The threat that worked in the wake of World War II was that of Soviet communism, institutionalized as the Cold War. It was in part for the purposes of the Cold War that the U.S. government began to foster the alleviation of Jim Crow, in order to polish its image as a free society internationally. The effect of the resulting civil rights movements was a more general upheaval that not only dispensed with segregation but threw out the Cold War ideology in its struggle to end U.S. intervention in Vietnam. At the end of the Vietnam War, it was whiteness that had to reconsolidate itself. While Black power and affirmative action were clearly recognizable to the white supremacist mind as threats to white coherence, a more pointed threat was needed to replace the defunct Cold War ideology for the mainstream.[12] This was the purpose of the war on drugs. It provided the crisis needed to legitimize the institution of police rule, a campaign to serve as the political background to police impunity and its reconstitution of segregation.

Police and government involvement in drug trafficking has been intimate and documented. Alfred McCoy (1991) wrote the first exposé of CIA involvement in heroin importation from Southeast Asia. Celerino Castillo (1994) has documented collaboration between Central American drug traffickers and the Drug Enforcement Administration, as has Peter Dale Scott (2003). Gary Webb (1998) wrote a well-researched exposé of the relation of cocaine trafficking in Los Angeles and the Contra war against the Sandinistas in Nicaragua, in which the CIA was shown to be involved. On June 19, 2008, the *San Francisco Chronicle* reported that since the beginning of Plan Colombia, a program to eradicate cocaine production in that country, coca production has risen 27 percent. The article also notes that the United States has knowledge of the tonnage of cocaine produced and exported here.[13] According to Catherine Austin Fitts (2001), drug trafficking in the United States at the end of the twentieth century amounted to roughly 10 percent of the GDP. The money is laundered inside the United States through electronic bank transfers, providing some nice capital for investors.

The "war on drugs" is a metaphoric war since a war cannot be fought against substances but only against people. Furthermore, this one occurs domestically rather than against a foreign power. It is euphemistically a war since it is fought by representatives of the law against people who, by law, are not permitted to fight back. It is a war carried on by imprisonment, a war of the government against its own people, signifying that the primary weapon in this war is the prison itself. And it is hypocritically a war since it deals with a situation the government itself has operated to create, complete with the proper denials. The devastation to people and communities that the prevalence and presence of drugs has wrought is all too real, however.

The benefits the police obtain from their involvement are extensive.[14] The most banal are, of course, monetary: the payoffs are enormous. Second, police connections to suppliers and pushers is perhaps just as important insofar as it provides a vast free informer network. Third, drugs tend to neutralize or disrupt the political and social coherence of a community (Webb 1998, 375). In the wake of the movements for self-determination and cultural autonomy of the 1960s and 1970s, the "stoning out" (as Gary Webb describes it) of such communities is of more than incidental interest to the police.[15]

But the fourth factor of benefit to the police is the misery of the people that leads them to turn to the drugs that are readily available. The presence of a drug market brings competition for control of that market and of the money generated by trafficking. People end up fighting each other, while the actual drugs produce strung-out and desperate individuals who turn to petty crime to maintain their drug consumption and to feed themselves. A tide of criminality emerges, confirming stereotypes of criminalization that had been created in advance. To stem this tide, police departments demand bigger appropriations from state legislatures. The resulting expansion over the years has made police departments the most powerful political forces in many urban areas (C. Parenti 1999; Martinot 2003a). That power is nationally coordinated and centralized through agencies created by the Law Enforcement Assistance Act, passed under the Nixon administration in 1973.

If there is a crime problem in the United States, the racializing operations of the police are at the core of it (not only as agents of its creation but because the de facto impunity of being a law unto themselves is of a criminal order). Racial oppression, impoverishment, imprisonment, and police impunity are all of a piece. Indeed, for most of white society, the increase in the prison population has become one of the arguments for further drug laws and racial profiling. Thus, the post–civil rights reconstitution of whiteness is a self-generating cycle. In the face of the criminalization of communities of color, more prisons are called for and built, again with a sense of cultural familiarity ("how else are we going to deal with crime?"), and those prisons then enhance the image of communities of color as criminal. Significantly, this is not perceived by and large as an extant injustice. It is the white consensus in solidarity with the police and prison industry that has allowed their untrammeled growth—a consensus whose content is white racialized identity.[16]

Three Eras

For those who remember Jim Crow, the sense of impunity that whites granted themselves as an ethic is wholly familiar. It was the thing that everyone took for granted, white, black, Native American, Chicano, everyone. And though the civil rights movements organized around real issues, such as voter registration, white impunity was their real target. That was the

astounding aspect of Robert Williams's movement in Monroe, North Carolina, or the Deacons for Defense and Justice, for instance. They armed
themselves as the only way to put that impunity in check. Now, since the
ethic of impunity has been shifted to the police, even those acts of self-
defense are criminalized.

What is special about an ethic of impunity is that it is both unbelievable
and familiar. Raw impunity is too uncivilized, so it gets disguised as law and
order. It hides too easily behind references to regulations and training manuals or excuses about "rogue" personnel. Once an ethic of impunity is able to
live under the cover of "law and order," it gains official sanction. And once
that happens, it trickles down to the population at large. Recall the dragging
death of Donald Byrd, or the torture of a black woman in a trailer by four
men, and other incidents whose racist dimension is evident. It is the familiarity of impunity that constitutes the core of its permissibility. The familiarity of the indictment of the black student in Jena who attempted to defend
himself is the mark of the machine that runs him down. Where does this
familiarity come from?

What justifies impunity and renders it familiar lurks in the cultural structure of the United States. It can be seen when we examine what is common
to the different eras of U.S. history, of which there are three. There is the
slavery era after the Revolution, the Jim Crow era after Emancipation and
the overthrow of Reconstruction, and the present post–civil rights era. To
see what is common to them, let us begin again with prisons.

Prison is the interface between the ethic of revenge, by which the judiciary operates, and the ethic of impunity, by which the white forces of
racialization operate. It is the icon and the model for segregation (we are
speaking about the United States; prisons exist in every nation, but they have
different meanings in different historical and cultural traditions), for which
"racism" is in turn the symbol. In the field of racialization, "racism" names
the confluence of the ethic of revenge and the ethic of impunity—revenge
against the mere existence of people of color, and impunity in enforcing the
rules of segregation. In both dimensions, white supremacy sees itself as acting defensively—defense against the transgression involved in racial equality,
and defense of its enactment of those "rules." If prison is the material manifestation or extension of both ethics, and the machinery of "defense" of both,
then it serves as the concrete institutionality of what "racism" only names.
Racism cannot be understood without addressing the confluence of the
ethics of imprisonment, revenge, and impunity.

Prison plays a central role in each era. In the present era, it is the context
in which police impunity and profiling do their segregating work. It valorizes
the criminalization of color accomplished by racial profiling, and it concret-

izes the performance of the police in their role as a reconstructed "color line." During the Jim Crow era, prison and the chain gang were the institutions that guarded the usury by which black rural laborers were held in debt servitude. And it served as an institution by which black prisoners were distributed between labor for the state and labor on plantations (see note 6). And finally, the slave system itself, being forced labor in its rawest form, can be seen as a prison system, and the slave's labor as prison labor. Indeed, the advantage of doing so is that it replaces the egregious pretension that it is possible to own a person and shows that to be mere (legalist) rhetoric. One cannot own a human being; otherwise one would not have to go to great lengths to prevent runaways or torture the person into obedience. To own something means it stays put under one's hand or one's ownership deed. Whites can rhetorically refer to bond-laborers as property because the laborer can be transferred from one person to another in exchange for money. But this only signifies that the alleged concept of ownership is a juridical relationship between whites and not a relation between an owner and a bond-laborer. Nevertheless, that metaphor of ownership marks the entire system by which white society defined itself.

These three forms of prison operation—as forced labor, the distribution of labor, and the reconstruction of segregation—constitute the center of the common structure of social domination of black people by white supremacy. In each era, the form of the prison changed because the form of racialization changed. And the form of racialization changed because U.S. society confronted a call for equality and democracy, which it resisted by reasserting white supremacy through complex campaigns of reracialization.

Each of the three eras begins with a document that calls the nation to an ethic of equality and justice. The first was the Declaration of Independence, the second the Emancipation Proclamation, and the third *Brown vs. Board of Education*. Under the aegis of each document, an anti-racist movement formed that took the document seriously and fought for the principles it enunciated. During the first era, there was a movement for the abolition of slavery; in the second, a broad support for the Reconstruction governments and the ethos of full citizen participation (black and white); and in the third, a mass civil rights upheaval against segregation to institute enfranchisement and opportunity for all. And in each era, the particular pro-democracy and pro-equality movement that arose was defeated.

The first era saw the rise of a powerful abolitionist movement. Its first successes were the outlawing of slavery or the provision for emancipation in the northern states in the 1780s and 1790s (in particular, in Pennsylvania, New York, and Massachusetts), either through court decision or state constitutional provision (Bennett 1969; Litwack 1961). But by the 1830s, a white supremacist populism had divided abolitionism against itself, into a "respect-able" and a radical wing. A major fraction of the movement shifted its atten-tion from the question of slavery's existence to toleration if it was not extended to the new territories. Slavery's extension became the issue of a regional struggle for hegemony in the federal government between the North and the South. In the process, the "respectable" (mainstream) elements of abolition-ism were led to compromise on the principle of equality and to accept the principle of disenfranchisement of free black people (Kraditor 1989).

Just as abolitionism faced a reactionary white populism (Martinot 2003b, 91, 107) as well as an obsessive political opposition from the plantation elite in the South, so Reconstruction confronted a white populist reaction from the beginning, involving the landowners, the media, violent para-military gangs, and the "defrocked" political leaders of the Confederacy and the Democratic Party. A campaign to overthrow the multiracial governments in the southern states began from the very inception of Reconstruction, led by white people who already had the principles of resegregation in hand. After the overthrow, they built the Jim Crow system through laws passed over a period of decades, accompanied by continual terrorism and violence against any people who defended the Reconstruction experiment.[17]

The present era has seen the defeat of the civil rights movements through a similar confluence of political forces, including government operations, the media, white populism, and police impunity. In the face of demands to end discrimination, the government established avenues for suing those accused of discriminating. Although this looked like a victory against racism at the beginning, it quickly became clear that anti-discrimination laws and equal opportunity agencies had the more profound effect of fragmenting the social movements and the communities that had brought them into existence and supported them. One sues in court as an individual; the collective politi-cal character of the movements was atomized by the individuating nature of court proceedings. The political energy of the movements began to collapse. Community demands for economic development were co-opted by govern-ment funding of social projects, creating a dependency on government money for those projects while not providing the capital for community economic development. And those social projects were eventually disrupted when the funding was turned off. It was in this context of movement atomi-zation that a white populism grew and provided the base for repeal of affir-mative action programs, as well as support for the police profiling and impu-nity from which the present vast prison industry developed.

Each era also witnessed the ideological twisting or warping of a central democratic principle held by the specific pro-democratic movement of the time so that it could be used against that movement. Against abolitionism, the Declaration's proclamation of "all men" was reinterpreted to mean only "all white men." The equality of citizenship implicit in Emancipation and the amendments that codified it was shunted into a rhetorical notion of "separate but equal." And the present era's attempt to rectify past discriminatory injustice through the institution of affirmative action programs was inverted to read "reverse discrimination."

That twisting of principle also reflected changes in the symbolization of "race" itself and how racialization is conceptualized. Not only have "minority" status and criminalization become the central symbols of contemporary exclusionism and inequality, replacing the overt modes of inferiorization of Jim Crow, but the resegregation produced by police and judicial impunity has been camouflaged by the legalist rhetoric of "colorblindness." Originating in court proceedings and new legal doctrine, the language of colorblindness presents itself as a way of proceeding with racialization without speaking about race.

If each era found a different way to reconstruct the social institutionalities of reracialization (prison, impunity, racial exclusionism) to undo the pro-democratic forces that sought to end the anti-democracy of white supremacy, each needed to involve the actions of the state in the context of a white supremacist populism. The reconstruction of the cohesion of a culture of whiteness, and the fostering of a form of anti-democracy, required the activity of both. In the context of state sanction of its activities, that populism could see exclusionism as democracy, impunity as justice, and prison as the symbol of social stability and cultural cohesion.

Goldberg (in the *Racial State*) focuses on how the state uses social control to maintain social homogeneity and, in meeting the self-proclaimed threat to it and to governance in general posed by heterogeneity, posits the "ethnoracial" other as a source of heterogeneity in order to counteract it (Goldberg 2002, 15). For instance, against the pro-democratic demands of the civil rights movements, which in Goldberg's terms would valorize heterogeneity itself in its multiculturalism, the state has intervened to reestablish a process of reracialization. In effect, the state that proclaims itself democratic engages in this essentially anti-democratic function. But with respect to the patterns of resurgence of white supremacy, there is more happening than a state guarantee of homogeneity.

In sum, for each era, it took decades to reestablish the anti-democratic institutions of racialization and to restore a system of social norms familiar to white racialized identity. For each era, reconstruction of a coherent white society involved similar social constructions: segregation, an obsession with incarceration, a decriminalization of the state and its populist context through criminalization of the racialized, and a warping of pro-democratic principles into an anti-democratic program. In this repetition of structures and political conditions across the three eras produced by pro-democratic moments of U.S. history, a general cultural process suggests itself. It suggests that the state as well as individuals and social institutions obtain their meanings and their ethics from the underlying structure of racialization. Though the concept of race can change with each social transformation, and thus transform the substance of what Goldberg would call homogeneity (and there is even a homogeneity to the white co-optation of the idea of multiculturalism [Goldberg 2002, 221–222]), the effect is the same.

During the first era, race was posited as a natural and untranscendable difference, which, in Jefferson's terms, meant the two peoples should live apart if both were free (Jefferson 1964, ch. 14). Even Lincoln upheld this notion in his debates with Stephen Douglas in 1856. After the Civil War, during which there had been a mass escape of slaves from the plantations to the Union army camps, together with the subsequent Reconstruction experiments, the concept of "innate difference" withered under its own patent irrationality. Race was then conceptualized as a cultural difference, not of capacity but of kind, for which the notion of cultural "progress" toward white norms and standards of civilization was articulated. Even the eugenics movement, with its genocidal desires, admitted to this shift of racial paradigm by focusing on individual cases for elimination rather than whole groups. Since the civil rights movements, race has been understood as a social construct, a social invention for the purposes of oppression. In that light, many white people think that it can simply be de-invented, rendered non-existent through "colorblindness," eliminating the oppression by eliminating the raciality of the oppression (Goldberg 2002, 222). This is the meaning of the Obama election for many whites; race and racism have been overcome. If Obama could make it, then the impoverishment of black or brown communities and the enormity of the prison industry must be a failure on the part of other black and brown people. White society and white people can claim to have nothing to do with it.

Some Questions

If a social process of racialization produces "race" differently at different times, then what is the actual nature of the "race" produced? There is, first of all, the structural commonality of the white supremacist resurgence in each era. There is a domain of ethics that renders the impunity that characterizes that resurgence both permissible and familiar. And there is a comfort in the familiarity that governs the violence and brutality by which the cultural cohesion of white society is reestablished. The criminalization of its victims and of the anti-racist activists of each era (e.g., abolitionists as subversive, anti–Jim Crow whites as race traitors, civil rights activists as communists) becomes the means of decriminalizing that brutality, rendering it acceptable if not virtuous. From within the very structure of this repeated warped logic, the question arises, what is it about the process of racialization that U.S. society cannot do without?

History teaches us that the forms of segregation, the outlawing of mixed relationships, the criminalization of entire peoples, the impoverishment and disenfranchisement of communities, all of which represent forms of social control—control over sexuality, control over personal freedom, control over economic sustainability, control over political involvement—will re-emerge in new forms of racialization each time the hegemony of white supremacy and the coherence of white culture are called into question. We see these elements of racialization emerging today in the campaign around "illegal" immigrants, not for the purpose of ejecting them from the country, since most are needed to do the work they do (mostly in construction and agricultural labor), but to keep them in place (Bacon 2008). Yet they are labeled "illegal" to present them as a threat. A vast white populism is generated to support their exclusion from humanitarian considerations, from social welfare, from driver's licenses, from education and health services, as a form of white solidarity defending itself against their trespass. (We look more carefully at this immigration in Chapter 5.) Violence is committed against them by the Minutemen populists or through ICE raids and arrests,[18] as well as border harassment that results in hundreds dying in the desert or being warehoused in indefinite detention. But conveniently, it is never enough to put a dent in the labor supply they constitute for certain U.S. industries.

In opposition to the inherent social autocracy the constant resurgence of white supremacy represents, the movements against both structural and institutional racism that have been initiated by the three historical documents mentioned, in their recurrent call to equality and justice, all present themselves as necessarily pro-democracy movements. Regardless of how autonomous they may have sought to be, they are inclusionary in standing in opposition to the coloniality of white supremacy. Their local struggles for rights and participation against the monopoly of white political institutions imply an undreamt-of form of direct democracy. Yet their pro-democracy project keeps getting stymied by familiar modes of exclusion, stereotyping,

and disenfranchisement. Every attempt by anti-racist movements to democratize social institutions, such as schools, health facilities, or welfare agencies, have met with institutional obstacles that are indistinguishable from
repression (Piven and Cloward 1977). These destinies, imposed by white
supremacy and its anti-democratic sense of entitlement, ever reconfigured
by the coloniality of power, have led many people to ask again, what is the
nature of whiteness and white supremacy that even in the face of the pro-
democratic ethics of the civil rights movements, it must keep coming back
and reasserting itself?

3

A Structural Concept of Race

The Recurrent Problem of Race

The question arises again and again: what is the nature of "race" that whiteness and white supremacy must keep returning and reconstituting its institutions of racialization? Race as a concept and a social structure has bequeathed us a difficult and horror-ridden history. For 300 years, it has presented itself as a machine of oppression, a political issue, a line drawn in the sand between citizen and non-citizen, and a central element in the struggle between pro-democracy and anti-democracy. How could we not know what race is?

Each time there has been an attempt to throw off the oppression of racism and white supremacy, a new concept of race and a new process of racialization has appeared. Its source is not something inherent in people. It occurs through the intervention of the state. Yet it is accepted by white people as a cultural structure of great familiarity. Though every call to eliminate racism has been a call to substitute a sense of "humanity" for the criminalities and dehumanizations of racialization, each call seems to get turned around by white supremacy, so that even the sense of "humanizing" gets reracialized. Whiteness keeps reappearing and thrusting itself on society as a "transcendental norm" (Yancy 2008).

·As shown in Chapter 2, after the civil rights movements threw off Jim Crow and placed the question of equality at the top of the political agenda, a new sense of racialization, a new style of racism and racial discrimination, and a new concept of race crept onto the social stage. Despite civil rights laws, despite disposal of the hypothesis that "race" was inherent, and despite millions of people trampling the old symbology of race into the ground under their feet, a new symbology emerged. One heard about it from the difficulty well-dressed respectable-looking black people had getting a taxi. One wondered about it as jokes and complaints multiplied about that new traffic violation, Driving While Black, to the point where it ceased to be a joke (see Chapter 2, note 4). One wondered about the universal occurrence of plain-clothes security guards following black and brown shoppers in supermarkets and department stores. One wondered about it as the number of black and brown prisoners rose and the United States built the largest prison system in the world. As the stories of torture in police stations, cries of forced confessions, and police beatings on the street (which amount to state-sanctioned torture) multiplied to the point where they could not be kept out of the media, one wondered what it was about race that this country could not seem to do without.

Previous anti-racist movements had attempted to undermine the idea that whites had special status and that their white skin privilege was both unearned and artificial. White people were informed that they too were a race and could claim no special status on that basis. But that proved to be an insufficient argument. For whites to think that they too were a race only valorized the concept of race as whites had invented it and allowed them to pretend that it had a foundation in something natural. It also places the relation of races on a horizontal plane, while the process of racialization that whites impose on others is by that token hierarchical, a vertical system of domination. Many whites have hidden their awareness of their hierarchical status from themselves by trying to think of themselves as simply human— which, in a white supremacist social context, is itself a form of white skin privilege, a luxury, as Yancy has pointed out, accompanying white hegemony (Yancy 2008, 44). It too is just another attempt to substitute the horizontal for the vertical. On the horizontal plane, one has simply to call for the tolerance of difference to stand in opposition to racism and its violence. To make a vertical hierarchy appear horizontal eclipses the oppression inherent in racism and elides the benefit, and indeed, the identity, the racializers receive from the process. It locates race where it is not, and does not locate it where it is.

In the context of race's pretended horizontality, it was thought that understanding race as a social construct in a political sense would be a step forward. If race had no basis in objective fact, then its only basis could be social discourse. But that conceptualization of race is also insufficient. It brings with it a certain simplicity. It allows some people to conclude that race does not exist at all, and if it does not exist, then nobody is a racist, since there is no "race" to hold against another person. But this again represents a white opportunism, escaping responsibility for what white supremacy has done in the name of its invention.

Black thinkers have long argued against the idea of the naturalness of the racial division (thinkers such as David Walker, Hubert Harrison, and Lucy Parsons). They tried reason, logic, and calls to humanity. It was only more recently, when a number of white thinkers (such as Ashley Montagu, Lilian Smith, and Gunnar Myrdal) offered their refutations, however, that the idea of race's naturalness began to dissolve for many white people. (Even the critiques of race are racialized.) Appalled by the criminality and the cruelty of white supremacy, they wrote about the irrationality and baselessness of the entire concept. They hoped that if one could show the concept of race to be fallacious and empty, white racism would see itself as without foundation and disappear.[1]

But it is not the alleged naturalness of the distinctions or differences that provide whites with their hegemonic position; it is their power to define. It is the hegemonic status of their thinking that determines the character that the field of races will take. One sees this in the white conception of multiculturalism (which differs from the multiculturality asserted by people of color). When people of color advance the concept, it is as a demand for inclusion, not in whiteness but in the society dominated by white exclusionism. But for whites, multiculturalism is not an alternative to white hegemony since it does not dissolve the exclusionist purity condition on which whiteness is constructed. When whites advance the idea of multiculturalism, it is to include the white exclusionism of their purity condition within the inclusionism of the multiculturalist concept. What people of color are telling white people is to back off from the hegemonics of their exclusionism by accepting the multiculturalist ethic. When white people include themselves as white, with their exclusionist purity concept intact, it is precisely their social hegemony they are refusing to abandon. Multiculturalism gets lost in the oxymoronics of including an exclusionism.

Those anti-racist whites who support the promise of democracy that multiculturalism holds out find the chaos generated by their desire to include their whiteness disconcerting and even unfathomable. Perhaps it is because they remain unaware of the exclusionism of the purity concept they seek to include with themselves. In that case, the reality they are not recognizing is the inseparability of the hegemonic mind and whiteness. To gain an awareness of the (their own) "hegemonic mind," since it is a manifestation of power, and of the power to define, white people would have to go beyond the notion of race as a social construct.

For any concept of race to truly represent the reality of racialization, it would have to include the verticality of the racial hierarchy and point to whites as the constructors of that hierarchy, that is, as the racializers. The racial differences between so-called races remains subsidiary to the difference between whites as racializers and the others whites have racialized, precisely because it is whites who produce those racializations. It is that difference that continually bestows on white people an interest in maintaining the social processes of hierarchical racialization. It is that difference which renders the social processes of racialization acceptable, while at the same time renewing the notion that racial divisions are natural (and therefore horizontal). It is the paradoxicality of white racializing logic which indicates that merely understanding the inventedness or constructedness of race is inadequate for comprehending the force of its resurgence, the desire of white people not to just be human but to be humanity.

In other words, there is more to fight for than humanity in seeking to replace the social system of racial categorizations that whiteness has foisted on the world. And there is more to fight against than merely the effects of racism on its victims. For a person to be white, other whites have to be able to apply that designation to them. That makes it a question of "membership" and of a social group that demands allegiance to itself. We who are anti-racist have to take seriously the fact that in opposing racism, we are opposing a cultural structure that not only divides us into races but serves primarily to unite white people in an exclusionary socius. To oppose racism is to oppose that unification and its anti-democratic solidarity. To be anti-racist for a white person means to break allegiance to whiteness, to abjure the purity concept on which it is based, and to stand opposed to the persistence of a social identity, that is, white racialized identity. In other words, it means to renounce one's membership in the white socius precisely because of its basis in the purity concept and its exclusionary ethic.

The question becomes how a white person who does not think he or she is doing anything to produce race can come to see his or her own actions, and those of others, insofar as they obey the underlying structure of racialization, so that the ethics of white hegemonics or domination engaged in the process of racialization can be discerned, discarded, and replaced by a pro-democracy ethics. This is not only the question of what "race" is but also the question of how we are even to apprehend a cultural structure as such.

Assessing the Problem of Race Philosophically

In light of this, the civil rights era itself becomes a historical conundrum. How was it possible that it did not result in a social climate in which racism was no longer ethically viable? If racism was a symptom of a racializing system like Jim Crow, and Jim Crow was ostensibly eliminated, why did the racial discriminations and prejudices not go away? What did we not understand about race and racism that it persisted? How did the Civil Rights movement become a ghost of itself, a mist of social change behind which new forms of racialized segregation (profiling, prisons, impunity, and disenfranchisement) appeared?

These questions have made new philosophizations of race necessary. The philosophical work becomes all the more urgent to the extent the political struggle can be seen as insufficient. A number of philosophical approaches have emerged in recent years. Robert Bernasconi (2001) has compiled some of the more significant texts on the question from the last 200 years. Lucius Outlaw (1996) has collected essays on race from various traditional philosophical perspectives. Lawrence Blum (2002) has written a book about "racism" in which he argues that it should be considered only in moral terms. Anna Stubblefield (2005) has responded by arguing that this is quite insufficient politically or historically—and thus morally inadequate. William Julius Wilson (1980) has argued sociologically for the "Declining Significance of Race," and Cornel West (1993) has answered that "Race Matters." Critical Race Theory has expanded on the idea of "social construct" (Crenshaw 1995). And Leonard Harris (1999) has compiled a volume in which he compares the two most prominent modes of philosophizing "race." David Roediger (1991), Charles Mills (1997), Theodore Allen (1996, 1997), Lewis Gordon (1995), Linda Bell (Bell and Blumenfeld 1995), Joy James (1996), Ruth Frankenberg (1993), Linda Alcoff (2006), George Yancy (2004b), Alexander Saxton (1971), and Noel Ignatiev (1995) have spearheaded a large effort to research the meaning of whiteness and how to combat the racial hierarchy and the many forms of oppression it conditions.

All of them, appearing 30 years after the civil rights movements, are bellwethers testifying to the fact that new forms of segregation have been developed and institutionalized and a new symbology of race has emerged to serve white supremacist ends. The ghosts of segregation not only still haunt us; they continue to dominate social and political policy. The new symbology embraces the fact that there are black generals, black cabinet members, and now a black president, all in the presence of increasing school segregation, racialized tracking of students, continuing neighborhood segregation, and black unemployment twice that of whites. If the police have come to reembody the color line, as I argue in Chapter 2, are they impersonating a ghost, or are they the avatar for a structure that simply went into hiding while black and brown people attempted to democratize the nation?

Let us take a look at the major dimensions of this new movement to philosophize race. Two approaches are prominent. They call themselves the objectivist view and the constructivist view. The objectivist view holds that there are objective differences between people, some of which are reflected in biological differences and some of which emerge from geographical origins. Though all humans exist in the same species, these differences reflect millennia of distinct adaptations to disparate global regions. What these differences do not imply is a hierarchy of social status or a social meaning inherent in those objective differences. In short, the objectivists argue, the concept of race exists because it makes reference in some fashion to real differences that precede it as a concept.

The constructivist view holds that the physical and biological differences that exist between people, though they or their ancestors originated in different regions of the planet, are wholly contingent and without inherent meaning. Under the skin, there are no differences. We all have the same capabilities, potentialities, and desires, and are subject to the same propensities to believe, to invent, to reason, and to evolve forms of community. Race, this view holds, is constructed as a disequalizing overlay on an inherent equality; its inherent meaning is the formation of hierarchies of domination whose strata are symbolized (or signified) by physical traits that are then appropriated and deployed as a racializing language. If color, for instance, becomes a central system of signifiers for race, then the terms for color, when used to refer to race, are used not descriptively but as socially categorizing instruments instead.

White supremacy, for instance, by nature and by definition, is objectivist. It claims that the white race is naturally superior and that whiteness is the mark or measure of that superiority. Other races, on the white supremacist account, fall short of white rationality, the autonomy of white subjectivity, and the ability to build or control social organization. For the white supremacist, a mixture of "blood," for instance, which means having a foreparent of color, is a corruption of the purity of white raciality and its inherent superiority. White racism, as the quotidian expression of white supremacy, is thus also objectivist. And racism, we should note, it is not simply an expression of prejudice or discrimination; it gains the power to be prejudicial and discriminatory from the social matrix of white supremacy that breeds it. In other words, white supremacy is also expert at ignoring the fact that it has historically imposed its rule on others by arrogating the power to define who others are.

White anti-racism must be, by nature and by definition, constructivist. For white people to abjure their hierarchical position, to refuse to assume white skin privilege, to reject it where they can, and to do battle with their own "hegemonic mind" as the manifestation of having been inculcated with supremacy as white, they would have to affirm that no aspect of supremacy was inherent in whiteness, and that all aspects were refusable or refutable. John Brown, in his hatred of slavery, saw the slave system as the instrument by which differences between white and black had been constructed. For Theodore Allen, a knowledge of the history of race is the history of its construction by whites.

But there is also an anti-racist objectivism. For many black thinkers, the objectivist viewpoint provides the possibility of thinking of race, and of reappropriating one's own racialization autonomously, for themselves—not as a compensatory mechanism but as an oppositionality totally distinct from a white point of view. Black objectivism argues for a solidarity to Blackness within an anti-colonialist framework that at once contests and refutes the white construction of blackness (and there is a similar call by Latinos to solidarity around *Latinidad,* or Native Americans around indigeneity, and other comparable forms of ethnic or racial solidarity issuing from the prior condition of having been colonized).

Albert Mosley, among others, argues for understanding the worldwide emergence, conjunction, alliance, and ideal of Africans in commonality as a single heroic vision of an anti-colonialist African race, a vast worldly African presence aware of itself as objectively African. It is a sense of African presence that began to stand forth in opposition to the nineteenth-century wave of European colonialism in Africa. As a vision, it also informed DuBois's thinking and his identification of a common African continent-wide, Atlantic-wide, and worldwide unity (Mosley 1999, 75). In his view, African unity resides in common descent, history, memory, and condition of having suffered the same "disaster and insult." For DuBois, it forms a common "kinship" for all the "children of Africa," deploying the concept of kinship as more than metaphoric for an African race (DuBois 1940, 116). But it goes beyond simply a sense of an "anti-colonialist race." Through the struggles against Jim Crow in the United States, the Negritude movement in Europe, and the African national liberation revolutions after World War II, this common kinship in Africa presented the world with a global entity, a melding together of those who had been scattered and dragged to the far corners of the colonialist system. That is, concomitant to "kinship" as an Africanist background, there was the kinship in struggle which constituted a politics of Blackness that participated in discerning that background. It was a common kinship that emerged from recognizing the implacability of the colonialist enemy, from the starvation, torture, and apartheid suffered from Algeria to South Africa, to the police brutality and police occupation of Black communities in U.S. cities.

Mosley adds to his vision a meditation on African philosophy, as reflective of an inherent psychology and world view (Mosley 1999, 84). For him, the rise of an Africanist consciousness is not the same thing as an African consciousness. When African solidarity bestowed a political existence on a racialized group in motion, it also expressed an underlying Africanist origin that had never been undone by transport, migration, or redefinition. African people could recognize each other as a people of common descent because they had all been told the same thing about the way they looked. What they did, in appropriating for themselves their African origin, was turn the way they looked into the way they looked at each other, a commonality of past and future.

Since white objectivism defines black people as deviating from the white account of agency and subjectivity while Black objectivism understands and encounters black people irrevocably as agents and subjects for themselves, Black objectivism and white (supremacist) objectivism are incommensurable. In other words, objectivism cannot be generalized to a point that no longer takes account of its own racialization.

Between the worldwide common descent that DuBois celebrated and the sense of Africanist consciousness that threads its way through traditional African thinking, more than a social construction emerges. It is a sense of descent that transcends politics, embracing all—those who had struggled uncompromisingly and succeeded, those who had stepped too far ahead in their revolutionism, and those who had stopped short in their struggles and opportunistically betrayed the process of liberation through a reconciliation with colonialism.

It was to this anti-colonialist race of Africanity that DuBois turned as a source of opposition to colonialism. Yet he necessarily oscillated back and forth between the raciality of Blackness and the politics of Blackness. He inhabits the former as a perspective in his book *Dusk of Dawn,* for instance, and he inhabits the latter in his novel *Dark Princess.* But to place the enemy's recalcitrance at the center of one's own being, to objectivize the colonist's evil as a source of self-objectivization, is to place oneself at the interface between self-construction as objectivist and the objectivism wrenched and appropriated from the colonialist construction of Africans and Africa (Mosley 1999, 75).

In that sense, DuBois is an example of the difficulty of living a clean disjunction between anti-racist objectivism and constructivism. Indeed, though their adherents may think that the two schools of thought are divided with little or no common measure, if we look closely, we can see that the difference is perhaps ephemeral and that we need both.

Objectivism and Constructivism

Leonard Harris's book (1999) places this entire question into useful confrontation. (And in the context of there being both a supremacist and an anti-racist objectivism, as we have seen, it is important to note that Harris is a black philosopher and an objectivist.) He organizes the book as a kind of forum for these two modes of theorizing. The important question facing the participants in this forum is, what does "race" mean? What is the reality of the issue in the first place? Is "race" a biological reality that has conditioned the way society has categorized people, or is it a social reality that has used biology as a way of legitimizing itself? If it is a biological reality, then why are the relations of "races" not the same in every country? And if it is a social reality among other hierarchical relations of social oppression, why does it need to mythify itself as biological?

These are serious philosophical questions, each with profound political import—though ordinary people who live the social reality to which they refer, and know these questions in their bones because they live them, might think they were somewhat frivolous. Is it not frivolous to take the inane irrationality that some people use to excuse their oppression of others and fill books full of endless thinking and debate about it? Ultimately, it is not, if that thinking is necessary not only to know but to articulate, to bring up out of one's bones, what one really confronts and how to configure and organize one's confrontation with it. The philosophical theorization of a complicated issue (and the complexity of race is demonstrated endlessly in the shape-shifting it exhibits from place to place and era to era) is what provides the language by which one can take what one knows (in one's bones) and stand it in the light of day and in the call to solidarity. Real political unity can form around only what can be stated and projected as program; it is populism that congeals around the unstated, or what is taken for granted. To combat injustice, mere solidarity is insufficient. The multiplicity of perspectives on the complexity of race need to be able to talk to one another, and for that they need a common language. Feeling something in one's bones is the first step, but only the first step. Answering the question "what does 'social reality' mean?" is a necessary second step if different people within the same society can see what they call "social reality" differently.

With respect to the two philosophical approaches to race already named (constructivism and objectivism), we are dealing with distinct schools of thought that, for Harris, are irreconcilable. That is, they are irreconcilable for him, since he gives irreconcilable definitions for them. For the objectivist, races are natural divisions in the human species based on some inherent objective trait (biological, psychological, geographical). The objectivist, he says, "can believe that there are groups, such as races, which exist independent of cultural and social ideas . . . [and] can consider racial groups as objective causal agents, that is, [that] race causes groups to exist" (L. Harris 1999, 18). The constructivist, on the other hand, "does not believe that groups exist independent of cultural or social ideas, . . . [and] can believe that races are constructed causal agents" (L. Harris 1999, 19). For the constructivist, races are "unnatural," culturally specific, and based on self-descriptions and social psychologies that are peculiar to the specific culture in which a particular concept of race resides; that is, race has no prior determined or determining definition and thus can change from culture to culture.

Harris's definitions are somewhat curious. He juxtaposes ambiguity with a definitional "absoluteness" in a somewhat eccentric manner. First, he phrases the fundamental or definitive moment of both objectivism and constructivism in terms of possibility—that the adherents of each school "can believe" what they do, suggesting that they do not necessarily have to. And then he ties those possible beliefs (or disbeliefs) to "ideas" that are seen as inhabiting a certain absolute determinate domain. For Harris, constructivists believe that human facts are "absolutely" dependent on contingent cultural ideas, as if to bestow on the process (of construction) a rigidity or inflexibility that he spares objectivism. That is, he reserves a certain sense of fluidity for objectivism. Objectivists "can argue [have choice in how they approach things] that the uses of racial categories are justified because they refer to objective realities," a possibility of choice he denies constructivists. That is, constructivists believe "the use of racial categories is never justified" referentially (that is, they have no choice in the matter). Absoluteness appears on the side of constructivism whereas fluidity, strategies, and tactics pertain to objectivism (L. Harris 1999, 443). One would think that it would be the other way around, with absoluteness pertaining to objects and the hardness of objectivity. But Harris admits he is (dare I say "constructs himself as"?) a "moderate" objectivist (L. Harris 1999, 442).

This confrontation of objectivism and constructivism, in which each sees the other as irreconcilable across the act of reference to race, has been around for a while. Anna Stubblefield describes one of its earlier bouts in her account of the now famous debate between Kwame Anthony Appiah and Lucius Outlaw (Stubblefield 2005, 70–98).[2] Appiah is an objectivist who argues that race (objectively) does not exist, meaning that no real reference can be made to it as such. Outlaw is a constructivist who argues that although race is a differentiation between people that is socially produced, one can make real reference to races insofar as they have been constructed.

There is a convenience to dividing philosophical positions in this manner, as Harris does. It provides a clear-cut distinction (like the difference between materialism and idealism). Indeed, it is reminiscent of that old philosophical dispute, which for two centuries has appeared in the pages and arguments and meeting halls of organizations from hard-line socialists to academic colloquia. For instance, is the exploitative nature of some social relations (such as the relation of capital to labor) real, having objective existence independent of the mind that thinks about it, or do those relations attain their sense of being exploitative only because consciousness sees them in a particular way? One is a materialist account of exploitation, that exploitation exists in the system of relations of production independent of the mind, and the other is an ideal account of it, wholly dependent on how those relations are conceived or defined. The irreconcilability between these philosophical positions then extends to issues of morality, philosophy, and culture.

But why would a clear-cut distinction in how race is conceived be necessary or desirable, and for whom? There are constructivists who argue that though race is socially constructed, it is not simply an idea; rather, it is produced by a complex process of economic, cultural, and social evolution in response to real historical factors.[3] Under Harris's definitions, the question of the "real" materials out of which race was constructed, including the structures and operations of power, could not be asked. Such a question would imply an underlying objective reality (though not a biological one) to which racial entities as constructed would make real reference. As Harris proclaims, "constructivists deny that races can exist as natural or objective entities" (L. Harris 1999, 20).

Perhaps the objectivists have to cleanly dissociate themselves from constructivism in order to define (against Appiah [L. Harris 1999, 267]) what "real reference" would mean. That is, when we refer to something, what are we really doing? And Appiah was able to make the argument he does because he restricts the domain of the referent to a very narrow arena (the bio-physiological). But hierarchies are socially real, and one can refer to them using a variety of terminologies to name the different strata of the hierarchy. When racial terms are used to refer to different social strata in a hierarchy, they engage in a real form of reference. In other words, the real issue, in the dispute between objectivism and constructivism, is reference, and not race. Objectivists argue that race has to exist as a real referent to serve a social purpose whereas some constructivists argue that the concept of race as constructed already serves (indeed, emerges out of) a social purpose (materially).

The Historicity of the Difference

To raise the issue of reference and the question of social purpose brings an additional issue with it, that of history. History has been one of the dimensions of this discussion of race all along. We live in a culture (the United States) in which the notions of whiteness and white supremacy are not simply produced in the moment but involve the historical idea of a "white nation." This idea begins with Benjamin Franklin in 1751 and in its vast trajectory includes the proclamation of a white nation in the Immigration Act of 1790, the Dred Scott decision of 1857 denying Black citizenship, and the need for constitutional amendments to give black people citizenship after the Civil War. The implication of this history is that the United States and its culture were produced by whiteness and supremacy. Whiteness and white supremacy are the very bedrock and foundation of its political, economic, social, and cultural structures.[4] Navigating the question of justice in the United States becomes a real problem, owing to its racialization. On the one hand, there is an inherent absence of any sense of justice in the incorrigible exclusionism exercised by whites toward non-whites, barring them from full participation. And on the other, contesting this exclusionism, there is the implicit and explicit demand for justice in the philosophizations of race under consideration here. In addition, it is precisely the extreme noticeability of Barack Obama's election as the first black president that marks the ineluctable continuation of that historical exclusionism. Were that exclusionism not extant, his victory would have been just another presidential election.

But history does strange things to the distinction between objectivism and constructivism. The colonialist conquest of the Americas is a story of whites constructing race and racial identities for themselves. By imposing racial definitions on Africans and Native Americans, the colonists sought to engender "fundamental" differences between themselves and the Africans and Native Americans. In producing this relationality, Europeans acted like constructivists, producing Africans and Native Americans in otherness as objectively real groups, to which a subhumanity could be attached (constructed) and then perceived there (objectively). By giving transcendental and transhistorical values to a real "us-not-them" paradigm, whites then saw the dehumanization they imposed on the others as providing "objective" testimony for a "real" subhumanity. It is in this sense that "whites" "do" race, as a social act (of exclusion and noticing the other as excluded, of "othering" and noticing the other as other). That is, whiteness is a performance of racializing activity. Nevertheless, insofar as whites have arrogantly superiorized themselves by these means, the white "objectivist" perspective emerges from its historical mists as something whites *constructed* for themselves, for which those they racialized were the means.

On the other hand, Africans and Native Americans discovered themselves having been constructed as objective groups by colonialist occupation. That is, their racialization at the hands of colonialism rendered them objectivist despite themselves (having to grasp and appropriate their raciality in their need for defense against the imposition of an "objective" raciality on them) and constructivist against themselves (seeing themselves made into conquered, victimized, and marginalized people).

The constructivists would say that race was not something discovered among people (for instance, among those colonized by Europeans); the objectivists would say that when Europeans discovered the difference, what they were looking at was race. When European colonialists then defined race (the constructivists would say that they "invented" it, and the objectivists would amend that to read "invented it referentially") to legitimize their theft of land and kidnapping of people for forced labor, they did so from a position of power. "Racialization" (the construction or appearance of people as divided into races) amounted to a complex socio-political act in the interests of power.

How can race exist if it was invented-or-discovered as a socio-political strategy? How can race not exist if that strategy has had the effect of enslaving, killing, segregating, criminalizing, and robbing millions in the name of race? The confluence of these two antithetical questions suggests that the disjunction between objectivism and constructivism is not very clear-cut.

Actually, it appears that the inclusion of the history of race inverts Harris's definitions. In his definition of constructivism, races are contingent on self-description, or their own construction of a cultural and communal cohesion and coherence (L. Harris 1999, 19). And objectivists see races discovering themselves, as it were, objectively as races. But in their colonialist operations, Europeans "discovered" others, and thus discovered themselves as objectively white through their self-definition as different from those others. When they racialized those others as non-white, they pretended to construct themselves as "objectively" superior by imposing an objective sub-personhood (socially and economically) on those others, whose discovery constituted the primary act of construction of their own (white) objectivity. And it is important to emphasize here that "discovery" is a name given to an act of construction of others that both imposes otherness on them and naturalizes that otherness as having existed prior to the act of construction called "discovery"—the same way biology has been used, in the constructivist account, to "naturalize" the concept of race that had been socially constructed. When Christopher Columbus first came to the Caribbean islands, he encountered human beings whom he chose to apprehend as different (enslavable, conquerable) rather than as people (humans) who warranted the same respect and honor he would give to any European stranger who spoke a different language than he. Thus, he constructed them as different and called his construction a "discovery" rather than an "encounter with a fellow human." "Otherness" is a choice that the person seeing another as "other" makes for him- or herself.

Harris's philosophical disjunction becomes still less tenable with respect to Native Americans in the United States. For instance, Native Americans today argue among themselves about who should be included in their societies—in part in response to federal legal intervention imposing new definitions (Garroute 2003). Is membership to be decided in terms of who can trace parentage and bloodline, or rather who can live the life and walk the walk? At what objectivist cutoff point does the percentage of "Indian blood" cease to be Indian blood? At what constructivist point does the maxim "If one can live like us, walk the world like us, think like us, take strength and heart from our ceremonies like us, and love the world like us, then such a one is one of us" cease to be sufficient? During the eighteenth century, there were many European settlers who went and lived the indigenous life, and found it more to their liking than that of the Puritan colonies (St. John de Crevecoeur 1981, 214). By the nineteenth century, however, the white settler mentality had become too consolidated, too rigid, and unopposable, as Herman Melville suggests at the end of his novel *Typee*. Today many indigenous persons (some as light as any white person) have said to whites, "We are not like you, and we live a life that you could not live, and could never understand." Part of that is the hardship of living and maintaining a tradition in the face of white U.S. genocidal assaults on that life. What part is objectivist if it changes with history? And what part is constructivist if it changes history itself? Both sides have adherents with respect to Native American thought, as does the community of black thinkers and philosophers. Indeed, Mosley points out that the split that occurred between Leopold Senghor and Aimé Césaire in the Negritude movement during the 1930s was over this same disparity (Mosley 1999, 77).

The definition of race and the power to define race through violence do not form a basis for enslavement and segregation, but they are their collective mask. They mask the inverse, instead, namely that enslavement and segregation are the basis for the definition of race and the power to define. For some constructivists, the imposition of that mask is the objectivity of race. Race begins with power and never stops making reference back to that power—what Clevis Headley calls "epistemic imperialism" (L. Harris 1999, 89). It is not that whiteness is the center of all discourses of race, but rather that the historical structures of racialization (of oppression, land seizure, and forced labor) and the imposition of social categorization on those racialized in the name of forced labor and segregation are at the ineluctable center of whiteness and white identity.

The idea that the term "race" could be without a referent is possible only if the power relationships that generate what are known as race relations are discarded and discounted. Power relations are real; indeed, one denies the reality of their effects only in the interest of a different set of power relations.

Nothing more emphatically testifies to the reality of power relations than opposition and resistance to their effects. Today, looking back, we can see seventeenth-century white "objectivism," constructed through white objectification of others, as the core of white self-description as white, while (some of) those who had been "constructed" as objective despite themselves (Africans and Native Americans, made into "Negroes" and "Indians") reconstruct themselves as "objective" races in order to give themselves alternate standing in their own eyes, and thus to stand in opposition to that imposed by white constructivism. The historical irony in this inversion is that the qualities of the constructivist are adopted by white objectivism for the purposes of social categorization and domination, while the qualities of objectivism are adopted by those suffering white racial constructions for the purposes of resistance, to throw off racial oppression. An intimate conjunction of these two approaches appears unavoidable. If the term "reality" has a different meaning in each philosophical system, there is nothing about race or racism that can be said realistically without using both meanings of that term.

The interweaving of these thought systems is not a dialectic, however; it has no synthesis. At best, it is circular. Each interpretation (system of definitions) is the foundation for the other. To dismantle the boundary between the two positions (which Harris had considered "irreconcilable"), one does not dispense with anything. Objectivism is historically constructed, and constructivism has an historic objectivity. The purpose of both approaches is to set up race in such a way that racism can be combated. It is anti-racism that is at the core of both modes of thinking.

I am not trying to build a bridge between these positions. None is needed. Their historical inseparability is the very source (in their colonialist origins), the prior condition, for their separation in the first place. But in light of the difficulty of maintaining the irreconcilability that Harris postulates, perhaps objectivism and constructivism are more properly understood as belief systems than as philosophical approaches. That is, they are forms of political praxis. Belief approaches the world with a choice of lens in hand, through which to view experience and history; it does not question experience and history as a way of arriving at a lens.

What this ultimately means is that there are white and Black objectivisms, and white and Black constructivisms, and each plays a different role in the politics and practices of race and anti-racism. In other words, like all things in a racialized society, philosophizations of race are themselves racialized. Race is something that one group of people does to another, and the other must find means of resisting this imposition if it is to survive. This is not to diminish the involvement of objectivism and constructivism in rethinking the post–civil rights situation in the United States. Far from it. It is to suggest the importance of both modes of thought.

What is important is that anti-racism recognize this interweaving. The strength of its critique of white racism cannot just be that whites are objectively a race along with others, but must be that white racialized identity has no other foundation than an entire history of oppression of those constructed as non-white for the purpose of constructing that white identity. What is objective in this is the apparatus of power that enforces this relationship (which has always been accompanied by a system of forced labor). And that apparatus changes in response to real historical conditions. The power of anti-racism must begin in solidarity with those who objectify themselves in resistance against their subordination at the hands of their construction, as a road to autonomy. One must accept both because both operate as tools or weapons in the struggle against white supremacy and the white racialized identity it hides in.

At the same time, one must oppose both. The objectivism of white supremacy has been the scourge of the earth. It has no redeeming values; it has destroyed that possibility in its murderousness and its destruction of whole peoples. At the same time, the constructivism of the white "purity concept" has to be opposed. In recalling the biological anomaly (of racialized motherhood), the irrationality that valorizes the non-parity between black and white motherhood advertises the unconscionable constructedness of the entire concept of "race," which remains indefinable without its purity concept, a concept that holds for no other "race." Only white self-definition (self construction as objective) requires it in order to exteriorize other peoples and to define differences among them. The very existence of race in general is predicated on the ineluctable necessity of this white purity condition. In that sense, the purity concept is a negative purity principle because it turns exclusion into substance in order to define whiteness by what it is not.[5]

The Question of Power and Race

By defining itself as the primary difference, whiteness defines itself as the power to define. This is the self-referentiality that chains the definition of race to the white point of view.[6] The social categorizations that the power to define engenders through its acts of definition do not refer to anything but the self-construction of that power and the self-referentiality of that definition. As a system of power relations, its symbolisms refer to the way it dominates all others. It is as a white point of view that the ghost of race haunts the pretense to colorblindness. Whiteness itself marks the real irreconcilability between the mask of colorblindness and the color-coded symbolisms imposed on people that mark the continued operations of racialization. That is what makes irreducible reference to political power.

Whether those symbolisms use biology or genetics or the segregationist recourse to criminalization as their foundations, they only become different aspects of the language of race by which white people speak to themselves and behind which the reality of race is constructed. This is the privilege given power; it can transform whomever it wishes into the language by which it then speaks to itself. Biology, constructivism, genetics, cultural solidarity, inherent psychology, and poverty all become the rhetoric of a structure of power that, in its power to define and impose its definitions, its social conditions, and its impoverishments, can transform those definitions into cultural norms and then perceive those norms as objective. White objectivism is simply another name for the power relation of white coloniality.

Power constructs, and what it constructs takes on the aura of fact. Its ability to do that is what makes it power.[7] Resistance or popular opposition constructs alternate power, and alternate power redefines. It redefines because it starts as fact—the social fact of organized political resistance. This is the power inherent in oppositional social movements. The struggle against hegemony and hierarchy can avoid neither the struggle for redefinition nor the struggle against the co-optation by power of what is redefined in its attempt to preserve its monopoly over language.

The objective fact of race is that it exists only by extension and expression of its white negative purity condition, dependent on what it is not. White subjectivity, insofar as it defines itself through the other as other, finds its center in that indispensable other. In other words, the center of white subjectivity, insofar as it understands itself as white, is elsewhere in the other, in black people, through whom whiteness defines itself as such. Black people are thus at the center of white subjectivity. This is the source of the obsession with black people that continually besets white people. And its violence is an expression of its absolute dependence on the other. Its violence is deployed to neutralize that dependence.[8]

But because its violence is self-referential, its impunity is essential. Impunity becomes part of the cultural fabric of whiteness, even attaching to the white identity of those who do not consider themselves supremacist. One sees it, for instance, in the dys-conscious tendency of so many white people to be continually speaking for the other, even to his or her face. That impunity is a fundamental aspect of the hegemonic mind. The hegemonic mind thinks that whatever it does with respect to other people (any people) is okay as long as it protects the sanctity of the person doing it. This is the nature of the structure of racialization. It is a structure that racializes U.S. politics, U.S. cultural structures, political parties, and governance policies and strategies.

On the Purity Concept in Relation to
Objectivism and Constructivism

In this philosophical context, let us look again at the role of the purity concept that has revealed itself at the core of whiteness and thus of its concept of race. We have seen that it exists in three different forms. In each of these forms, it is a different kind of exclusionist idea. In its political guise, it refers to the primordial hermeticism of the colonizer and the racializer. It names the insularity on which both have to insist in order to be what they are. But that means the purity concept is self-contradictory. It assumes that race is inherent and objective, while presenting itself as necessary for the construction of its existence.

In its biological guise, the purity concept precedes both objectivism and constructivism because it is a conceptual necessity for the definition of race in the first place. For white people, women, sex, and purity are inseparable, not because the women have to be pure but because white racialized identity can define a biological (objective) existence for itself only through its social control of women.

And in its cultural guise, as the self-congratulation that white supremacy heaps on itself for being objectively the best and the mightiest, the purity concept loses itself in the other because power is always a disguised dependency on the dominated. That is, only through the imposition of a predefined racial purity is a white objectivist sense of race possible. But that means the white objectivist sense of race is only a power position, a coloniality, even when white people think they are just speaking about themselves.

In all its guises, the purity concept is anti-democratic. It violates the democratic principle that the people affected by political decisions must have the opportunity to participate in constructing, formulating, and making those decisions. Those who have been subordinated or demeaned or derogated by their racialization at the hands of whites have never participated in the social decisions to do all that to them. That is, the purity concept is the source for the anti-democratic essence of the concept of race itself. All acts and structures that produce a presence of whiteness, because they necessarily include the operation of a purity concept, are then anti-democratic, inherently excluding those not white from their white operations.[9] The purity concept is the way race as white domination is produced by coloniality; it is the way race as white racialized identity produces coloniality; and it is the possibility of there being a culture of whiteness that can form the substrate for a concept of race. If the concept of race as white supremacy still expresses itself in the maintenance of segregated housing and neighborhoods, the defeat of affirmative action, and a hostility to mixed-race relationships, it is referring back to an entire history of racialization. As such, the purity concept becomes the mediation between racialization as historical and history as racialized.

Insofar as whiteness is in essence anti-democratic because it relies on the purity concept, all those who call themselves white, and who identify as white, objectively form an anti-democratic group. In accepting whiteness as their tradition, they position themselves within a racializing culture, and thus as belonging to its process of racialization. This does not depend on whether they adopt a supremacist ideology or not. It accompanies their whiteness. This whiteness does not depend on their looks; whiteness is a social and cultural construct that conditions how they act as white.

To be democratic, to believe in democracy, in a racialized society like the United States, one has to abandon the purity concept in all its forms and at all levels of its operation. This implies that anti-racism has also to be, at every level, anti-colonialist, but in addition opposed to all identification with whiteness, since that is, itself, an identification with the purity concept.

The most essential alternative to the coloniality of whiteness for white people is to guarantee the autonomy and sovereignty of formerly colonized people, and of anyone subordinated to whiteness. It is not simply to be anti-racist in the sense of opening society to toleration and inclusion in political structures that are white. People of color have to be able to determine for themselves who they are, free of any imposed hierarchy. This would imply the freedom to decide whether to integrate into white society or to preserve a sovereign community as continued defense against white supremacist exclusionism. For instance, "Black power" is an option that black people developed in the course of their struggle against the murderousness of white supremacy. To adapt their racialization as black to their own sense of identity as Black was an expression of their autonomy. Thus, it is pro-democratic. Their ability to develop diplomatic and solidarity relations with African independence movements, and anti-colonialist movements anywhere in the world, was another. For Latino communities, Chicano identity, the Spanish language, and the ability to develop independent relations with the nations of Latin America or elsewhere in the world play a similar role. For Native Americans (of both continents), this has involved a struggle for national sovereignty, the unhampered ability to practice and teach their indigenous languages and religions and to form diplomatic and cultural ties with other indigenous peoples everywhere, as well as with other anti-colonialist movements. These too are pro-democratic movements.

To escape white supremacy, a white person would have to both guarantee and respect the choices communities of color make for themselves. That is the fundamental principle of anti-colonialism. The fundamental principle of anti-racism for whites is not simply that people not be discriminated against because of their race. It means that those (whites) who have racialized themselves through the imposition of a social categorization on others must stop doing so. They must act to put an end to all processes of racialization, which means figuring out how to end having an interest at any level (political, social, ancestral, cultural) in race and racialization and how to end their preservation of white racialized identity.

What This Means for White Anti-racism

A number of white people have tried to formulate a sense of anti-racist whiteness. Each effort centers on a change of terminology, so that whiteness and white racism can be seen in a different light while still granting whiteness and white identity their existence. Lawrence Blum (2002), in casting racism as a moral problem, changes the term "race" to "racialized group." Greg Moses (2005), who wants white people to take responsibility for being white, advocates whites naming themselves white so they cease hiding behind the unmarked assumed perspective of whiteness as the social norm. Blum falls prey to what Moses points out by seeking a "race-neutral" perspective on racism, and thus ignoring the distinction between the racializers and the racialized. Leslie Carr (1997), in his argument against the idea of "colorblindness," substitutes the concept of "nation" for that of "race," in order to see racism as a form of national oppression or colonialism, in which there are colonizers and the colonized, and a national liberation can be thought of for the colonized. For Joe Kincheloe (Kincheloe and Steinberg 1998), whiteness is an identity vacuum, always in crisis because contested by those it oppresses through their racialization. Though he wishes to steer white people out of that crisis toward a "progressive multiculturalism," he begins with a sense of threat to white identity, and thus feeds his idea of multiculturalism back into the essential structure of white racialized identity, with only the ideology of multiculturalism to offer as an alternative. These changes in terminologies are mainly attempts to bring anti-racism out of the morass of thinking of race as a field of groups rather than a hierarchy. Racism then simply runs around on this field causing trouble; and one is saved the trouble of looking at what the structure of racial hierarchy really is as a social and cultural structure. The assumption contained in trying to resolve the problem of racism or white supremacy through a change in terms is that it is still an individual thing and can be resolved on an individual level.

Whether one seeks to construct an anti-racist whiteness or abandon whiteness as such, as other people have advised, both efforts remain futile. A white person can of course abandon his or her white racialized identity or change the terms of racism while sitting in the living room. But as soon as one walks back out into the street, that whiteness will be reimposed by the people out there, just as it was before. Whiteness cannot be abandoned, because it is given by others. They have to agree to its abandonment. And the terms for race or whiteness cannot be changed either, because they name a relationality that is internal to the language that others speak and who then must also agree to the change. Nothing can happen without a social movement to transform the operations of racism, and it is the strength of that movement that will determine what kind of change in the structures of racialization will occur and what they will be called when they are changed. In the meantime, whiteness brings with it, from the rest of white society, a sense of privilege and hegemony.

The dilemma for anti-racist whites is that they cannot say they are not white, because they are; but if they identify themselves as white, they invoke an identification with the institutionalities of whiteness, the purity concept, supremacy, and the criminalization of the racialized. It marks the fact that whiteness has made itself white by derogating others through disrespect, prohibition from participation, and social depriviliging. It is the structure of racialization by which whiteness is given that must be dismantled, so that white racialized identity, with its purity concept, no longer has any cultural foundation for itself. This is not a question of terminology or language; it is about the transformation of a cultural structure. We have still to figure out how to do that, but first we have to see that structure and figure out how to stand in opposition to its operations.

The structure of racialization is an invisible "hand" that "wields" people, setting them against each other. It is a white hand that weaponizes white people in order to deploy them against those it has racialized as non-white. The struggle for democracy requires that we eliminate that hand to free the racialized from their racialization and to free white people from their weaponization as a form of dehumanization.

4

The Political Culture of Whiteness

The State and Racialization

So far, in mapping the outlines of the structures of racialization and the preservation of white supremacy, we have examined specific forms of institutional state power and of white racialized identity, both in the present and historically. At no time has either the original invention of whiteness or the reconstitution of white cultural coherence and supremacy in the wake of a pro-democracy movement occurred without the intervention of the state. Specific institutions of power have been central to this process, taking different forms at different times. These have included prisons, forms of police and populist impunity, and legalist or para-political disenfranchisement of people of color. Central to it all has been the use of a political paranoia, also taking different forms at different times, as a means of either weaponizing white people in the furtherance of racialization or rallying mass popular support for the actions of the state. This paranoia has been instrumental in the reconstitution and consolidation of white racialized identity, its sense of white solidarity, and the legitimation of violence against those seen as a threat to the coherence of whiteness. It both facilitates and justifies the inverse logic by which the aggressiveness of white violence is transformed into a form of self-defense, a self-decriminalization of violence through the criminalization of its victims. Today, decades after the civil rights movements, there is still neighborhood and school segregation, employment and judicial bias, and white popular support for the dissolution of many of the programs and agencies that the civil rights era brought into effect.

At the same time, since World War II, the United States has continually intervened militarily in other nations, claiming to "bring" democracy to them, for the purpose of either "stopping communism" or policing violations of "human rights" in those other countries. Decisions concerning this aggressive exercise of military power, however, have been outside the purview, influence, and decision-making capacity of the people, either in the United States or in the assaulted nation. None of these interventions has been voted on. Indeed, since the Korean War, Congress has abrogated its constitutional responsibility by granting blanket war powers to the president. And no element of foreign policy has ever been submitted to a referendum of the people. That is, interventions to bring democracy elsewhere have been a specifically undemocratic practice by the state.

In light of the undemocratic essence of the structures of racialization observed in U.S. domestic history, two questions emerge: Does a comparable structure appear in its international interventions? And what is the cultural basis for the support those interventions have received from the U.S. mainstream?

The Problem of Interventionism

During the 1840s, the United States intervened in Mexico, first with the settlement of Texas and then through war, resulting in the acquisition of what is now the southwest part of the United States. From 1991 to the present, the United States has twice intervened in Iraq, first by massive destruction of its social infrastructure through aerial bombardment and then by direct occupation through military conquest. These constitute the endpoints of a 150-year period over which the United States has aggressively intervened in other nations more than a hundred times.[1]

Both interventions were unprovoked. Mexico offered no threat to the United States, which simply wished to extend its slave system to Mexican territory. In 1991, Iraq had invaded Kuwait with the knowledge of the U.S. government.[2] The United States nevertheless assaulted Iraq to drive it out of Kuwait, in order to seize Kuwait for itself and establish a permanent military base there.[3] Whereas the first instance couched itself in a new ideology called "Manifest Destiny," the second projected a form of self-defense it called "preemption." The first occurred at a moment when the United States was beginning to spread west over the continent, and the second at a moment when the United States had attained political and economic hegemony over the entire planet. Though the original watchword of a "civilizing mission" in Mexico, insofar as it meant bringing slavery, may appear anachronistic to us now, the contemporary idea of "bringing democracy" should at least appear self-contradictory.

Indeed, the contradiction in "bringing democracy" through intervention is more than procedural or rhetorical. It is a self-subverting project. If democracy means that a people collectively determines its own destiny, then it has to be sovereign in its destiny in order to democratically determine it. The interventionary act by a foreign power cancels that sovereignty by definition, rendering "democracy" therefore impossible. Yet from the annexation of Mexico to the occupation of Iraq, this rhetoric of self-valorization, despite its contradictory character, weaves itself through the textile of U.S. political life, with a degree of general acceptance that attests to its cultural familiarity.

With respect to the congressional and socially extant debates on the annexation of Mexican territory in 1846, it took the form of a peculiar dilemma: Should the United States annex or colonize the Mexican territory? Many people (the electorate at that time was essentially white) opposed annexation in favor of colonization because they feared that accepting Mexicans as citizens would corrupt the racial purity of Anglo-Saxon society (Horsman 1981, 231). Those who opposed direct colonization feared that the autocratic tasks and agencies of colonial administration would corrupt the purity of U.S. republican institutions. In either case, the status of the people who inhabited the territory in question was a secondary consideration, subordinate to one form or another of ideological purity or sanctity. The issue, far from being the welfare of the people inhabiting the territory seized, was the structural effect that seizure would have on white U.S. society. That is, the effect of "bringing civilization" to other lands was to be judged with respect to the purveyor, the United States itself, rather than the recipient (Horsman 1981, 240). The primary concern was "purely" self-reflective.

The fact that the colonial or interventionist project itself was already a corruption of alleged democratic principles was not considered. And the idea of Manifest Destiny, that Anglo-Saxon society was ordained to settle and dominate the continent, was also not in question. The debate was never over whether to attack Mexico as a sovereign nation, but only when and how (Horsman 1981, 236).

In the congressional debate, annexation was deemed preferable if the land could be considered empty; thus, no new citizens would have to be accepted as a result of the takeover. To meet this requirement, a mere act of redefinition needed to be imposed on the current residents. The actual existence of inhabitants on the land (Mexicans and indigenous societies) was categorized as a form of corruption of the land itself (reducing them to non-entity status—if not depriving them of life), a problem that might exact a moderate toll for taking the land as a resource. "Bringing civilization" or "democracy" to the land would then primarily involve settlement by whites, their mission being the implanting (or importing) of a white society (which, for many, meant importing slavery as well) rather than the enabling of a form of "democratic" civil society to flourish among its present populations.

In other words, the "civilizing" or "democratizing" project consisted in conflating the U.S. self-image with the practice of "clearing the land." It meant to racialize the land (render its inhabitants subhuman) in order to deracialize the territory as an emptiness (Horsman 1981, 167). Ultimately, the prior inhabitants were reduced to varying forms of servitude or forced labor.

An analogous situation has unfolded with the occupation of Iraq. Though the announced rationalizations for invasion referred to both "rescue" from tyranny and "self-protection" from a non-existent threat (e.g., WMDs, a nuclear program), the act of "bringing democracy" involved the massive destruction of the former social infrastructure of that nation. Both the 1991 bombing and the murderousness of the invasion took on the aura of "clearing the land." The bombs dropped on Iraq in 1991 amounted to the conventional equivalent of six Hiroshima-sized atomic bombs. Among the first targets were electric power stations, desalinization plants, and sewage treatment plants, that is, civilian infrastructure (Clark 1992).

After the land was occupied, contracts were given to a small select group of U.S. corporations to rebuild that infrastructure, among which Halliburton and Bechtel were the principal beneficiaries. Their operations then filled the void created by the invasion's destructiveness, a "re-population" of Iraq with (corporate) entities of EuroAmerican origin and construction, to which the surviving Iraqis would be subservient through direct employment. It amounted to a corporate annexation of the Iraqi economy, an imposition of the multinational corporate institution on the Iraqi populace and its society. The economic goal of the invasion was to privatize Iraq's public assets and local resources. (Indeed, Iraq's oil resources were divided up among the major oil corporations long before the invasion, in secret sessions held during February 2001, whose records Vice-President Dick Cheney never agreed to release.)[4] Though the cause of "bringing democracy" to those bereft of it was proclaimed to be the purpose of the invasion, the real participants in that "democracy" were the corporations implanted on the "cleared land."

With respect to the popular support the invasion received, it appeared to be immaterial that no legitimate cause existed. Though a global opposition to the projected invasion arose before the fact, all proposals to negotiate any differences with Iraq were openly rejected by the U.S. government with little domestic objection. It did not even matter that UN inspectors had found no weapons and that this was widely known (Mokhiber and Weissman 2003). The violence against an imagined threat which informed the invasion after it began was apparently sufficient to solidify popular acceptance. That is, there was a cultural familiarity for the U.S. citizen in the impunity deployed in the intervention's self-arrogated policing function ("we can't just stand back and watch Hussein run roughshod over his own people; we have to do something"). In one gesture, Manifest Destiny was extended on a global scale and the sovereignty of nations erased. For the ethic of violence that supported the invasion, the "roughshod" violation of other peoples was of no consequence.

When, after years of occupation, the United States expressed its intention to maintain a number of military bases in Iraq, it signified that its alleged project of "handing over the reins" to a sovereign Iraqi government was a metaphor for another form of annexation. If this annexationist project eventually does not pan out, leading to an actual agreement to leave Iraq, it will be because of the implacable and resourceful resistance to the occupation by the people of Iraq. But that is simply the aspect of the situation that, in interventionist political lingo derived from the Vietnam experience, gets called the "quagmire."

The impunity that aggression claims for itself in these interventionary adventures has broader implications, however. Impunity signifies an arrogation of right and power to conflate policing functions with peremptory judgments on how other sovereign nations are to comport themselves—with respect to their "democratic status," for instance. In Nicaragua in all the elections since the dictator Somoza was overthrown, the United States has judged the electoral process defective and invalid to the extent one of the participants was a socialist party (the Sandinistas) and that party won (Chomsky 1991). In such judgments, the United States reveals that the ethics of a white supremacist approach is not a thing of the past. It constructs itself internationally through the ideological obeisance it demands from other nations—which the editors of the *Gulf War Reader* call a *pax americana* (Sifry and Cerf 1991; Klare 1991, 466). No sooner did Russia attempt to diplomatically resolve U.S. plans to assault Iran in 2006 than the U.S. government declared Russia a threat to democracy and initiated a plan to place missiles in Poland and the Czech Republic.

Under the operation of this ethics, a host of constitutionally elected governments have been found derelict and subject to detrimental economic policies and political hostility. One could list the governments of Arbenz in Guatemala, Sukarno in Indonesia, Allende in Chile, the Sandinistas, and Chavez in Venezuela, among many others. The actual participation and will of the people of those nations becomes secondary to U.S. determination of their situation. In imposing itself on the internal relations of those nations, it "disappears" the people behind that determination, a form of ideologically "clearing the land" and repopulating it with U.S. hegemonic oversight. Thus, the "purity" of its purpose to bring "democracy" to benighted peoples still only redefines the self-referentiality of U.S. control of others' lands and destinies. Popular resistance to U.S. judgment then gets consigned to either ignorance or criminality, to be met with raw power, as the ultimate prerogative of impunity.

A self-referential sense of purity and a self-arrogation of impunity are two sides of the same coin. They are what constitute the actual structure of U.S. "messianism." The interventionist ethic constitutes the international form that the messianism of white supremacy has taken.

The Legalist Rhetoric of Intervention

A juridical dimension to this interventionary project is revealed if we look at the recent invasions as an "attack sequence." Starting with Grenada in 1982, there have been military assaults on Nicaragua (1982), Panama (1989), Iraq (1991), Yugoslavia (1999), Afghanistan (2001), and Iraq again (2003). Each one violated a central principle of international law. Not only was each an unprovoked attack on a sovereign nation, in violation of the UN Charter (to which the United States is one of the original signatories), but each killed many people (hundreds in Panama, thousands in Yugoslavia, tens of thousands in Nicaragua, over a million in Iraq), did serious damage to an economy (at times creating a toxic environment through the use of depleted uranium in Serbia and Iraq), and created an internal refugee situation in the victim nation, also in direct violation of international law. Each one pretended to bring a criminal to justice, suggesting that in this attack sequence the criminalization of the target was more directly (i.e., less analogically) related to the white supremacist criminalization of those it racializes. And each received overwhelming support in the United States, at both institutional and popular levels. Let us look at the structure of these invasions.

The invasion of Afghanistan was ostensibly to arrest Osama bin Laden, for ostensibly having organized the events of September 11, 2001, though the FBI admitted it had no proof of a connection. Instead, the United States was charging him for the August 7, 1998, bombings of U.S. embassies in Tanzania and Kenya,[5] though apparently not seriously, since the "warrant" could easily have been served in July 2001 when he was receiving dialysis treatment in the American Hospital in Dubai. Instead, in violation of international law, Afghanistan was bombed, with enormous civilian casualties and without stated political goals beyond "getting bin Laden." Whole villages were obliterated. Thus, a military campaign was launched whose massive technological violence led only to "clearing the land" of any coherent political organization. All to arrest one man?

After the Taliban were removed from government, an interim administration was invented by pasting together various warlord factions that had previously been kept in check by the Taliban and whose rule was foreseen to be worse than the Taliban they replaced. While Afghani women spoke out against the invasion, knowing their situation would not improve, they were nevertheless used to propagandize for the invasion with messianic rectitude.[6] Indeed, messianic purpose is always better served by gratuitous action and an absence of express political goals.

Domestic objection to this assault remained small. What little there was received inordinate censure or repression. Public figures who spoke against the attack were vilified (e.g., Bill Maher). People were fired from jobs, students who wore anti-war T-shirts were suspended from school, university professors were sanctioned, and so on.[7] The internal atmosphere thus matched the vigilante mentality (impunity) of the invasion itself.

What was missing, of course, was real judicial legitimacy. The government's reference to international (UN) legalisms was deemed sufficient by politicians and the media to both symbolize and authorize the illegal intervention. Insofar as popular acceptance rendered its illegality ignorable, legalism and militarism could simply authorize each other in the name of anti-terrorism.[8] The hiatus between an absence of evidence (for what happened on 9/11) and a military policy that simply shouted, "Let's get him; we know he did it," signified that mainstream opinion needed no evidence for its "revenge." What vigilantism is as a procedure, interventionism is as an ethic; what both share with the structure of racialization is the assumption that impunity itself is sufficient evidence. Furthermore, given that the assault had been planned since July 2001 (two months before 9/11),[9] the government's ability to marshal support in the absence of reason or logic meant that the popular response was a cultural rather than a political phenomenon.

Each one of the interventions in the attack sequence makes a similar call to legalism and displays a similar hiatus between policy and legitimacy. Grenada, for instance, was invaded in violation of the Caribbean Treaty in order to enforce the treaty in an internal dispute between political leaders in that country. In the course of the invasion, a governmental system was annihilated.

The United States invaded Panama militarily to arrest a Panamanian, Manuel Noriega, for having violated U.S. law. The invasion was clearly in violation of the Organization of American States charter, which guarantees the sovereignty of American states.[10] Noriega was returned to the United States, tried, and jailed, while Panama was left to bury its dead (300 killed, 3,000 men, women, and children wounded, and 18,000 homeless, according to Physicians for Human Rights (1991, 4–5). Why Noriega, a Panamanian citizen, could be held accountable under U.S. law, given that the U.S. Constitution holds only for U.S. territory and no Panamanians participated in the writing or deciding of U.S. law, was never explained. No treaty existed that would extend U.S. law to other sovereign nations. For the U.S. government, jurisdiction over a drug trafficker overshadowed, as an act of impunity, the absence of legality in capturing him.

Nevertheless, a number of law theorists came forward to provide legal justification for these assaults. Anthony D'Amato, of Northwestern University Law School, for instance, argued that "sovereignty," in the case of Panama, was of no legal consequence in the face of the human "right" of "Panamanian citizens to be free from oppression by a gang of ruling thugs." That is, treaty conditions "are far less important to international law than the actual customary-law-generating behavior of states." The Panamanians being shot at by invading helicopters from a U.S. aircraft carrier perhaps more clearly understood what the term "thugs" referred to than did D'Amato. He nevertheless continued: "The U.S. interventions in Panama and, previously, in Grenada are milestones along the path to a new non-statist conception of international law that changes previous non-intervention formulas such as Article 18 [of the OAS charter]" (D'Amato 1990, 516).

Thus, D'Amato gives certification to "unwritten" (extra-constitutional, or non-statist) law, to a system of "precedents" in the process of being created (that is, without precedent), based purely (and unfortunately) on the acts of the powerful, of military might pure and simple. The actual precedent (for "non-statist" law) then becomes an arbitrary conflation of U.S. law with Panamanian law, an allegorical "internationalization" of U.S. (national) law unilaterally extending U.S. (statist) jurisdiction over other sovereign nations, in violation of international law. In the name of an alleged purity of purpose, it imposes invented procedures through violence. It is this "internationalization" of U.S. law that was then extended to the 1991 bombing of Iraq and later to the 1999 bombing of Yugoslavia, for the purposes of seizing Kuwait and Kosovo, respectively.

The Culture of Interventionism

The Iraqi resistance that responded to the 2003 US invasion placed the U.S. occupation in crisis. Impunity works only so long as its presumption to uncontested power prevails. The ethos of impunity, because it presents a threat to all other nations, cannot afford to appear at all vulnerable. When it gets caught in the contradiction of advocating democracy while suppressing it at every turn, both in policy (the actual suppression of Iraqi newspapers, self-organized elections, labor unions, and free speech [Gourevitch 2003; Bacon 2003]) and in the inherent character of intervention itself, that facade crumbles. The coherence of domestic support dissolves through exposure to the lies and pretexts on which the invasion was based. And the failure to gain control of Iraq's oil, owing to the resistance of both Iraqi unions and guerrillas, which was deemed the necessary source for financing the war, reveals the criminal nature of the adventure. The crisis resonates with the same dilemma that beset the United States over the annexation of Mexican territory in 1846.

Why does the impunity of such destructiveness, and the destructiveness of such impunity, get popular support in a nation that prides itself on valuing the inviolability and sanctity of the individual and of national sovereignty? What is the real dynamic of that popular support? It is not economic gain. The attack sequence does not provide economic benefit to its domestic supporters among the populace. The economic projects—control of resources, and corporate investments that may be at stake—have no direct connection to social conditions in the United States. Indeed, military adventures have so absorbed the economic resources of the United States that health and education facilities at the state level are in a condition of advanced decay. Furthermore, the connection between corporate investment and mainstream social conditions was broken in the 1970s and 1980s with the deindustrialization process, from runaway shops to the growing outsourcing of much of U.S. manufacture. Support does not arise from political advantage; the people of the United States do not gain from the territory occupied (the Canal Zone, Kuwait, Kosovo, Iraq, Afghanistan). Neither economic interest nor compelling "logic" explains the support given by ordinary people in the United States.

Indeed, the official justifications have consistently been self-contradictory. The 1989 invasion of Panama to arrest a citizen (Noriega) of that nation for having violated U.S. law renders the concept of law empty in the name of law. In Iraq, the principle of sovereignty was invoked with respect to Kuwait only in order to cancel it for both Kuwait (through subsequent U.S. occupation) and Iraq (through destruction of its social infrastructure). In Serbia, humanitarian purpose (to stop "ethnic cleansing") was invoked to render Serbian terrain uninhabitable (through the use of depleted uranium and the massive toxicity produced by bombing chemical plants) and to "cleanse" Kosovo of Serbians. Milosevich was charged with human rights violations in his own country, though NATO's involvement in Serbian internal affairs was swept out of sight.[11]

Ultimately, no non-contradictory logical connection is even possible between "humanitarianism" and militarism. One can write "humanitarian aid" on a bomb, but when dropped on a village from 30,000 feet it can only amount to mass murder. To think "humanitarian mass murder" is to think criminally, within the arrogance of impunity and its self-proclaimed "purity" of purpose. The technological violence of U.S. interventionism recalls Joy James's observation that there is always a genocidal dimension to white supremacy, as well as a violently enforced allegiance to it (James 1996, 46).

To explain the political support these aggressions receive domestically, we must explain the cultural ethic at work in them. Three elements have generally been coordinated in each assault. The first is an arbitrary criminalization of a nation, symbolized by the demonization of its leadership (in the case of Serbia, Milosevich was demonized; in the case of Afghanistan, the Taliban were demonized).[12] There is an arbitrary character to these demonizations, accentuated by the existence of parallel situations in other areas which the United States simply ignores—for instance, during the 1990s, East Timor, Guatemala, or Chiapas. Though the Zapatista presence in Chiapas was attacked by Mexico in a manner much more severe than Kosovo by Serbia, it remained off the political radar and ignored by the media. The implication is that the alleged "criminality" of the "target" leader (i.e., Milosevich) was not the reason for the assault on Serbia, but instead a rhetorical pretext.

Second, there is immediate benefit from a demonizing rhetoric. By proclaiming the target nation criminal, the United States implicitly decriminalizes the violence it uses against the other nation and attributes to this violence a form of "virtue." The responsibility for the assault and its destructiveness is shifted to its victim. The terrible hardships to ordinary people wrought by the economic embargoes on Cuba, Nicaragua, Zimbabwe, and others get blamed on the local leader. Not surprisingly, this ethical inversion has actually been normalized as law in the United States. It is called "vicarious liability." For example, if a police officer fires into a car to stop it from being driven away and kills the passenger, the driver and not the police officer who shoots will be charged with murder. This vicarious liability ethic is what was at stake in the famous Bear Lincoln case (Fukurai 1998). Violence and destructiveness become self-legitimizing, a "law unto itself," with all the advantages of impunity.

Third, the issues of social justice, or of human rights violations, used to rationalize an intervention are given standing in the arena of public debate only to the degree authorized by official governmental policy. That is, they become political issues only to an extent beneficial for official policy. When anti-war protests raise the issues of human rights with respect to the intervention itself, they are moved to the margins and not permitted to disrupt the official media debate or impair the rubric of the intervention's self-decriminalization. The wrongness of the Iraq war became worthy of public discussion only after the administration decided it was an issue. Before that, Congress merely rubber-stamped what the administration claimed, and popular debate on the war was muffled, suppressed, or clouded in oxymoronics (for instance, the claim that aggression is really self-defense).[13]

In short, the practice of political impunity and the easy deployment of violence that stand behind the legalist rhetoric and the inversion of criminality all condition and legitimize each other. The pretense to legalism legitimizes impunity, impunity legitimates violence, and the ostensive necessity for violence provides legalistic authorization. Its cyclicity is what disguises the ethical inversions (the self-decriminalizing criminality) at work in each instance. The political sanctity that this cyclic structure imparts through its hermeticism obviates the need to open its ethical claims to scrutiny. It is precisely its self-referentiality that bestows on the government the ability to equate its arbitrary acts with political principle.

If interventionism needs no explanation or extant political goal beyond its rhetorically machinated and militarized response to its own criminalization of another, then messianism becomes a sufficient rationale. Indeed, the ability to recast the other's defense as aggression in order to render one's own interventionary aggression defensive makes a programmatic or explanatory political purpose all but impossible. Thus, it is the development of a social solidarity in support of the adventure as a function of the ability to criminalize the other that is itself the achievement of the adventure's goal, the confirmation that its paranoid perception (that the other is a threat and therefore criminal) was real. While there are in each case material benefits to be gained, such as the seizure of resources or geo-political positioning, we are examining why the populace of the United States, which does not benefit, would support the adventure.

What we arrive at is that U.S. interventionism exhibits all the elements, in their cyclic configuration, that we have observed for white racialized identity, namely, a concocted paranoia whose rhetoric both criminalizes and demonizes, an aggressive violence that renders the paranoia real, and a call to solidarity to decriminalize that violence and substitute a messianism for an apparent absence of political purpose. Interventionism becomes another element of the structure of racialization that we are examining.

The self-referentiality of this cycle, its self-legitimizing character, not only explains why the absence of intelligible or meaningful political goals is acceptable to people—and perhaps even desirable, if recognizable goals, as in the case of Iraq, would imply confronting the unscrupulousness of establishing military bases. It also explains why the unspokenness of political goals is familiar to people, a primary element of its acceptability. The goal lurks in the silent reference to what goes without saying. The intervention becomes the goal itself, just as racial segregation in neighborhoods and schools remains a goal in and of itself. With respect to the bombing of Iraq in 1991, removing Hussein was not a goal, since his continuance in power was essential to consolidating U.S. occupation and control of Kuwait. And the embargo was essential for ensuring that Iraq did not recuperate its economy. Popular support for both the war and the embargo suggested that death and devastation were sufficient rationales.

It is true that opposition to U.S. interventionism has existed and has attempted to reveal the contradictions within the government's rhetoric. But opposition is generally impotent because those who protest do not understand the priority that violence takes over democratic principles for the culture of whiteness. For instance, the Vietnam anti-war movement made the assumption that if the facts of what the United States was doing in Vietnam were known, then the people of the United States would be outraged and bring the government's aggression to a halt. That would have been the logic of democracy; the idea of national sovereignty should have been sufficient to curtail the intervention. But that approach did not work. The assumption that an informed populace would live up to the principles of democracy and sovereignty proved wrong. Even with vast dissemination of facts, opposition proved consistently ineffective insofar as democratic principles were superseded by the acceptance of the war and of violence as a necessary goal in itself.[14]

The absence of outrage signifies that something would be abrogated for the United States as a culture if those principles of democracy were fulfilled, that is, if the sovereignty of others was respected. The anti-war movement's strategy was self-contradictory in assuming that some common ground existed between the principles of justice and the government's rhetoric of self-legitimization, that is, that discussion was possible on the ground of principles. But that is like assuming that justice and impunity can share a common domain of conversation, which they do not. Justice is predicated on the notion that the principles of justice must precede the act to be judged. And impunity (self-justification), which means being a law unto oneself, predicates itself on its own actions as the source of its principles. Under the operation of impunity, justification is inherent in its own acts, a priori. Discussion ends before it begins. In other words, strategies of opposition to institutionalized impunity based on democratic principles operate against themselves because they rely on a social ethos that in practice has been supplanted by an ethos that encases that opposition in its own messianic self-valorization. Such opposition succeeds only in valorizing the impunity and messianism it opposes. To assert the principles of sovereignty in opposition to U.S. interventionism is to valorize the "moral" foundation for that interventionism, which remains U.S. sovereignty and its interventionist impunity.

The Two-Party System and Black Disenfranchisement

If interventionism characterizes the U.S. persona internationally (and it cannot not characterize it insofar as all other countries, once aware of the impunity inherent in the intervention, would have to recognize that they too could become targets, should their sovereignty by chance stand in the way of U.S. interests [Chomsky 1991, 283–291]), then what characterizes the inner nature of U.S. politics that express itself thus? Historically, the state structure that the United States has sought to export to other nations consists of an electoral process, a two-party system, a separation of branches, and a specific form of representation. To export this system, as the United States has done in Japan, El Salvador, Peru, Chile, Iraq, and others, implies that the United States sees a certain purity in this system.[15] It not only marks the assumption that democracy can be exported, as the substance of a messianic civilizing mission, but ignores the sheer contradiction in that approach (the impossibility of democracy without sovereignty).

We can obtain some insight into the two-party system by tracing the operation of the purity concept within it. In the historical debates around Manifest Destiny and the assault on Mexico, which occurred at the time the two-party system was evolving, the purity of democratic institutions was a political concern, as we have seen above. The two-party system also emerged in the context of debate on the virtues of political parties and whether or not they accorded with the Constitution (Leonard 2002). On both counts, the process of party formation produced a structure similar to that of white racialized identity.

Political parties were not originally encouraged by the founders when they wrote the Constitution, nor was the existence of parties recognized in the original Constitution. For the most part, the founders considered parties to be conspiratorial cabals that would skew the uniformity of the electorate and warp citizen participation in political power (Leonard 2002). This was, of course, unrealistic. To run for national election, one has to have a support structure for one's campaign, and one has to establish a national presence for one's candidacy and program. For this, a political party is necessary.

Of the several issues that drove politics toward party formation, slavery was the most important and contestatory. The issue of slavery's abolition had been implicit in the first paragraph of the Declaration of Independence, and a movement calling for an end to slavery had formed around the principle of equality. The first Pennsylvania Constitution of 1780 abolished slavery. The ensuing dispute and hostility over the issue led to the writing of a second constitution in 1790 (after the U.S. Constitution was ratified), in which slavery was re-recognized, with provisions for gradual emancipation. Other states followed suit in this gradualism. Only Massachusetts ended slavery outright in the 1790s. On the whole, during those first decades, the Declaration's principle of equality had currency if not effect, and free black people in the North generally voted along with whites (Litwack 1961, 77).

The Democratic Party was the first party with national presence (Cunningham 1957). Its main constituency was the plantation South and the slaveholders. It had adherents in the North, particularly in the working classes, because it had emerged in opposition to the Federalists and their adherence to the interests of capital. To contest this party in either legislative or electoral arenas, other political parties became necessary. Between 1800 and 1840, a multiplicity of parties formed: Whig, Liberty, Know-Nothing, Free Soil, and Workingman's parties, with a spectrum of anti-slavery positions (abolition, non-extension of slavery to the new territories, gradual emancipation, transportation of free black people to Africa or to Central America, and others). Against the Democratic Party, which held national hegemony, mere alliances or coalitions among these groups were inadequate.

As a national party, the Democratic Party was the first to face the political problem that accompanied national presence. Its northern members could not simply support slavery outright and get a hearing or a following. What they could do was advocate for strict segregation and disenfranchisement of free black people (Litwack 1961, 84–93). The party's strategy was to engender harsher anti-black attitudes among people of the northern cities and to create social and economic constraints on black people inhospitable enough to dissuade slaves from fleeing north in an attempt to find freedom (Tise 1987).

By the 1820s and 1830s, this campaign bore fruit. A northern populist movement developed against voting by free black people. There were white riots in the 1830s in Philadelphia, Cincinnati, and Boston whenever black people attempted to exercise their franchise. By the 1840s, most states had amended their constitutions to disenfranchise free black people. Even in Massachusetts, the first state to eliminate slavery, where black suffrage had not been banned, mobs of whites in 1850 drove away from the polls any black person who attempted to vote (Litwack 1961, 91). In other words, white feeling about black people voting tended to get more hostile and actively antagonistic as time went on.

For the most part, this hostility did not stop black people from trying to vote; they came back, petitioning, organizing, and proselytizing for a truly democratic sense of citizenship. Even as they were being disenfranchised, free black people struggled against the slave system through abolitionist societies, speaking tours in Europe, and yearly conventions to push for suffrage, as well as by moving to Canada. They also fought against the African colonization schemes by refusing en masse to sign up (Litwack 1961, 25). But their participation in anti-slavery politics remained minimal because any party that would open its activities to black people would lose white votes.

The 1830s were also the period when the abolitionist movement was the strongest. Parallel to the disenfranchisement movement, its demand for the end of slavery grew more radical. What the proposal to emancipate black people from their forced labor crashed against was the other fundamental principle in the Constitution, the guarantee of the right to property. The ethical issue concerning enslavement as such drowned in the morass of debate over who or what would compensate the slave owners for their loss of property and capital. Various complex and convoluted plans for gradual emancipation were passed in several northern states, providing for years of servitude in which the bond-laborer would work off the loss to the "owner."

The white excuse for the disenfranchisement of black people during the 1830s and 1840s was at the core of white supremacy. Whites feared that if black people formed a voting bloc or third party, they would potentially obtain a tie-breaking vote in close legislative contests and thus gain the balance of power (Litwack 1961, 76–82). In such a circumstance, black people would have control of legislative policy, something that was anathema to the white mind.

It did not matter that black people had no party of their own or that electoral redistricting was controlled by white people. This paranoia took precedence. In fact, African-Americans at the time were quite conscious that the influence they might wield electorally was limited principally to the local or ward level, without extension to state legislatures. They realized that to extend their influence beyond that would have required a third (Black) party, an option generally rejected by black political groups because it would have meant sacrificing what influence they did have within the major political organizations, on which they relied for even tenuous connection to state policies. When the Liberty Party brought together various anti-slavery movements in a fairly strong coalition in 1840 in a still fluid political arena, many African-Americans hesitated to support its program, though it bespoke their interests, thinking it might antagonize both the Whigs and the Democrats, on whom the issues of slavery and enfranchisement would concretely depend (Litwack 1961, 88). Even throughout New England, prior to black disenfranchisement, no independent Black political parties appeared, nor did Black caucuses form within the existing parties. In short, when communities of free black people sought political expression, it was within channels, and they tended to establish the same kind of party loyalties that whites did.

The Two-Party System and White Paranoia

Here again, we confront the elements of white racialized identity, translated to a socio-political structure by which whites organized their society. The idea that a "black vote" would be a swing vote was a way of establishing a threat by which white supremacy could organize a defensive social alliance. Even with no actual experience of such a thing as a "black vote," and in the absence of extant issues with a clear racial component aside from that of the franchise itself, the mere invocation of a thing called a "black vote" as a threat was enough to give it political objectivity and coherence and to make it a sufficient pretext for refusing black suffrage. Thus, white racialized identity asserted itself self-referentially to bring about an anti-democratic agreement to exclude the imagined black vote, as a form of socio-political violence. That is, the three dimensions of white racialized identity (paranoia, white solidarity and coherence, and violence) were at work. Indeed, these same factors can be seen to be at work in a similar manner in the 1970s movement to repeal affirmative action as a form of reverse discrimination, or a quota system undermining white entitlement. The populism of the opposition and the violence of its exclusionism were the same. In effect, it was the white obsession with noticing that black people voted, rather than how they voted, that transformed itself into a so-called black vote in the white mind.[16]

In other words, the "black vote" was produced or invented by that obsessive white act of noticing. Had there been no segregation, and no obsessive white noticing of "black people," voting or not, there would have been no "black vote" as such, nor a black interest in counter-exclusionary protests. Herein lies the white self-referentiality that renders the issue a true paranoia. If a "black vote" had existed to express "black interests," the primary interest would have been to end their exclusion and denigration, that is, to eliminate the conditions for the possible existence of a "black vote." But nothing in the historical situation dissuaded the advocates of disenfranchisement.

White paranoia imagined black political involvement as an alien influence, an alien threat, against which it defined politics as white politics (McManus 1973,184). Indeed, though the vote against the black franchise occurred without the participation of black people, it was nevertheless proclaimed to be the democratic will of the people. In other words, it signified for the white mind that "democracy" was to be a purely white prerogative and that the democracy envisioned by white people was a white democracy (McManus 1973, 184).

This drive to disenfranchise black people grew out of the central dilemma confronting party formation in the United States. In order for a party to become politically significant, it had to be able to establish a national presence for itself in a society wracked with regional conflicts. During the pre–Civil War decades, there was nothing concerning the major issues of slavery and abolition that could be advanced in a forthright or principled manner in all regions of the country. That is, no uniform stance could be adopted nationally without antagonizing one region or another of the electorate. To establish a national political presence, in order to have national influence, a party had to reduce its program to what was arguable in all areas. The effect was to eliminate any principled ideological positions from party rhetoric. National political issues had to be reduced to expediencies, opportunisms, and lowest common denominators. And this was especially true for the politics of slavery and anti-slavery. The anti-slavery movement had to present itself as being anti-black so that the white vote would not flee to the Democrats (as Horace Greeley pointed out at the time [Litwack 1961, 88]). Even Lincoln did this in his debates with Stephen Douglas. And the pro-slavery party had to downplay its defense of slavery in order not to lose its northern wing, on which it depended to strengthen the structures of segregation.

In other words, as the anti-slavery groupings gradually coalesced into a single national association (which became the Republican Party in 1854), both sides of the issue of slavery had to appear anti-black and pro-white in some fashion. What they found they could agree on was opposition to black suffrage.[17] This provided the opportunity for the anti-slavery faction to proclaim an anti-black position, and for the pro-slavery faction to express antagonism to black freedom without having to openly defend slavery in the North.

It was in the context of this arena of agreement and consensus that the issue of the extension of slavery to the new western territories presented itself. Between the pro-slavery Democratic Party and the variety of anti-slavery movements, it was the one issue crucial to deciding regional hegemony which could be debated in any area of the country. Both sides could speak in advocacy without having to proclaim opposing principles that would not be arguable everywhere. The pro-slavery faction did not have to defend slavery; it simply had to advocate opening the territories to it (democratically). The anti-slavery faction did not have to present moral arguments or contest the right to property; it simply had to advocate proclaiming the territories to be a home for free labor (Almaguer 1994, 32–37).

Even white abolitionists fell prey to thinking in these terms of white consensus. The original abolitionist project began to break down as it accepted the notion that black people had to prove something. They too mouthed the ritualistic doctrine that black people were lazy, untrained, unprepared, uncivilized, condemned to poverty, and so on (ignoring the genius and capability for social organization displayed by black people in merely surviving the constancy of white hostility, as DuBois has pointed out). Those abolitionists who did not were labeled radicals and marginalized (Kraditor 1989). No one suggested that it was white people who needed to be improved, or who needed to prove themselves ethical by recognizing the criminality of their racist enterprise or the immorality and anti-democracy of their segregationist stance.

Thus, debate on the destiny of the territories formed a common ground in which the two movements of whites could establish a national presence for themselves as parties, in the context of agreement on the one issue that provided the political arena for it, namely, their solidarity and consensus on black disenfranchisement. This became the central dynamic that brought a multi-party situation to consolidate itself as a two-party structure. In other words, expansionism, the exporting of a specific political structure to other areas of the continent, as a prototype for late twentieth-century interventionism, was the dynamic from which the two-party system was constructed, intermeshed with the political expression of the structure of white consensus.

As the history of that period has been canonically written, the issue of the expansion of slavery to the territories was directly subsidiary to the conflict over which region of the nation would have control of the federal government. From 1800 to the 1856 election, the federal government was for the most part in the hands of the South, as the major economic power of the nation through its export of agricultural products, its landed wealth, and its economic stability. The industrialization of the North constituted a threat to the South's hegemony. As the eastern seaboard slave states stagnated owing to soil depletion, the South needed to extend itself to new pro-slavery areas. And the North opposed this expansion in its bid to gain federal hegemony. All that is fairly sound reasoning concerning U.S. history. What I am arguing is that the way the specific issues of slavery and the territories were formulated obeyed a racialized logic, and owing to that logic had a specific formative effect on the development of U.S. political institutions.

That process of formation itself had a structure. It reflected the structure of racialization and culminated in a particular political form that did not originate, for instance, on the European continent. European political systems, based on a definition and consolidation of nationality out of ancient cultural traditions, could permit and support ideological parties and political formations on a national level because they formed part of a common cultural ethos. Thus, a multi-party system in which elected representatives could be held to their party's program became the political tradition. Slavery and its regionalism made ideological positions untenable in national politics in the early nineteenth-century United States, and hence established a tradition of pragmatic rather than principled politics, with elected representatives having greater autonomy from either their party or their constituencies than was the case in Europe. The party system in Europe grew out of the gradual enfranchisement of class and cultural ideological forces while in the United States it grew out of the disenfranchisement of black people as a racialized group.

In sum, the form that political differences took during the moment of consolidation of the two-party system was based not on how to implement constitutional democracy but rather on how to organize white hegemony and how to structure white politics, for which black disenfranchisement was the necessary background. The white supremacist issue of black disenfranchisement was transformed into a common political language in which contesting political positions could talk to each other on a national scale. Rather than subordinated to regional politics, race became the overarching political language in which parties framed issues with respect to each other across regions.

In other words, rather than be a way to make democracy efficient, the two-party system formed around how to make democracy exclusive, as a way to make the structure of white hegemony efficient. What was preserved and sanctified by this confluence of political parties was the purity of the state as white. And in the process, what was truly at stake—the real anti-slavery and anti-segregationist interests of black people—was rendered politically ignorable by white politics.

In that sense, as a structure of disenfranchisement through non-representation, the two-party system can be considered a white institution. As a conjunction of white politics and black disenfranchisement, the two-party system became the envelope for the motifs of the messianism of that era (Manifest Destiny) and the interventionism of this one ("bringing democracy"). It constitutes the political landscape in which white people can find

residence for their general support of the government's interventions elsewhere in the world because it already expresses white racialized identity as
necessarily nationalist through its provision of an institutional identification
with the state. It is in the context of the two-party system that governmental
decision becomes the embodiment of national identity and that white-
identified people are brought to confuse policy with patriotism or nationalism. It is in this sense that anti-war protesters are accused of treasonous
opposition to the nation as such. And conversely, although Obama started
receiving many death threats after his election, his legitimacy was clearly
established through his being embedded in the two-party system, to which
he related as a whole in his initial attempt to bring about bipartisan involvement in economic crisis management.[18]

The alternative would be a system of proportional representation, one in
which the people would discuss political issues in their communities and
workplaces first and then elect representatives to represent those discussions. (The present system works inversely: people elect representatives, and
it is those representatives, rather than the people, who then meet and discuss
political issues.)

The Futility of Third Parties

What remains most salient about the two-party system today is its continued
function as a mechanism of disenfranchisement. This function is not only
available for deployment, as in the presidential election of 2000 in Florida,
which required the collusion of election officials, police, and both political
parties (Palast 2002); it is built into the structure of electoral districts. For
the most part, they are single-delegate, winner-take-all districts. If the winner
in a two-party contest assumes the role of representing the entire district's
electorate, those who belong to the losing party end up without representation, except through the largess of the winning party. To lose is to depend
on patronage rather than representation. This implies that representatives
represent the party that wins rather than the people who voted. In other
words, it is only through party organization that citizens can have an influence on political policy, meaning that the political needs of the people can
be expressed only through one of two leaderships.

But expression is still far from representation. In single-delegate districts,
an elected representative does not have the ability to effectively represent.
Electoral districts are composed of a multiplicity of interests, such as businesses, labor, landlords, tenants, ethnic communities, cultural groups, ideological groups, and racial communities. No single delegate can represent
them all, especially since conflicts of interest exist between these groups in

various forms. Each representative ends up representing no constituent interests well while at the same time getting absorbed into the matrix of a legislative body composed of other delegates facing the same inability to represent. Too often, this means that the representative goes to the highest bidder, which is generally a corporate interest or a specific interest organization (such as the association of prison guards in California, reputed to be the most powerful lobby in that state [Holwerda 2006]).

To be absorbed in a legislative body of representatives who cannot represent means to be immersed in a hermetic situation. To promulgate or promote a specific policy, a delegate must proceed by organizing a voting bloc among other representatives, and not by organizing the constituents whose interest would be fostered by that policy. A delegate can advance a particular project only by horse-trading projects with other delegates. The political content of the project, and its relevance to a constituency, becomes secondary to this "barter system" because of its separation from constituencies. Ultimately, as hermetic, an assembly of delegates attains interests and purposes of its own, disassociated from constituencies other than those that can afford a vast lobby apparatus. Such a legislature operates by focusing on itself and what it can accomplish as a group acting in its own interest. Representation then gets reduced to lip service to representation.

In short, there is a structural disconnect between constituencies and governmental bodies that locks all constituencies out of representation and participation except those with large financial resources. That structural disconnect is the direct effect of the confluence of the two-party system and the single-delegate district.

The irony of this situation is that it places popular, principled, yet financially unendowed constituencies, such as anti-racist or anti-interventionist movements (which will generally be stymied by the traditional and indispensable white solidarist consensus of both party leaderships), in a position where they need to form a third party, while the system's very structure condemns any third-party efforts to futility. Two major obstacles exist to forming a third party. The first is the traditional monopolization of the political field by the two major parties. The second is the "lesser-of-two-evils" idea. Both emerge from the confluence of the two-party system and the single-delegate district.

When a movement organizes a third party in order to accomplish in the electoral arena what the two major parties will not address, it is usually composed and led by people who emerge from one of the major parties, the one that is in general closest to the position advanced by the third-party effort. It calls on people from that party to join its alternate campaign. To the extent its call is successful, it ends up weakening the party that is politically closer to it and thus strengthening the other, the one politically more distant. When election time comes, the third party's candidate is assured of defeat (except in a very few unusual cases), because many of the people who support the third-party candidate will vote for the major party from which he or she emerged, as the lesser of two evils, in order to ensure that the other, more inimical party does not win. Weakening the lesser-evil party by voting for the third party (thus by implication strengthening the more-evil party) only makes the policy situation worse (what the third party was trying to correct in first place), while voting for the lesser-evil party destroys the third-party effort.

The lesser-of-two-evils problem is actually a euphemism for the inability of a mainstream political party to uphold a political or ideological principle. The need for national or statewide influence, the inability to represent legislatively, and the need to express political interests through a party apparatus rather than through the representative of a constituency all militate for rejecting political principle in favor of instrumentalities and expediencies.[19] Ultimately, there are only two interests that are consistently represented in this single-delegate two-party system, and they are the two interests that do not require a choice between parties to gain representation: corporate interests and the sanctity of white racialized identity. For instance, the United States decided to pull out of Vietnam, which had become a "quagmire" because the Vietnamese resistance was undefeatable (unless the U.S. military simply murdered half the population), only when two historical factors came together. The first was the repudiation of the war by major corporations because military spending had destabilized the international dollar. The second was the popular acceptance of the idea that the war was immoral and a mistake, an idea that contested the sanctity of U.S. (white) nationalism. While this fell short of seeing the war as an outright criminal endeavor, such a failure was also due to that same identity sanctity.

It is not beside the point that the "lesser-of-two-evils" slogan first appeared in the 1820s around the question of emancipation (Tise 1987). Given the choice between slavery and emancipation, between continuing the imprisonment of black people in forced labor or freeing them and thus creating communities of free black people, the former was considered by most whites to be the lesser of two evils. In other words, historically the lesser-of-two-evils idea refers to a traditional white consensus. In a fundamental sense, it is white consensus that has become institutional through the two-party system, allowing no inclusion of others (alternate parties) from outside its political supremacism. The two-party system is constructed to preserve the purity of white politics and the equation of white political identity with white national identity.

Where anti-war and anti-interventionist movements have generally failed in their project is in predicating their actions on the premise that the United States is a political state rather than a racialized entity. The problem for anti-interventionist movements is how to stop relying on "democratic" sentiment to discredit the mystique of interventionism and instead rise in opposition to its injustice. What those movements have not seen is that "democratic sentiment," as white, depends on that interventionism for the preservation of its racialized identity. Any program for justice (such as respect for other countries' national sovereignty) has negative capability insofar as it will crash against the self-justifications of the paranoia and violence of which whiteness is constructed. If a truly democratic ethic existed, it would have long since countermanded the aggressiveness of U.S. interventionism. But it could return the nation to the paths of justice only by abandoning the preemptive messianism of whiteness itself and its paranoid requirement to intervene. Being merely anti-racist is insufficient to this task. It is the underlying structural foundation for racism, the structure of racialization itself, that must be dismantled.

The Boundaries of the United States and Immigration

The Boundary of Whiteness

White democracy is a democracy based on exclusionism and an organizational monopolization of political participation. Its exclusionism originates in a paranoia, a sense of white solidarity, and a valorization of disenfranchising violence. It pursues its contemporary operations through a prison industry, interventionism, and police impunity, by which it preserves the white cultural cohesion for which the two-party system is the political expression. These are the means, not the ends, by which a white unity is constructed.

The two-party system emerges out of an historical and internal process of disenfranchisement, and it reflects that process structurally in its everyday operations. Interventionism produces an external form of disenfranchisement by destroying the sovereignty necessary for democracy in the areas assaulted. If the former establishes an ambiguous and shifting boundary between those it includes, who monopolize the political process, and those it excludes, the latter establishes a similarly ambiguous boundary by extending the ostensive national boundary of the United States out over those areas it invades. This double fuzziness of the U.S. boundary has been brought into relief as a political terrain in itself, and no longer a geographic line, by the attacks on Latino laborers who are labeled "illegal," who work in substandard conditions, are barred from social or political participation, and are instrumentalized as a new source of fear for white society. It is indeed ironic that a nation involved in internationalizing its own national legal structure would see fit to label as "illegal" those who come to its territory to work.

To understand Latino immigration, and the nature of the "illegality" imposed on it, we must understand the nature of the boundary by the crossing of which they are brought into existence as a group.

Borders That Are Not on Maps

In Oscar Handlin's account of immigration in *The Uprooted,* a second implicit border—in addition to the official border of the nation—makes its shadowy appearance. It is the border that he names "alienation." Writing sensitively from the perspective of the immigrant, Handlin presents it as a social barrier erected by the poverty to which most of Europe's new arrivals to the United States were condemned for roughly a century and a half, bruising them psychologically as they crashed into it and its categorization of them as strangers. Some well-heeled immigrants stepped easily over this border while those who had nothing but their labor to sell found it hard and grievous. Even the modes of exploitation were unfamiliar compared with the ones they had left behind. Often coming from rural areas, these immigrants understood agriculture better than industry, and industrial labor stranded them in their pauperization (Handlin 1951, 272). Many saw the way their accents caused judgmental scowls on others' faces as the doors of employment opportunity closed in their own. They crowded together in small apartments in order to pay the rent. Some vulnerable immigrants even allowed themselves to become an unwitting football kicked around by party politics. As often as they were told they would never make it as "Americans" because they were too lazy and too parasitic, they were also accused of competing in the market unfairly and taking jobs away from "American" workers. They looked at "America" through this pall of xenophobic prejudice as if from afar, while finding themselves in the midst of it and unable to extricate themselves.

Under the locutions of Handlin's pen, the force of this second border seems to occur automatically, as if it had happened to people before, or perhaps had never stopped happening. And indeed, it continues, appearing again in contemporary complaints about Latino immigration, leveled at those who risk their lives to cross a dangerous border for U.S. employment. These immigrants already know they will work jobs that white people rarely accept, simultaneously being accused of not wanting to work. They too encounter the shadowy second border and form culturally oriented communities to keep from starving psychically.

This unspoken internal border had previously appeared in the form of a different anti-immigrant movement even earlier than those explored by Handlin. During the 1800s in Pennsylvania, and later in other northern states, an anti-immigrant sentiment had expressed a similar concern about unwanted people who did not want to work, who would take others' jobs, and who were dirty and uncivilized. A segment of the public demanded that Pennsylvania's borders be closed to these immigrants. Oddly, the guards who would close this border were not to be stationed at the main port in Philadelphia but instead along Pennsylvania's southern border with Virginia and Maryland. Its target was not European immigrants but runaway slaves seeking freedom from southern plantations.[1]

This "anti-immigrant" movement was not driven by respect for the Constitution's clauses on fugitive slaves;[2] in 1847 Pennsylvania enacted a law of non-compliance with the federal policy of returning fugitive slaves (Turner 1911, 238). Nor did it reflect a fear that free African-Americans would become a political force; populist mobs and lawsuits were adept at preventing African-Americans from voting or having their votes counted from the early 1820s until African-American disenfranchisement was written into the Pennsylvania Constitution of 1836. Indeed, anti-black riots occurred in Philadelphia every year from 1831 to 1836. The very continuity of the violence suggests it was not fear that drove the white mobs but rather the intentional enactment of an unwritten social policy. As Leon Litwack points out, both pro-slavery advocates and white abolitionists participated in enacting segregationist regulations because the two groups agreed that a separation of the races was desirable and that integration resulted not in the "elevation of the degraded, but the deterioration . . . of the better class" (Litwack 1961, 66). In other words, these immigrants seeking freedom were perceived as a corruption of the purity of white "American" society. And the "nation" being delineated and defended by this internal "border" was the "white nation." What drove this early anti-immigrant movement was white nationalism.[3]

Yet the form and effect were so similar to that second hidden border appearing in Handlin's descriptions that they beg comparison. Like the new arrivals from Europe who landed in debt and were dependent on others, these refugees from slavery were thrown together in dehumanized conditions by a society that did not care how they lived. Forced into overcrowded slums, they were charged with being biologically inclined toward uncivilized living and self-imposed segregation—in much the same mode as the impoverished European immigrants (Handlin 1951, 272). In cities such as Philadelphia and New York, the impoverishment of runaway slaves only increased the poverty of the free African-Americans who already lived there (Turner 1911, 158–167), for they competed with each other for work that was withheld. Their destitution increased white hostility and segregationism. To be "accused" of poverty was to be accused of cultural inferiority, which these African-Americans then in turn suffered as a denial of employment. A bond or tax was levied in many cities on the Black community itself as a budgetary preparation for foreseen social care or welfare. Some ordinances required African-Americans to prove free status and often barred them from attending educational institutions (Litwack 1961, 70). These ordinances created an environment in which many whites granted themselves license to commit violence or to threaten it arbitrarily. In 1829, mobs assaulted Black communities in Cincinnati so severely that 50 percent of the African-Americans left for Canada.[4]

The overall African-American response was to form clandestine networks of Black organizations and mutual aid societies. Safe houses, later known as the underground railroad, were founded to facilitate escape from the South (McManus 1973, 263). And this highlights a significant distinction between the paths traveled by these different groups of migrants—the European immigrants and the escaping black bond-laborers. People escaping plantation bondage had to make their way across terrain infested with patrols, bounty hunters, and white people who simply believed that black people needed to be kept chained to hard labor. Few of these whites thought sympathetically of the physical torture or perhaps death awaiting those fugitives they might be party to returning to bondage. In contrast, among the hardships many Europeans encountered while traveling to a port to book passage to the United States was a hostility that only sped them on their way. And even if, in some cases, they were refused entry into the United States, they might return to destitution and possible dislocation in a European port far from their original home, but that destitution and dislocation did not come with additional punishment.

After the Civil War, many poor European immigrants had their tickets furnished by industrial agents in order to throw them into debt and debt servitude in the United States until their passage was paid off (Handlin 1951, 67); the steel, mining, railroad, and packinghouse industries were foremost in this practice, using debt to keep their labor force in line. For black escapees, the inverse was the case: they found only tenuous safety after arriving in a "free state." The threat from both fugitive slave-catchers and kidnappers who sold fugitives (and often free black people) into southern bondage permeated the culture. Black communities in the northern states, facing the possibility of the sudden seizure or disappearance of family or community members, often constructed elaborate security networks.

Jack Johnson and the Color Line

But let us speak of the nature of the white border itself. At the end of nineteenth century, the operations of that unspoken interior border can be seen in unmistakable terms in the life of Jack Johnson, as presented in a PBS documentary titled *Unforgivable Blackness: The Rise and Fall of Jack Johnson* (Burns 2005).[5] Jack Johnson was a black heavyweight prizefighter at the turn of the twentieth century. He was a quick and powerful man, an indefatigable boxer who emerged from the illicit fight circles of Texas during the 1890s. At the time, mixed matches, white and black, were forbidden under Jim Crow. Yet Johnson's name got around as the man to beat, and white as well as black challengers showed up to try to do so. Johnson defeated them all, at times ending up in jail along with his white opponent when the police decided to take a hand in the matter. Though Johnson remained undefeated, he reached an impasse, a boundary he found difficult to cross, when he challenged the heavyweight champion for the title. For years, the white title holders refused to fight him. John L. Sullivan, Jim Corbett, and Jim Jeffries in turn declared they would never let the title be taken by a black man. Their refusal demarcated an inner sanctum of championship as a domain to which Johnson would always remain an alien, a stranger, a man without a visa.

The fear (or cowardice) this expressed, and the unspoken premonition it contained, bespoke a fragility about white dominance that infected even that ultimate of "manly" sports. All the usual racist rhetoric was used. Johnson was the one called a coward, or lazy, or ignorant of the sport by those who feared to fight him, while in the same breath he was vilified for having issued his challenge in the first place. Only a blind obsession with whiteness and the sanctity of white society could engage in such double talk with a straight face. Provoked by Johnson's mere existence, the hegemony of white identity revealed a fragility and an obsessiveness that lurked within it like a specter.

Yet these white champions were spared the pain of confronting the meaning of their refusal by a vast outpouring of support and valorization from white society in general. The white press, white politicians, the white crowds who followed the sport, as well as average people on the street, concurred and honored this refusal and further denigrated Johnson's existence. Even that "man of the people," Jack London, chimed in on the side of white sanctity against Johnson's power and talent.

Nevertheless, Johnson met these assaults with equanimity and wit. He seemed to have an unwavering intuition of how to out-maneuver the white investment in segregation and the denigration of black people. Along with his talent in the ring, he showed a sense of dignity and an independence of personal comportment that was unflappable. His words bit into the fabric of the society that sought to exclude him, as he metaphorically kicked down its little white picket fences.

Intent on getting a title fight, Johnson chased whoever was champ around the country and even to Europe, repeating his challenges and publicizing the rebuffs. Finally, Tommy Burns (the title holder in 1908) was shamed into accepting the challenge. The fight occurred in Sydney, Australia. Johnson won the fight and the title with ease.

In the wake of his success, the attacks on him kicked into overdrive. White society responded (through press editorials and political statements) by disparaging him for his lifestyle, for the money he was winning, and for the women with whom he related—special note was made of the fact that many of the women closest to him were white. A defense of white hegemonics consumed the nation in a mass panic. Threats were made on his life, though he was not physically attacked. The white nation engaged itself in the task of finding a challenger, a "great white hope," to take the title back. All who were thrown at him, Johnson demolished.

With no new viable talent on the horizon, the former champion, Jim Jeffries, was coaxed out of retirement. The fight occurred in Reno, Nevada, in 1910. Surrounded by thousands of white people, all clamoring for his blood, Johnson answered the taunts of the audience with a smile. He toyed with Jeffries for fourteen rounds, often holding him up when he started to go down, to punish him for his earlier craven attitude and to wear down the crowd. Gerald Early (interviewed in the PBS film) suggests that if Johnson had just gone in and knocked Jeffries out in the first round, which he clearly could have done, there probably would have been a riot. When he finally put Jeffries out of his misery, the audience had become quiet, sick and tired of watching the inevitable. Johnson emerged without a scratch from the fight.

But the moment the news of Jeffries's defeat was broadcast, race riots occurred in dozens of cities around the United States. As Johnson returned home on the train to Chicago from the fight, hundreds of black people were beaten, shot, lynched by mobs, and burned out of their houses around the country. Editorials appeared warning black people not to think that they had gained any new stature or human standing as a result of Johnson's victory. Tortured and panicked by its own fragility, white nationalism's self-generated sense of its own lost stature and human standing appeared able to reinstate itself only through a spate of wanton violence and anti-black criminality.

Nevertheless, against these attacks, Johnson constituted a beacon of autonomy and self-respect for Black communities all over the United States. Beyond his talent in the ring, he showed an independence and ability to throw off the white boot heel that demanded obeisance. But if Johnson thus provided African-Americans with a renewed articulation of their entitlement to citizenship (simply on constitutional grounds, not to mention the claim authorized by their centuries of forced labor), the resultant assaults and riots demonstrated that Johnson's existence itself constituted a form of violence to the social coherence of white society—not unlike an aggressive act by a foreign power.[6]

In short, Johnson's experience further demonstrates the real content of Pennsylvania's earlier anti-immigrant movement. Both disclose a boundary of whiteness that was of much greater importance than the boundary to be found on a map.[7] The commonalities of these two histories suggest that whiteness was the real substance of that second border that haunted the subjects Handlin portrayed, whose form he could only label "alienation." Handlin's immigrants were just not-quite white.

The White, the Not-Quite-White, and the Not-White

Handlin does not address the subject of white identity. He never investigates in depth what was being preserved by the "nativism" by which anti-immigrant sentiment styled itself. His narrative leaves out the subject of escaped slaves as immigrants, despite their own analogous "uprootedness." Yet it had been against black people that the structures of discrimination the European immigrants encountered had been honed. It had been pro-slavery sentiment that had set them in place, ready to be shifted to the new arrivals—or not, depending on the whim of "nativist" sentiment. The machinery of exclusion and segregation, the accusations leveled against both groups, and the contorted and inverted logic used to rationalize both forms of discrimination impacted them similarly. While the form of this border of exclusionism and violence appears in Handlin's narrative, what adumbrates the content or substance that he omits, that is, its fundamentally racialized character, its delineation of a white nationalism, are the experiences of Johnson and, earlier, the escaped slaves.

Ultimately, the European immigrant groups who initially suffered from cultural exclusion and alienation found that second border porous for themselves. A mode of racialized integration into U.S. cultural membership (as white) awaited them (albeit sometimes across one or two generations). In contrast, the border that African-Americans continually encountered was one they could not cross without massive movements to break it down, such as the civil rights movements of the 1960s. For Handlin, these differences are incidental. At most, he explores the psychological significance of African-American experiences of alienation. Although the experiences of alienation and exclusion of the two groups are significantly different, they are not unrelated. The permeability of one boundary and the durability of the other implied that the European immigrant had the option to cross the ethnic border by offering to become a guard on the racialized border.

Handlin's sensitivity to the ethnic border and to those who collided with it is acute. It allows him to adopt the immigrant point of view rather than that of the "nativist." It is what inspires the insightful humanism of his book. In taking the European immigrant's perspective with respect to nativism, however, he too finds himself able to cross over that "nativist" boundary and to position himself on the side of the white nation with respect to black people—a stand he also takes with respect to the Chinese exclusion movement. He speaks of African-Americans and Chinese from afar, and no longer with a refined sensitivity to their perspective. He does not distance himself very well from the theories or theorists (foreign and domestic) of biological race inferiority, to which he gives brief mention (Handlin 1951, 275–279). He understands that for European immigrants, movement was possible toward enfranchisement. But he leaves untouched the fact that African-Americans were always being torn away from it—by state constitutional provisions before the Civil War, by systems of poll taxes under Jim Crow, and by the disenfranchisement attendant on the massive felony charges and racialized sentencing that today throw ever more people of color into the largest prison industry in the world.[8]

Although it is easy to generate metaphors about black people as immigrants in their own homeland due to the similarity of their treatment with that of European immigrant groups, significant differences remain in terms of the integration and prosperity of both groups. European immigrants eventually found they could cross the hidden boundary of "alienation" by aligning themselves with forces of racial exclusion, those that imagined black people as permanently immigrant in the country of their birth. They had only to become "white," a process that meant performing acts of "nativism" and abandoning the ethnic cohesion that attended their "alienation." Most often, this meant distancing themselves from black people and evincing a scorn that, when amplified, was a fully articulated anti-black racism. As Toni Morrison (1992) has pointed out, the process of rearticulation as white has worked for all groups of European immigrants. Adopting the anti-black ethos that united the "white nation" was the condition for admission beyond that second border.[9]

In bypassing the "other" immigrant movement without notice—and in having the luxury to do so—Handlin himself retraces the European immigrants' own mode of internal passage. Focusing on the national boundary that gets drawn on maps, he excludes what that "other" border, the "color line," signified by its existence. Writers such as W.E.B. DuBois and Frederick Douglass, among many others, had to play Handlin's role in telling the story of African-Americans who were refused permission to cross the color line,

Douglass as an escaped slave and DuBois as a raconteur of the conditions of the freed slaves re-enslaved in debt servitude after the Civil War.[10]

These two internal borders are not unrelated, despite their tangible differences. To the extent that a border is a technology of national existence, both the racialized and the "internal" border of "alienation" are part of the machinery of white cultural self-definition, a portal to be opened or tightened, racialized or deracialized according to the economic and cultural requirements of the moment. That is, behind the process of racialization and the alienation of "the uprooted," there is a single complex social structure that materializes through its performances of border defense: the structure of whiteness.

Jack Johnson's victory, the civil rights marches, the freedom rides, the voting registration drives, the children enrolling in schools in the wake of *Brown vs. Board of Education* were all met with a white populist defense. The intensity of white resistance to these events illuminates the threat it felt in the face of such racialized border crossing. The reprisals taken for Johnson's victory, the movement against affirmative action, the refusal to recognize the Mississippi Freedom Democratic Party at the Democratic Party convention in 1964, and the media-politician mob that barred Lani Guinier from appointment to a civil rights administrative post in 1993 (see note 7) all had the aura of indictments for trespass. In its defensive responses, white nationalism indicated that these transgressions had called its boundary and its very identity into question.

But they do more than that. These "border defenses" occur in a juridical context that has since taken the form of police profiling, brutality, and impunity toward black people that white society has generally found acceptable. That acceptability, beyond the ongoing empirical derogations of black personhood, signifies a purpose. The forms of exclusion enacted through white segregationist "border actions" are not merely erected in defense of a social framework but serve to racialize white people as white. Against the fragility of white racialized identity, the need for white social solidarity and allegiance is the real import of this second racialized white border.

Latinos and the Second Border

Today a new anti-immigrant movement has emerged against Latinos. It is a populist movement that includes rancher patrols, enjoys the support of many unions, and has spawned chauvinist or white nationalist para-military groups such as the Minutemen, who have terrorized Latino communities in the midwestern and southern states and have taken it on themselves to build a fence along the Mexico-Arizona border. Like the anti-black, anti-immigrant movement of the 1800s, this contemporary one seeks to prevent Latino immigration through a variety of laws, reorganized residency controls, a militarization of the border, and violence (e.g., the use of vigilante and SWAT team tactics against Latino communities). It has made border crossings dangerous in the same manner black escapees from slavery were. Thousands of Latinos have been shot or have died of hunger and thirst in the desert trying to get across since the 1980s.

Most migrant Latinos since about 1990 have crossed the U.S. border not to settle but to earn money to send back home to family and community.[11] This is far afield from the motivations of the African-Americans who moved to Pennsylvania in the 1820s. While the latter moved northward with the goal of never returning, the former migrate largely with the intention of going home after having saved some money. Most Mexicans, in fact, return home after an average of three years in the United States (Airola n.d.; Amuedo-Dorantes, Banzak, and Pozo n.d.). In this respect, Latino immigration also differs markedly from the immigration that Handlin describes. Most Europeans who immigrate do so with the intention of residing permanently in the United States and integrating themselves into white society, while Latino immigrants who come to stay often find integration barred in ways that parallel the segregation faced by African-Americans.

Latino immigration reflects the consequences of interventionism described in Chapter 4. To the extent corporate investment in Latin America is untrammeled and unbothered by taxes, royalty payments for resources, or labor unions, it functions as a direct source of impoverishment of those nations. During the period from 1930 to 1980, capital was generally invested in extractive industries. Using the cheapest of labor, the resources extracted were taken to the United States for its own industrial purposes. The rate of profit on investment in Latin America during the 1950s was 20 percent, meaning that an investing institution would recuperate its investment in five years. The profit from this process remained with the extractive firms, and the "host" nation received little from the enterprise. U.S. industry then returned manufactured goods to those countries, selling them at a second level of profit and thus extracting more wealth from them through marketing (Beals 1963). In effect, U.S. corporate investment functioned as a vast "vacuum cleaner," sucking up wealth from the poor and depositing in the pockets of the rich, an impoverishment machine that has left those nations destitute, their economies prostrate and defenseless against further corporate exploitation.

Since the 1990s, with the imposition of NAFTA, this process of impoverishment of Latin American societies has escalated. Under that treaty, no hindrances by either government or native capital were to be allowed to multinational corporate investment. And trade barriers were ostensibly eliminated. But because state subsidies to farmers were to be stopped by the treaty while subsidies to large corporations were not, agricultural goods such as corn, which were produced by corporate agribusiness, could be subsidized and exported from the United States to Mexico to undersell the small farmers who depended on their corn crop. Those farmers were then driven into poverty and unemployment, with little option left but to go north looking for work to support their families (Bacon 2008). In general, Latino immigration into the United States represents an attempt by Latinos to follow the money taken from them through U.S. economic exploitation of their own countries.

There is a closer historical parallel between Latino immigrants today and the roles played by African-Americans in the nineteenth century. In 1800, the U.S. economy depended on slave plantation production of agricultural goods for international trade and credits. And similarly, today the U.S. economy depends on Latino agricultural labor both for international trade and credits and for domestic fruit and vegetable products. Various economic disruptions have resulted from government raids or roadblocks against Latino agricultural workers. In one case, when immigration agents intercepted Latino workers traveling to northern California to harvest cherries in 2006, the agents were later sued by the cherry growers because the crop rotted on the trees. The arrest of twenty-one workers in the onion fields of Vidalia, Georgia, prompted thousands of workers to abandon the fields at the height of the harvest season. When a raid on a North Carolina town arrested twenty-four undocumented workers in the fall of 2004, inciting thousands of workers to leave or go into hiding, the town lapsed into depression because all economic activity stopped.[12]

Latino immigrant motivations differ markedly, of course, from those of escaping slaves before the Civil War. But their living conditions as laborers are similar to those of black tenant farmers after the Civil War. Many black agricultural workers, freed from slavery, found themselves thrown into a pseudo-enslaved condition called debt servitude by the crop lien system. As described in Chapter 2, the farmer would mortgage his crop at the beginning of the growing season at usurious rates in order to purchase seeds, tools, and subsistence supplies to carry him over to harvest time. The bank or commercial establishment owning the mortgage would seize the crop at harvest time, sell it, put the money toward interest and debt payment, and return to the farmer anything that might be left. If nothing was left, the farmer ended up deeper in debt. Thus, the farmer was tied to the land. Attempts to escape the trap of this debt by going elsewhere meant prison and the chain gang if caught.

Insofar as many undocumented Latino workers are paid subsistence wages, often in scrip, and housed under guard in labor camps (mostly on the East Coast), they live in forms of social constraint similar to those of black sharecroppers.[13] Attempts to escape, to form unions, to demand human rights, or to receive the social services to which their labor and taxes as workers entitle them run the risk of arrest, with arbitrary and often indefinite detention (without due process), by immigration authorities. Thus, undocumented workers, like black tenant farmers, are tethered to labor under extreme duress.

On the other hand, Latino laborers today have the possibility of escaping to cities where large Latino communities serve as havens, offering social networks among which to hide, obtain information and documents, and begin a more independent life.[14] Similarly, the vast migration of black laborers to northern cities after the 1880s to work in factories gave rise to communities that provided havens against the trap of debt servitude.

Latinos, like black citizens, face police profiling. Migrant laborers with Latino-looking faces or Spanish surnames are subject to harassment by Immigration and Customs Enforcement (ICE; formerly the Immigration and Naturalization Service). Raids on places of employment or neighborhoods are an ever-present threat. (See Chapter 2, note 18.) Any organized attempts to better their labor conditions expose workers to arrest, deportation, or indefinite detention (in violation of the Constitution). African-Americans face a parallel situation in the arbitrary felony charges often imposed on them, that is, the felonization of misdemeanors to induce plea bargaining and easy imprisonment, as described in Chapter 2. The immigrant has no access to basic civil rights, such as courts, trial procedures, or due process, while in the hands of immigration authorities. Though African-Americans are today granted the legal benefits of citizenship, discriminatory practices within the legal system often undermine them.[15]

The Common Structure in Anti-immigration

The conceptual thread that runs through these different immigrant landscapes spans the space between historical and contemporary forms. It signifies the underlying cultural structure we have been outlining here, especially the elements of forced labor, an ethos of imprisonment linked to police harassment (profiling), and an impunity (whether official or white populist) that is often deployed as an arbitrary form of terror. (See Chapter 2, note 6.) Today the massive incarceration of black (and Latino) people has embedded both these groups in an ever-expanding police-prison complex (described in Chapter 2). These are the structures that are common to the alternate borders engendered by anti-immigrant movements.

In effect, there have been three forms of anti-immigration, each one corresponding to one of the three eras of U.S. history: against escaped slaves during the slavery era, toward the alienation of European immigrants during the Jim Crow era, and a form of racialization of Latino immigrants during the present era. The historical position of these anti-immigrant movements suggests that they are critical elements in the defeat of the pro-democracy movements (abolition, Reconstruction, and civil rights) that mark the beginning of each era.

Conversely, the analogy between the color line of segregation and disenfranchisement (the original racialized border), the "internal" ethnic boundary (immigrant "alienation"), and the servitude to which Latino immigrants are subjected by the official and populist anti-Latino movements suggests they are technologies of the same cultural structure, which has deployed them variously during the different eras in order to define itself through them. Operating across those eras, they conjoin as a form of the state that produces them and is produced by their conjunction. The state of a white nation that defines itself (racially) behind one border is then the same nation that defines itself (nationally) behind the others.

Borders are the limits and delimiting elements of a state, the state of power, the power to define, the definition of political constituency, and so on. What those many borders generate in the United States is a state that functions both legally and against its own laws in sanctifying those borders, in a manner that recalls the impunity sanctifying U.S. interventionism. While these borders are conceptually incommensurable, with none being coincident with the border drawn on maps, they function in parallel ways with respect to the same social entity (white society) and the same underlying cultural structure that deploys them as its technology.

In effect, white racialized identity, as the content of that white "social entity," is given socio-cultural coherence by the racial boundary, and in turn gives a (white) "national" character to the "internal" alienating boundary that accompanies it. If that "national" character has a certain spectral quality, it is because it resides in a cultural rather than a geographic domain.

The Para-political Nature of White Populism

In these terms, the white articulation of the issue of Latino immigration takes on a strange, schizophrenic character. Latinos remain essential to the white economy, yet are to be excluded (deported or imprisoned) in the defense of the white boundary guarded in the name of the national boundary. That schizophrenics expresses the para-political character that white populism exhibits in its actions against not only immigrants, but black enfranchisement, affirmative action, and the like. The para-political is that which takes on certain attributes of the state yet operates beyond the state, freed to an extent from the constitutional bounds that are placed on the state.

During the Cold War, certain organizations, such as the American Legion and the Veterans of Foreign Wars, harassed people whom the government had named un-American. People were hounded out of jobs and neighborhoods and terrorized into silence by such harassment. Though it was, in general, unconstitutional and anti-democratic behavior, the government could say it had no control over it. Similarly, today, Latino immigrants and residents alike are the targets of white populist harassment in the name of hunting for those the government defines as "illegal," and the government can likewise disclaim responsibility.

Handlin mentions the specter of this populism, but he does not understand it. Speaking of the KKK in the 1920s, he says, "It was not so much because they hated the Catholic or the Jew that the silent men marched in hoods, but because by distinguishing themselves from the foreigner they could at last discover their common identity, feel themselves part of a meaningful body" (Handlin 1951, 280). Handlin is of course being too parochial here. The KKK was indeed anti-Semitic and anti-Catholic; but the identity · its members rendered *meaningful* for themselves by marching together under their hoods was a white identity, which had been honed and constructed through their violent and never silent racialization and oppression of black people. For Handlin, to exclude the KKK's central focus (black people) in his description is to position himself, as we observed above, within a white racialized identity.

What he misunderstands is the necessity for a threat from some recognizable and racializable quarter, and a populist presence in confrontation with it as the expression of a defensive solidarity, one that can guard the white border of U.S. society. Whether it is the KKK during the first quarter of the twentieth century or the White Citizens Councils of the decades following *Brown vs. Board of Education,* the anti-immigrant movement against escaped slaves in the 1820s or the Minutemen today, the function is the same. It is that function that was enacted by the thousands of whites who poured out to witness Jack Johnson's fights and to scream for his blood while others rioted and killed black people across the country.

From the slave patrols to contemporary police profiling, from police impunity to the militarization of the Mexican border, from the criminalization of African-Americans to the indefinite detention to which immigration authorities can subject their arrestees, from the migratory labor camps to the prison industry, there is a sequence of analogous structures that re/produces itself through borders, walls, and color lines. In each case, government action creates a paradigm that white populism then parallels in its para-political operations.

For all the people who feel the brunt of this white populism (black people, alienated Europeans, Latino immigrants), there are degrees of impoverishment and segregation. Similarly, there are degrees of development of cultures of resistance for survival. For all, there is a profound cultural structure that they confront which drives these processes of harassment and guardianship. Its surface contour is not just racism but a white exclusionist sanctity whose fundamental operation is a self-decriminalizing criminalization of those others.

The Question of Cultural Structure

The present discernible panic over the possibility of a "non-white majority" in certain areas of the country is bringing these incommensurable borders into yet closer proximity in a socio-cultural sense. Generated in a context of fear, laws pinpointing Latino immigration have been passed to deprive immigrants of humane social services and education. State laws depriving them of driver's licenses have been passed, as if to childishly and petulantly harass them while recognizing their presence and forcing them to work under conditions of greater immobility. A harsh misanthropic scorn is directed at those people traversing the border to find work (some of whom die).

The concern that people of color could become a majority is not a concern with democracy. In a truly democratic political environment, a shift of majorities should not be a problem, let alone be a source of callous misanthropy. The concern is an anxiety about the sanctity and coherence of white hegemony and its underlying white racialized identity. It means that its political coherence and identity can be preserved only if whites remain the majority. It is tantamount to claiming that for whites, democracy is white, as a political structure, and that it can continue to be a democratic structure only with a white majority. If the coherence of white culture is what is in question, then Latino immigration will be perceived as a threat of subversion of white society's sense of its own purity, both socially and in its whiteness. Its panic resonates with the fear expressed in denying a black man the opportunity to become boxing champion. It preserves itself even after a black man is elected president. It is this same ethos that obstructed the integration of European immigrants into U.S. society until they figured out how to be white. In other words, the political substance that lurks under

the interweaving of "immigrant/racialization" borders is the cultural structure of whiteness.

A cultural structure is more than a way of thinking, a mindset, or a way
in which disparate elements of human experience render themselves coherent as knowledge for members of a society. It is also a relation of social
practices that cohere as common understanding, as both a regularized pat-
tern or norm of social thought and the production of that thinking itself. It
defines the proper and the ethical through acceptance of those social practices.[16] Discerning its operations is important analytically insofar as it provides the ability to understand those who reside within its framework and
see the world through its contours. But more importantly, for those who
reside within its framework, it is essential to grasp those contours if they
wish to see beyond it, to perceive how their own cultural structure scripts
their own thought and behavior.

Insofar as the structural relations examined here involve the police, the
judiciary, and so on, it is important to recognize that these departments of
governance do not constitute cultural institutions as such. The cultural is
what is reproduced in their modes of operation and in the structure of their
activity rather than in their institutional existence. Police and white populist
impunity, a prison industry based on a revenge ethic, the permissibility of
indefinite detention and police torture, arbitrary assault or arrest, the stereo-
typed criminalizations of African-Americans, the doctrine of an "illegal" person are what express the underlying cultural structure of white society
(regardless of whether all the persons enacting these practices are in fact
white). White (para-military) populism (both police and civilian) is granted
authority by the cultural structures that organize and govern it and provide
it with familiarity rather than statutory legitimacy. The waves of lynchings
that have swept the United States at various times, toward which the police
have traditionally turned a (complicit) blind eye, have depended on this
cultural legitimacy (familiarity). Although the para-military and the "para-
political" draw the same rhetorical legitimacy from reference to official jurisprudence, their authority grows out of the recognition given them by members of their society. Indeed, it is their innate familiarity that makes them
acceptable.

Insofar as white identity and the coherence of white culture depend on
certain institutions, those institutions express components of the structures
of racialization. Historically, the social manifestations of the structures of
racialization have been the means by which white society has produced itself
as white over against others it has defined as non-white for its self-racializing
purposes (Martinot 2003b, ch. 4). There are, of course, many ways for white
society to make itself white. In his seminal work on the variety of forms of

the construction of whiteness in California, Tomás Almaguer has revealed different forms of white self-racialization with respect to Mexicans, Native Americans, and Asians (Almaguer 1994). The Mexican land grant owners of California were alienated from their land through a juridical attack on local entitlements. A federal requirement for property deeds was instituted, despite the absence of such legal instruments for those land grants. Often incapable of meeting the new requirement, the land grantee lost the land, reducing him to second-class status with respect to the white settlers armed with their federal statutes. Native Americans, on the other hand, were declared by fiat to be non-human and were hunted, killed, or enslaved with a barbarity that white culture nevertheless managed to use to proclaim itself non-barbaric (civilized). In effect, those who were indigenous to the territory were transformed into foreigners, in a process by which the white settlers "nativized" themselves on that land. Finally, as Alexander Saxton has argued, it was against the Chinese laborers brought to build the railroad that white workers in California defined themselves as the working class through a populist anti-Chinese labor movement—and thus defined the working class as white (Saxton 1971).

The structures we have explored exceed simple prejudices. What is at stake is a conception of the United States in which its social and political system has defined itself in a racialized manner. The fear of a non-white majority, focused on Latino immigration, is a fear generated not only by the fragility of white racialized identity, or its dependence on those it racializes, but by its need to preserve the state and its political institutions as white. It is to ensure that although black or brown people join parties, run in elections, get elected to office, and vote on measures, they do so within white institutional structures. That is, they function within those political structures as if given a certain "residency," or "green card," to work at pre-specified levels of institutionality or governance. The mere presence of black or brown persons in white political structures does not change their racialized character because the whiteness of these institutions is structural. This holds for Obama and the presidency as well. The structure in which black or brown people participate remains a white structure because each black or brown face remains a "minority" face. This is why, for many white people, each black person elected to office is said to represent all black people (and each .elected Latino to represent all Latinos, etc.), instead of being viewed simply as a Black or Latino voice in the halls of government, which would assume a greater degree of parity and equality.

The border that anti-immigrant movements defend is a border that circumscribes and protects the operation of the structures of racialization which constitute the foundation for both white culture and the white nation.

The purpose of the structures of racialization is not simply to define and exclude non-whites from full social participation, but to redefine, reconstitute, and reconsolidate white racialized identity in the face of its own fragility and dependence, and to decriminalize its acts of protecting that fragility by turning its dependency into a determination to dominate through a repression and criminalization of all resistance to its hegemony. Fragility requires violence, police impunity, an ethos of imprisonment and forced labor as its first option toward those the white nation racializes. While the people racialized differ over time, bearing different histories and locations, they all reside in a similar structural condition—as "other" to the white nation that depends on them economically and culturally.

In these terms, a fundamental aspect of anti-racism becomes how to rescue white people from the dependency and fragility to which their white racialized identity has condemned them.

6

The Dual-State Character
of the United States

Introduction

A national border is part of the technology of a state as well as the edge of a nation. The several internal and unmapped boundaries we have encountered have shown themselves to constitute the technology of a white para-political entity and the edge of the white nation, residing within the United States under the auspices of the official constitutional state. That alternate entity, which moves beyond the limits of the political while expressing and socially instituting policies culturally, that is, manifesting what is taken for granted in the white culture, forms a mode of para-political state.

White Populism and the State

Let us return to the historical event that Jack Johnson's life became. In the wake of Johnson's 1908 victory over Tommy Burns in Sydney, newspapers and commentators called on Johnson to return to his place in the racist hierarchy, and they counseled black people not to think more highly of themselves because of Johnson's victory. That is, Johnson's status as a beacon of self-respect and personhood for black people required a special response. When white populism failed to stop him and he did not return to his place, white society turned to more stringent (and strident) measures. The state was enlisted to find an indictment. (See Chapter 5, note 6.)

In 1911, the government concocted a fraudulent (and illegitimate) charge against Johnson under the Mann Act. The Mann Act prohibited the transportation of women across state lines for immoral purposes. The government warped the intent of the law by focusing on trips Johnson had made across state lines with a white girlfriend. Since the woman was white, Johnson's intimacy with her, though of mutual affection, was proclaimed by definition (a priori) to be "illicit." Again, a woman was instrumentalized for the state's political purpose: to reconstitute the coherence of white society in the face of the threat posed by this one man.

The government's first attempt failed because Johnson's current lover, Lucile Cameron, refused to testify against him. The FBI then procured the services of a former lover, Belle Schreiber, to accuse him of Mann Act violations. It did not matter that the journeys to which she could testify occurred before the Mann Act had been passed and thus could not justifiably (or constitutionally) be used against him. Evidently, for the white state, warping the law for the repression of a self-respecting black person (or person of any color) trumped all principles of jurisprudence or justice. We see a similar corrupt pragmatics at work in the cases of Mumia Abu-Jamal (Lindorff 2003) and Leonard Peltier (Messerschmidt 1983), who are still in prison. The government got its conviction of Johnson, without constitutional or evidentiary grounds or justification. And after a brief flight to Europe, Johnson returned and served a year in prison. In effect, white populism was able to wield the constitutional state for its own purposes.

This is not an isolated incident. The obsessive racialized solidarity between a repressive social populism, the political structure, and the media has effected itself again and again, even up to the present. We have recently seen it war against Ward Churchill when he happened to put his finger on what made the U.S. economy tick: its financial administration of the impoverishment of the third world for corporate enrichment.[1]

Churchill, a Native American professor of ethnic studies at the University of Colorado, has been a severe critic of the racist foundations of the United States, its colonialist history, and its genocidal policies toward all Native Americans. At one point in 2004, he was invited to give a lecture at an eastern college. A single derogatory remark by a nationalist white talk show host about one phrase in a three-year-old article, taken out of context, was all it took to elicit a call for his blood. The shock jocks, newspaper editorials, special state investigative commissions in Colorado, and even his own university administration all joined the mob. Few had read his work: some said they did not have to, while others said that they would go over it carefully enough to find what they needed to fire and disgrace him. When academics and high government officials go into frenzies over a shock jock's turn of phrase, it is not because they are shocked but because they are already primed for posse duty, and need only a single rabid word to mount up and hit the trail.

The attacks on Lani Guinier and Mumia Abu-Jamal have been mentioned earlier. (See Chapter 5, note 7.) Mumia Abu-Jamal was a journalist who wrote and spoke about police violence against the Black community in Philadelphia during the 1970s. The police took the first opportunity to frame him for the murder of a police officer. Despite the bigotry and prejudicial corruption of his first trial, the availability of evidence of his innocence to both the court and private citizens, the proof of withholding evidence by the police, and the recanted testimony by witnesses, the politician-media-police mob that labels him a "cop killer" keeps him on death row without access to a fair retrial. At all levels of the judicial process, a false prioritization of formal procedures over the substance of his innocence or the interests of justice has been used to prevent him from introducing the evidence of his innocence or contesting his tainted conviction (Lindorff 2003).

Conversely, there is a white obsessive defensiveness in the silence that has greeted the egregious assassinations of Black leaders (e.g., Malcolm X, Fred Hampton, Malcolm Ferguson, George Jackson) and the frame-ups of Assata Shakur, Geronimo Ji-Jaga Pratt, Kevin Cooper, Ruchel Magee, and many other autonomous black persons. It manifests itself today in the acceptance of a prison industry into which people of color are shoveled and warehoused through racially enhanced sentences and the vast system of victimless crime laws of which the accused have become the victims. As stated earlier, and worth repeating, the United States has the largest prison population in the world, both in numbers and per capita, 75 percent of whom are people of color. (See Chapter 2, especially note 3.)

It is not the existence of these politico-populist mobs that is astounding (and to remain silent in the face of a "mob" action like the assassination of Fred Hampton is to be part of the mob), but the fact that they are so ready to swing into action or to maintain their supportive silence.

Frantz Fanon argued that a decolonized subjectivity, that is, a former colonized subject who had brought him- or herself to think and act autonomously, is seen by the colonialist state as an act of violence against itself.[2] Johnson's life itself was perceived as an act of violence directed at the coherence of white society. Johnson's equanimity in the face of racist taunts and his breaking the color line as a public figure were interpreted by white society as a whole as doing aggressive damage to its identity; hence, no one was prosecuted for the attacks after his 1910 victory.

The form of "Fanonian" personhood that Johnson embodied and symbolized is not limited to men or to specific kinds of characters. It can be applied to anyone who emerges from the many underclasses of U.S. society to provide an example of human autonomy in a struggle against coloniality. The Fanonian men and women who have emerged in the United States are legion. Fannie Lou Hamer led the Mississippi Freedom Democratic Party in 1964 against the political monopoly of the regular party. Marcus Garvey, in mobilizing whole communities to change the political nature of U.S. urban space, led a decolonizing movement against the white monopoly of that space. Gregorio Cortez, mythified in song and film, symbolized the undefeatable spirit of resistance. Let us include Angela Davis, Leonard Peltier, John Trudell, the American Indian Movement, Adam Hakim, Elizabeth Gurley Flynn, Mother Bloor, Mother Jones, and Big Bill Haywood. Some are white; all present a form of courage against injustice that has elicited, in various forms, the howls and calumnies of a threatened white corporate society. The panic and obsessiveness expressed becomes an additional lens, a further insight into the inner workings of the structure of racialization.

Contra-state and the Para-political State

Let us invent some terms with which to speak about these things more pointedly. Issues lose focus when fragmented into individual incidents, even by the mere act of listing them, as in the preceding paragraph. Each incident, each Fanonian individual, becomes an isolated case when taken out of context. Context has to be named and described to provide the commonality of content, the source of paradigmatic existence that conjoins them.

Let us use the term "contra-state" to name the domain of existence of those people whom the state or para-political populism sees as a threat to itself. In the sense that Johnson's life encountered a form of proscription and arraignment at the hands of both officialdom and white society at large, he lived what could be called a contra-state life—a life whose every move was apprehended as anathema (and thus a threat) to white socio-political norms.

Personal and communal autonomy is one of the attributes of the contra-state. It is not secessionist or separatist since that would render the notion of autonomy, whether communal or individual, irrelevant by removing it from the context in which autonomy functions as a form of resistance. Instead, the salient fact attending a person in a contra-state role is precisely that person's insistence on autonomy of life and thought within and against the coloniality of the surrounding white society.[3] It is, as well, a clear indication that the nation is anti-democratic (regardless of its proclamations or intentions). Democracy, after all, is based on the principle of autonomous and independent persons coming together to make collective decisions concerning their destiny. It is the suppression of that autonomy that testifies to the social dimension of white coloniality and anti-democracy.

What Johnson's life demonstrates is that a white supremacist frenzy lurks deep within banal daily racism or populist prejudice. It has a political content that overflows the bounds of official governance while remaining closely linked to it. At the behest of this hidden frenzy, unlegislated rules are enforced; punishment is exacted for the crime of existence; social standards are violated with impunity, as if they did not apply to the social order. They emerge as political operations that do not get named "political" because their coherence is extra-legal and self-legitimating.

If this para-political populism has a political content, it is that it occupies itself with its own rules, judgments, punishments, and impunities, which emerge from its inchoate mass obedience to what is taken for granted, namely, the properness of the racialization of society with white supremacy as its norm and hegemonic model. In other words, it takes on the attributes, in virtual form at least, of an alternate state. It takes on the virtual aura of a state insofar as it imitates the operations of a constitutional state through multiple political performances designed to conjoin its members within a common social context, which is a social identification with whiteness. That is, it secretes itself within the constitutional state of official governance, lurking behind legalisms and the rhetoric of official jurisprudence (rules, judgments, and bureaucratic ethics) while reserving for itself its unofficial status. Thus, from behind the traditional modernist nation-state governed by constitutionality (rules), legalist rhetoric (judgment and punishment), and officialdom (bureaucratic or formal ethics), this self-defined, alternate para-political state emerges as an unofficial enforcement of white entitlement and white social cohesion.

It has no practical social policies other than the ideology of white supremacy, whose enactments and violence remain its mode of self-definition and self-expression. It has no juridical form other than the white allegiance and white solidarity it engenders for itself in order to dominate people of color. Its juridical acts or practices consist of the violence and depravity it grants itself and finds permissible against those others through whom it defines itself as white. In particular, it represents a cultural polity that structures itself through those forms of violence. It legislates sexuality (in an unwritten and informal sense). It even becomes the arena in which severe disagreements over how to deal with certain individuals or groups (e.g., Johnson or the Panthers) can be debated. And it views the existence of someone like Johnson as an invasion, as if by a foreign power. What confronted Johnson and the Black community first was this para-political state with its vigilante indictments and punishments.

As a mass populist social entity, this para-political state operates according to unwritten cultural standards and administers its violent enactments through an ethic of white racialized entitlement. Its inner cohesion is constructed by individual acts of identification with that ethics and its insistence on white supremacy. It substitutes white allegiance for the Constitution, permissibility and impunity for legality, and supremacist norms for legislation.

The constitutional "state" is the entity that handles official rules, formally derived punishments, and ideal-conforming ethical judgments. Its operations and attributes exhibit a collection of political functions along five conceptual lines. The first is a demand for solidarity from its social membership (citizenry) around cultural norms; second is a common expectation of political performance by those citizens; third, a sense of permissible violence pursuant to political goals; fourth, an enforcement of common (political and personal) standards of comportment among its citizens; and finally, a defense against external aggression. This was the state of officialdom that turned a blind eye to the game of illicit boxing from which Johnson emerged. (And in so doing, it acceded to the demand by the para-political state that the sport of illicit boxing be allowed to exist for its own entertainment and its propensity to gamble, and as a general arena for the discharge of aggressions.)

The para-political state, on the other hand, decided when and how Johnson's personal comportment violated its social standards, especially his intimacy with white women. It was what led the charge against Reconstruction, affirmative action, and civil rights in general. It is the primary force for coloniality in the United States insofar as it is dedicated to the reduction of people of color to second-class status as social objects for itself. It is exclusionary insofar as it organizes social actions to maintain segregation (not only during the Jim Crow era) and to support the reconstitution of segregation when needed—for instance, its support for police impunity in the present era. Thus, it becomes the active agent in maintaining what George Jackson (1970) has characterized as the subcolonial status of communities of color (internal to the United States, exploited as sources of cheap labor, and used as special markets).[4]

Johnson's entire life as a boxer was a confrontation with these two state structures. It was the para-political state that first saw his existence as a form of violence against itself and, in perceiving Johnson to be in violation of its white cultural sanctity, viewed its own aggressions as a defense of white society. It was the para-political state that induced the constitutional state to break its own rules in order to arrest and convict him. In that sense, the constitutional state did violence to itself at the behest of the para-political state. In other words, Johnson's contra-state character became a real threat to the constitutional state insofar as he, in his mere existence as a powerful athlete, turned the constitutional state against itself through the para-political state.[5]

The para-political state is the state in which those who are white-identified, and who affirm their "white racialized identity," are claiming membership. It is through their identification with that state that whiteness gets its social and cultural substance and meaning. The para-political state is not a racialized state but the state of racialization. It acts consensually within a white supremacist cultural framework. The entire history of vigilante para-military activities—the lynch mobs, the current border Minutemen, the KKK, the hard-hat attacks on anti-war demonstrators during the Nixon administration—are the activities of the para-political state. Its violence and judgments trump the legalisms of the constitutional political structure, and its criminality is either acquitted (as were Amadou Diallo's killers) or slighted in punishment (as was Tom Coleman of the Tulia travesty [see Chapter 2, note 8]). It can call on constitutionality when it needs more than self-legitimization. And insofar as the complex relationships of white social hierarchy and white hegemony, which constitute cultural structures rather than political issues, must be maintained, the constitutional state is always ready to grant tacit and unspoken legitimacy to the para-political state.

The constitutional state, of course, has its own well-known forms of state violence—the army, the police, the courts, and the prisons—which it deploys to maintain what it calls "law and order." But police actions against black people—including profiling, arbitrary arrests, and torture, which transcend legality and law enforcement—represent para-political violence. Though the police remain officials of the constitutional state, their actions cross that boundary to the alternate, para-political realm. In this sense, the police constitute an interface between the two states. Police profiling traverses this boundary by replacing the search for a suspect with an act of police suspicion that then searches a target group for the possibility of charging a crime.

The legitimation and authorization that the white para-political state receives from the constitutional state has long historical precedents in the enactment of traditional white supremacy.[6] It appeared in the Constitution's original support for slavery (Wiecek 1977), the juridical valorization of white supremacy in the Dred Scott decision, the contemporary trampling of black women's child-bearing rights (see Chapter 1), and the judicial and populist movement to abolish affirmative action. In the persecution of Jack Johnson, the constitutional state conceded the para-political state's perception of his existence as an act of violence, and the latter welcomed the former's distortion of its own principles in his prosecution. Each state becomes a buttress for the other. And indeed, many forms of violence characteristic of one or the other actually overlap between the two: the torture of black and brown suspects in police stations, the standard use of SWAT teams to serve arrest warrants for non-violent crimes on black or brown suspects, the invention of a prison industry to replace Jim Crow segregation with the geographic separation and disappearance facilitated by the prison wall.

Because it resides between two states, police criminality (like the wanton shootings of Amadou Diallo or Sean Bell) is beyond reform by its victims or their community. Attempts to act through the constitutional state will not affect the norms established by the para-political state, which remain out of reach of the constitutional state. Conversely, to attack the para-political state will result in criminal charges levied against the anti-racist persons who do it by the constitutional state. By extension, any political opposition or reformism with respect to the constitutional state will necessarily be inadequate, since the para-political state will be insulated behind it, equipped with a political force of a different order against the reformers. And radical or revolutionary confrontation with the constitutional state will bring about no transformation of the para-political state, which will be the constitutional state's main force of defense against that radicalism. Indeed, the para-political state will probably perfuse the ranks of any radical or revolutionary movement, if only in the unconscious internalization of white hegemony by white radicals.

It is the existence of this para-political state that will survive the symbolic undermining of white supremacy by the Obama election. It is true that many white people, mostly young, supported this final break in the color line, just as they had accepted Colin Powell and Condoleezza Rice, Mayor Dinkins and Mayor Washington. But none of these officials contested the coherence of the constitutional state, since they gained their elections to office through it. And none of them sought to hinder the operations of the para-political state, whether populist or police, since they were forced to restrict their activities as state officials to that which was legal for the constitutional state. Each was therefore isolated and surrounded by a white management, a sub-management, a network and matrix of white people involved in politics, with whom to work. What the para-political state feels as a danger is that Black and Brown communities might attempt to build on and concretize the cultural sense of autonomy and self-respect that these officials, and the Obama election in particular, might have given them.

In other words, what the Fanonian character of the persons we have noted above suggests is that autonomy of personhood and community is what most existentially subverts the power of the para-political state. It does not provide the confrontation with constitutional political structures that resistance movements do, but it destabilizes the identity of both states at once.

Existence in an Allo-cultural Domain

Though Johnson stood in opposition to this para-political state his entire life, it was not through any intended opposition. He simply insisted on his own autonomy, dignity, and self-respect. That was who he was. It was the para-political state that proclaimed him to be living beyond its cultural framework, as a result of which a contra-state existence was thrust on him. If the para-political state has to respond to someone like Johnson (or any other Fanonian individual) with denigration, demonization, mob force, or violence, it is because it has defined those individuals as violence incarnate, perceived as aggression personified—as happened to Lani Guinier and Ward Churchill. This is the white para-political ethic. After the denigration or demonization begins, there is nothing the person can do to throw it off. They are wholly renarrativized by the generalizations in the attack. Similarly, when the police instruct a movement to keep its demonstrations peaceful, there is no response the demonstrators can give that will convince the police that they are peaceful because the existence of the demonstration is already an act of violence unless specially governed by police hegemony.

But if this is the case, the lives of Fanonian individuals must truly represent an alternate state of cultural being. In accepting the contra-state character given them, they are thrust onto a cultural terrain that is beyond political and social norms, even of the constitutional state. This alternate terrain has nothing to do with the law. The law, in its constitutional function, deals with individuals and how they have acted, not with how they are presumed to act (by the para-political state). The judgments of presumption by which the para-political state administers itself may perhaps call on the constitutional state when necessary, and that can at times lead the constitutional state to violate its own norms. But the alternate terrain of contra-state existence is constructed as incommensurable with that of the constitutional or the para-political states. As a domain for the affirmation of dignity and self-respect, in whatever way it can defend itself against the political repression of coloniality, it involves a return to the human, a process of humanization, that stands in contradiction to the racialization that is the stock in trade of both states.

If the structures of racialization are central to the cultural coherence of white society, then for those racialized by that society, an alternate domain of cultural existence can be said to be the first principle, the first foothold from which to contest these structures and their institutions. It would have to be a space of alternate culture where the racialized can rehumanize themselves and construct an autonomous culture of humanization. For the para-political state, humanization that it does not control as "white humanism" can only signify standing in opposition to racialization in a way that will appear as violence to its domain of racialization. Though a culture of humanization simply represents a cultural alternative, it will nevertheless be charged with criminality by the para-political state. This is what has happened to the Black power movement, to the Puerto Rican independence movement, to AIM, to Ward Churchill, to Sami al-Arian, and so on. And it is what Fanon articulated so forcefully in *Black Skin, White Mask.* (See note 5 above.)

Let us call this domain an "allo-cultural" terrain (*allo* meaning "other" in Greek). It is where those who have been racialized and generalized by the endless performance of whiteness at the hands of members of the para-political state can think and act autonomously, even in the middle of the white supremacist society that condemns them for it. The "allo-cultural" is not a geographic but a social and ideational terrain.

The autonomy that Johnson or Guinier inhabited represented a violence for white society, not a criminal violence as such, but "allo-cultural violence." Since it did not appear as criminal violence, it had to be ideologically and rhetorically criminalized in order to be attacked as a form of (threatened) violence.[7] (If we think back to the demonization of leaders of nations in which the United States sought to intervene, we see the same structure. The one act that Cuba committed with respect to the United States, for which it has been endlessly attacked and vilified through the demonization of Fidel Castro, was its uncompromising insistence on its sovereignty.)

For Fanon, violence is the fundamental language that colonialism speaks or thinks. Anti-colonialist violence is thrust on the colonized by their every attempt to be human, to achieve their own subjectivity. It is the nature of domination that there is nothing the dominated can do autonomously that will not be seen as violence. And when the coloniality of power, in whatever guise, attacks that autonomy, it will see itself as acting in self-defense. This is the character coloniality gives itself in refusing to recognize the autonomy of the other, a character that can only enmesh coloniality in its own morass of violence. We saw this happen with the attack on the Branch Davidian compound in Waco, Texas, in February 1992. This is also what has happened in Iraq and Afghanistan. It is the very essence of impunity, exemplified in the horror of the Guantanamo prison, for instance, that breaks with half a century of international law and centuries of human moral development, authorizing itself with the flimsiest of terminological inventions ("enemy combatant," a term that criminalizes defense of one's own nation or culture against U.S. invasion).

If the purpose of para-political violence is to reduce the allo-cultural subject to object status and obeisance, the purpose of allo-cultural subjectivity is conversely to retrieve autonomy against para-political violence.[8] These two processes, though sounding inverse, are instead incommensurable. There is no common dimension, no common thought or act of language or communication that will have the same meaning for both. The latter affirms a humanity that the former cannot apprehend because the former thinks and speaks a language of racialization that predefines and generalizes people, and thus cannot know them in their appearance as real individuals. For instance, the para-political state assumes that black people are inferior and sees their refusal of that inferiority as an act of violence against itself. Black people conversely see their inferiorization by the para-political state as an act of violence against themselves, to be responded to with refusal. The two sides may use the same words to describe this situation, but the words "inferiority" or "refusal" have no common meanings between them. What is self-affirming for one side appears as an act of violence for the other. For communities of color, para-political violence is gratuitous. For the para-political state, any sense of dignity in a person of color is seen as rebellion.

For communities of color, there is an inability to convey their situation to most whites, because most white people hear through their own hegemonic reasoning and assume that "justice" is understood as white justice. When whites speak of justice, many people of color may hear it through their experience of para-political justice and thus hear it as racialization.[9] It is not that whites suppress dialogue intentionally in order to preserve their hegemony (though some do). Dialogue is existentially vacuous a priori for members of the white para-political state because it approaches the other through its assumed power to speak for the other. Dialogue can occur only between autonomous persons who can think and speak for themselves.

In sum, an allo-cultural autonomy of black and brown people is what is implied by the white para-political aggression and its attribution of violence to them. Against this, what autonomy potentiates is the construction of alternative political structures, as a mode of instituting the refusal of obeisance to the para-political state that autonomy implies. Alternate political structures have always existed in the United States. The early Black churches, the underground railroad, worker's cooperatives, the Farmer's Alliance, Black power, the Black arts movements, AIM, La Raza, the Tijerina movement, the Mississippi Freedom Democratic Party, Aztlan, the IWW, radical industrial unionism were all forms of allo-cultural autonomy.

In a profound sense, what the Zapatistas have taught, as an indigenous movement (not wholly alien to what Jack Johnson represented), is what the transformation of political space into an alternate political culture could look like. Beginning with an alternate knowledge of themselves as indigenous, with an alternate decolonized epistemology toward the world, they have constructed an allo-cultural terrain (Esteva 1998). Their autonomous municipalities represent an allo-cultural violence for the constitutional (Mexican) state, which can see that allo-cultural terrain only as subverting its own sovereignty. Zapatista autonomy uncompromisingly refuses legitimacy to the Mexican nation-state, precisely because the Mexican state cannot see (behind the blinders of its own sense of threat) what indigenous sovereignty represents. That refusal is its response to the Mexican state's refusal to grant subjective and political autonomy to indigenous peoples, but instead to continue their colonization.

If whiteness and the institutions of white racialized identity occupy a dual state, with dual borders and a dual way of looking at or philosophizing race, all in parallel and alternate to the official state and its political structures, it suggests that the structures of racialization, for which white people are the active racializers, are the most fundamental cultural structures in the United States. They have duplicated (at least virtually, that is to say, culturally) all social institutions as their means of operating under the cover of officialdom.

And thus, for anti-racism and the decolonization of the white mind, it is essential to grasp the importance of a domain of allo-cultural being from which to contest the para-political state. It is perhaps the failure to understand the depth of racialization in this culture, and thus the need for an allo-cultural domain, that has led to the ultimate failure of all anti-racist movements and processes up to the present. Even in the present, racism and white supremacy are considered ideologies that in principle could be refuted. Most anti-racists have thought that argument and laws passed by the constitutional state were a place to begin, without seeing the essential futility in this. But the dependency inherent in racial domination, and the violence in the ethics of racialization that drives the para-political state in all its racist acts and assumptions of white supremacy, is not an ideology but a cultural structure that must be dismantled.

Rebellion and Autonomy

The concept of alternate political structures is inseparable from the question of rebellion. But as Fanon has pointed out, there is a difference between rebellion and cultural autonomy. Rebellion is vertically oriented and acts strategically, while autonomy is allo-cultural and acts with a horizontal self-germinating communal orientation. For the colonized and the racialized, autonomy is the necessary response to racializing de-subjectification, as it is to all forms of coloniality. Rebellion can only initiate the process of re-subjectification; it cannot foster the cultural terrain in which community and subjectivity can restore or reinvent themselves. It needs an extant power against which to throw itself, or against which to say no. Rebellion occurs against an institutionality, such as a constitutional state. But it has no strategy against the ephemerality and non-organization of a para-political state. Toward the latter, rebellion can only be reactive as it makes its sporadic appearances. (This marks one of the inherent insufficiencies of rebellion for its project of political transformation. Reforming the constitutional state will not change the para-political state, which will then reconstitute a constitutional state for itself. And the para-political state will persist as long as it has the constitutional state to hide behind.)

While rebellion directly opposes the political domination of power structures, autonomy does not. Its focus is elsewhere, in constituting allo-cultural structures, a process for which the refusal of para-political presence and violence is a basic assumption. Thus, it is through its existence that a social movement for allo-cultural autonomy becomes a direct rejection of the para-political state.

Whiteness can interpret allo-cultural autonomy only as a threat since it depends on those it racializes being dependent on itself. White supremacy and its para-political populism operate according to a cultural ethos (and an ethics) that is existentially alien to de-colonizing autonomy and to the refusal of domination that self-recognition and human dignity entail (Fanon 1967). This is why a para-political ethic, such as racism, is irrefutable; there is no refutation of a dependence on violence and impunity, or of the self-decriminalization of coloniality's criminalization of the "other." Rather than seek to refute the para-political ethic (racism) or reform the constitutional permissibility of white supremacy, allo-cultural autonomy signifies the construction of a social "elsewhere," out from under white supremacist dependency on the racialized. This was the core of the original call for "Black power" (Carmichael and Hamilton 1967). Not only does autonomy's refusal generate a Fanonian subjectivity, but it allows people to make of themselves something other than what had been made of them by white para-political domination. Instead of the dialectic of power and counter-power of rebellion, it deploys the incommensurability between autonomy and dependency against the para-political state.[10]

Autonomy and rebellion stand in a symbiotic relation to each other. Each opens political space in which the other can operate. Communal or allo-cultural autonomy depends on the power of rebellion to defend it against the constitutional state's repressions, and rebellion depends on the ability of autonomy, of alternate political structures, to subvert and undermine the para-political state. All successful guerrilla struggles of liberation from colonialism have exhibited this symbiosis between liberated territory and continuing guerrilla struggle within the territory controlled by colonialism (e.g., China, Cuba, Eritrea). It is the conjunction of the two, rebellion and allo-cultural autonomy, that can stand in absolute opposition to the structures of racialization and white supremacy. The sit-ins and voter registration organizations that participated in the formation of the Mississippi Freedom Democratic Party (MFDP) constituted the dimension of rebellion against segregation and disenfranchisement that allowed the MFDP to become a terrain of alternate political structures, while conversely the allo-cultural autonomy of community that developed through the MFDP gave socio-political strength and authorization to the anti-segregationist organizations that carried out the rebellion (C. Mills 1997). During the sit-down strikes against the auto industry in 1936 that produced the UAW, it was the support of the community, which came together with a new sense of cultural presence as a class-oriented community, that protected the political presence of the unions in the factories (Kraus 1985). This also happened in many of the factory takeovers in Argentina between 2004 and 2007.

Allo-cultural communities are the unavoidable responses to the para-political state. They are often the first level of struggle, manifesting in their autonomy a transformation of the political space that goes beyond rebellion to the construction of a re-subjectified identity. Though movements such as AIM, the IWW, Aztlan, and various "Black power" organizations (for instance, the Panthers or Robert Williams's movement in Monroe, North Carolina [R. Williams 1962]) have seen themselves in rebellion against the constitutional state, their lasting political effects have been to reveal the potentialities of autonomy for throwing off the para-political state, in rejecting the norms of para-political obedience and obeisance. In this, they produce modes of community sovereignty (which can take the form of anything from a political movement to the emergence of worker cooperatives and community-oriented "restorative justice" movements) that pose an alternative to the dominating sovereignty of constitutional state institutions.[11]

Dual-Class System

Is it possible for there to be a dual-state structure in the United States and only a single unitary capitalist class structure? Can even an ephemeral form of state, such as a white supremacist para-political state, revealing many of the characteristics of a constitutional state, exist without some economic shadow or antecedent on which to rely, if only culturally? What would be the material or economic foundation for it otherwise? If no constitutional jurisdiction has refused to valorize para-political violence, what is the class nature of that violence? Does it take the constitutional state itself as its foundation? Does this duality of state structure divide along class lines? Or are there two class structures, each of which is governed by its respective state?

Both forms of state, and both forms of "state" violence, have existed and expressed themselves in tandem since the beginning of this nation, even up to the present. In the wake of the civil rights movements, the para-political state and the constitutional state walked hand in hand in new ways, with new explanations for their actions. We have seen the automaticity of this dual violence. It occurs in the forgiveness of white violence and the criminalization of black self-defense in Jena, Louisiana. In New Orleans after Katrina, white people foraging for survival were extolled in the media, and black people doing the same things were criminalized, both in the media and by the varieties of troops sent in to patrol the flooded city. It appeared in the pseudo-belief that defeating affirmative action was struggle against "all discrimination" and not the restitution of previous 100 percent white quotas. Can all this have occurred without some "material" (class) substrate?

Let us return to the antecedent formation of a class structure in the wake of Bacon's Rebellion. Theodore Allen (1997) has provided us with a powerful tool for understanding how economic organization developed in the colony. What stabilized the extreme exploitation of the slave system was the organization of what Allen has called an intermediary control stratum (ICS). The slave patrol in the early 1700s, the enforcement mechanism for the slave system (as described in Chapter 1), was the first form of ICS. Its dual task was to stop runaway bond-laborers and repress autonomous organization among them. Its violence, directed by a colonial need for solidarity against a self-constructed and self-generated threat of labor rebellion, was instrumental in producing the social unity (across class and wealth distinctions) among the European colonists that formed the foundation for white identity and the cultural structure of whiteness.

Exploited by the elite, the laborers and farmers of the patrols functioned as both economically and culturally productive. They fulfilled the former function simply as laborers in the colonial economy. In their latter function, they became the force that consolidated the social coherence of the colony and the consensus within it on the "virtue" and legitimacy of the slave system. As an ICS, the patrols formed a wall of exclusion against black people and for inclusion of white people. They were the mechanism whereby a white hermeticism was produced that crossed class lines and made a social identity around whiteness possible. Gratuitous violence against black people has been, from the beginning, the medium of coherence for white society.

This sense of functioning as a "control stratum" carried over into the early formation of a working-class consciousness after the Revolution (though T. Allen [1997] did not extend his concept of a control stratum beyond its function in the formation of the "white race"). One can see its operation among white workers in the northern states in the decades following independence. White skilled workers in the North sought forms of organization that would preserve their social status and the dignity of their crafts as well as define a political role for themselves as a class in the new political situation.[12] At the same time, they excluded free black workers from their organizations and from many job sites, though these workers had worked for many years in the same crafts, with skills comparable to those of the white workers (McManus 1973, 183). Shops that hired free black skilled workers were often boycotted and struck by the white workers to force the firing of black employees.

Competition was one of the reasons given for this exclusion. The white workers claimed that free black workers offered unfair competition. But the notion of unfairness made reference only to the hiring of skilled bond-laborers who, as slaves, had had to work for lower wages and harsher conditions and were unable to establish independent relationships with employers. If the black bond-laborer degraded shop conditions, it was white owners who were the source of that, both the employer who took advantage of the black bond-laborers' absence of options and the white "owner" of the bond-laborer, who benefited from the wage the bond-laborer earned. In ignoring that fact, the white workers were essentially holding the black workers responsible for their own enslavement. And in charging free black workers with similar "unfairness" of competition, white workers were holding the enslavement of the bond-laborer against the free black workers (DuBois 1935, 28; Martinot 2003b, 90). At the same time, white workers accepted European immigrants into both unions and job sites (though not as readily during times of economic crisis). In other words, they assigned greater importance to white social cohesion than to the labor solidarity (across racial lines) that would have given their organizations greater political power and influence through numbers in the new states. That is, they refused to abandon their earlier role as an ICS.

By excluding black workers as competition rather than joining and coordinating with them, white workers of northern urban and industrial areas not only created them as competition, they reduced their own power as a political force. What invested this double truncation of the white workers' position was their presumption to define themselves as the working class, at a time when the vast majority of workers in the United States were black, working under forced-labor conditions on the agribusiness plantations of the South. In effect, they were defining the working class as white.[13] At the same time, they were participating in the development of the prototype structures of segregation that would later become Jim Crow, not only in employment but in voting rights and political participation.

Ultimately, without access to skilled employment, the black workers gradually lost their skills and were reduced to unskilled status. The economic differentiation this created amounted to a process of proletarianization of black workers at the hands of white skilled workers. Black people had little political recourse to this exclusionism. They could only turn to autonomous social organizations, community unions, churches, and the like, which had to remain partially clandestine to survive. In some cities, Black worker cooperatives were developed. The Black ship-caulkers' cooperative in Baltimore is one example (P. Foner 1976, 15). But often their churches and community halls were subjected to vandalism and arson, targets of the proletarianization process. And Black communities were scapegoated by race riots, in many cases sparked by attempts of black people to vote (Ignatiev 1995; Laurie 1980).

In other words, in acting to proletarianize black workers in ways that they themselves were not, white workers produced a class difference between themselves as white and black people in general. That is, they redefined their contemporary political role to reflect their earlier traditional role as a control stratum, continuing the slave patrol function in different terms. The other side of the black proletarianization process was white workers' unification of white society itself. In other words, they constructed their class consciousness as workers in primary allegiance to white society rather than to working-class solidarity.

This is one reason that white racism has historically worked so well as a weapon (in the hands of the ruling class and political leadership) against working-class organization in the United States. Its real strength is its ability to deploy a tradition of white worker access to social standing and white solidarity, for which racism's ever renewed hostility and exclusionism toward black people is a means. It is that internal white inclusionism, bounded and guarded by an exclusionism that held hostility and violence at the ready in order to maintain the hermeticism of white space, that is the real power of white racism. Though nineteenth-century white workers understood that their essential strength lay in numbers, and "class solidarity" was the watchword of labor organization even then, they chose to weaken themselves as the price of a ticket to status as white. Most continued to support slavery in the South, fearing the labor competition from masses of freed slaves to which they would be subject owing to their own inability to form lasting worker cooperatives. White racism, the decision by white workers to define themselves as the working class, and the class collaboration that is implicit in the white inclusionary cross-class consensus of white society are three aspects of the same thing (T. Allen 1969).

White workers thus became productive in a dual sense. On the one hand, they produced capital values as exploited workers. And on the other, they produced the cultural coherence of white society. They were both marginalized as an economic class and fully integrated into the coloniality of white society in its relation to black people in general.

In playing their dual role historically, white workers have developed a dual-class consciousness with respect to themselves as workers. On the one hand, they live a class consciousness as workers dependent on their solidarity as workers. And on the other, as an ICS, they live a consciousness of being a part of a "ruling class" in class collaboration with the elite that grants them recognition as white. At times, their working-class consciousness has come to the fore, and they have extended solidarity to other workers across racial lines. But at other times, for the most part, they restore to themselves their role as ICS, at which time their white solidarity within the racialized class system trumps their class consciousness as exploited workers.[14] This priority was clear during the 1860s with respect to the organization of the National Labor Union (NLU). Black workers, in the wake of the Civil War, started organizing and petitioned to join the NLU locals. They were told to form their own black locals. Though the NLU claimed to recognize black workers as workers, it still refused to include them organizationally. Common cause was proposed only out of a pragmatics rather than a sense of class commonality: "If we don't make friends with them, capital will use them against us" (Commons et al. 1910, 9:159). When these black locals met in convention as the National Colored Labor Union, and accused the NLU of breaking the class solidarity it had advocated by excluding black workers, the white workers who reported this found it unintelligible (Commons et al. 1910, 9:243–245). Like the craft workers of 1800, the white workers primarily thought of black workers as a threat and addressed them as an "issue" only to neutralize that threat.

Had an extensive and successful worker's cooperative movement appeared during those years, it would have extricated white workers from their double role, their double consciousness, and the class collaboration in which that embedded them. A system of cooperatives could have obviated the problem of competition by absorbing all workers, black and white, into an alternate economy that would have guaranteed both jobs and income. But white workers either hesitated or refused to form cooperatives, abjuring the autonomy it would have provided, because that would have broken their bargain as a control stratum with the white elite by which they gained recognition both as producers and as white. In effect, on a cultural level, the role of white skilled workers in producing a coherence for white society trumped their production of themselves as a political force. And on an economic level, white solidarity trumped class solidarity, as it typically has ever since.

In terms of the dual role that white workers have played, the outlines of a dual-class structure begin to appear. On the one hand, there was a white class system consisting of a traditional capitalist structure in which white workers labored as exploited producers of capital values for a capitalist elite. And on the other, there was a racialized class system in which black (and brown) workers were excluded from political participation and more intensely exploited economically through their proletarianization by white workers and the entirety of a white solidarist society. That is, the proletarianization of workers of color stood in relation to white society as a whole, whose coalescence in white cultural coherence set it in the role of a "ruling class" toward them. And the structure that divided these two class systems was the ICS, which, as a control stratum, was the instituted force that in guarding against inclusion of people of color, produced the inclusionism of white society as a ruling class over them. In the duality of this class system, race, the relation of racializers and the racialized, becomes indistinguishable from a class relation.

If, in 1800, the majority of black workers were working as bond-laborers on plantations, in 2000, these racialized workers over which white society extends its domination includes most of the third world areas of the globe, where EuroAmerican corporate capital exploits them. The ICS for this globalized system is much more complex than its original form as patrols or exclusionist white skilled workers. Today it involves World Bank and International Monetary Fund control of international financing, a protectionist and often xenophobic labor union leadership in the United States and other industrialized countries, local capitalist classes in the subordinate nations, and EuroAmerican control of international trade.

In sum, there is a duality of class structure that supports the dual-state system we have described. It has its origins in the slave system, characterized by a dual role for the white working class as exploited and as a control stratum (or part of one as the role of a control stratum became more complex). And it persists in the capacity of white society to act as a ruling class in that racialized class system that reflects itself as a para-political state.

In these terms, the civil rights struggles that changed the face of race and racialization during the 1950s and 1960s can be seen as hard-fought class struggles within the racialized class system. It was by changing the face of racialization that the civil rights movements brought about a change of symbology for "race"—terms such as minorities, Democratic Party constituencies, high school tracking, and criminalization have all become euphemisms for it. As with every class struggle, one of its results has been to propel many black and brown people into the middle class and into the professions (e.g., law, medicine, finance, corporate management)—but never in large or unharassed numbers. Many people of color have been absorbed into electoral organizations, governmental institutions, and security apparatuses (military, commercial and residential security, local police, though not international mercenary corporations). What this has produced for the Black communities is a brain drain, leaving them even more defenseless against their present abandonment by capital investment. And on the other hand, while the Democratic Party has touted itself as the representative of communities of color, and of the oppressed, it need do nothing for the population of color it has coaxed into being a constituency for itself, since black and brown people have nowhere else to go politically. All that indicates is that the Democratic Party has become an essential element of the ICS in the wake of the civil rights era.

What this suggests is that class relations in the United States cannot be understood without taking the form of the ICS into account as part of the analysis. Class relations must be seen as varying from epoch to epoch as the form of the ICS changes in response to political changes resulting from forces and struggles in the racialized class system. Though the ICS has changed over time, from patrols to white skilled worker exclusionism to para-military anti-black mobs (KKK and others) to urban police forces and SWAT teams, its function has remained the same: to subdue, repress, and control the working classes of color, and to alienate communities of color from political participation.[15] Today there is an anti-immigrant movement, one of whose roles is to open all Latino communities in the United States to harassment and disruption in order to keep them politically subordinate and in docile acquiescence to their labor (Bacon 2008).

Conversely, one of the roles of the labor unions, both craft and industrial, has been to keep black and brown militancy and activism contained within organizations that structurally function within the white class system, and thus subject to the structure of class collaboration built into working-class thinking within the white class system. The unions are basically populist organizations with a corporate structure, in which the executive stratum monopolizes leadership and organizational direction. There is a top-down demand for allegiance and obedience to the contract, as well as an imposition of responsibility. Black union members, whether as rank and file, officers, or leadership, find themselves having to struggle against the whiteness of the union structure and the lopsided sense of solidarity (black in solidarity with white, but very little the other way) at the same time that they participate in common union struggles for workers' rights against employers.

The alternative, which has appeared momentarily at different times, is a unionism that functions on a collective democratic (non-corporate) basis, organizationally linking workers in their place of employment with the communities in which they live. This was one of the characteristics of black unions organized after the Civil War. Today only the longshore local in Charleston, South Carolina, which is a mostly black union, attempts to function in that way, as a union and a social center for the community. One of the characteristics of unions that categorizes them as white institutions is their separation from community. To become active at the community level would constitute an abrogation of their role as ICS.

Toward a Theory of Decolonization

The function of the white para-political state is to constitute the matrix of coloniality in the United States, for which the structure of racialization is the central organizing principle. Because the state is dual, and the class system it governs is dual, trapping white workers in dual incommensurable roles, traditional class analysis as inherited from Europe is insufficient (but not unnecessary). Neither the para-political state nor the inherency of the ICS to the construction of the racialized class system is definable within traditional terms or concepts derived from European historical experience or its capitalist class relations. Because it falls short of addressing the complexity of this power matrix, working-class (socialist) consciousness remains inadequate to either anti-capitalism (struggle against the constitutional state in the white class system) or anti-colonialism (struggle against the para-political state in the racialized class system).[16] What a politics of racialized working-class consciousness might be, what a strategy of class struggle in accord with the racialized class system would look like, and what an analysis of white working-class participation in the ICS would have to admit have no precedent in Europe. Only the English colonization of Ireland contains antecedent elements relevant to the U.S. experience, but there the factors that would pertain to the dual-class systems as they appear in the United States are on separate land masses (T. Allen 1996). The consensual solidarity the ICS gives to white society across class lines in the United States, which defines the ability of white society as a whole to function as the ruling class in the racialized class system, is wholly beyond the ken of traditional European class analyses. The idea of merely transforming class relations, as per continental European concepts or experience, though necessary as a theory focused on alleviating the exploitation of labor, would be insufficient for eliminating the ethos of violence and impunity that constitute the white para-political social order.

To translate European concepts of class organization or class struggle to the United States, we would need to recognize three things. The first would be the idea that the active resistance, anti-coloniality, and autonomy of people racialized as non-white by the para-political state constitute the core of the real class struggle against capitalism. Second, the participation of white people in the para-political state, even though it may involve class struggle in the white class system, is in reality a form of class collaboration and participates in "ruling class" activity in the racialized class system in its refusal to abandon white solidarity. And third, the virtual possibility of white people decolonizing themselves, jettisoning their participation in white coloniality and their identity as participants in white solidarity (whether that means abandoning whiteness or constructing a progressive white identity free of racism) would be the first step toward their moving across the line of class struggle in the racialized class system and entering into real working-class solidarity with the exploited of the racialized class system. But only the first step. White decolonization, white working-class abandonment of its role in the para-political state and the ICS, involving a refusal of white allegiance, are the necessary preconditions for working-class struggle in the United States.

Capitalism is a profitability machine exploiting labor and the planet as mere resources. In the United States, its structure of internal coloniality appears as the structure of racialization. That is, the entire structure of the coloniality of power within the United States (patriarchy, individualism, heterosexism and homophobia, the property ethic and its subsidiary "family values") is organized by the processes of racialization. Racialization constructs the exclusionary dividing line between white society and all allo-cultural communities (including the "counter-culture" and the social movements). For whites, that dividing line, and its central discourse of racism, has traditionally valorized para-political violence as the foundation for the cohesion of white culture. Historically, the structure of "democracy" as it has been understood in the ruling white class system has been a structure of alienated representation, inseparable from the structure of racialization. It has at all times included an ethics of ICS exclusionism, often with violence, as central to the para-political preservation of a racialized social order, the substitution of populism for political participation, and the legislation of sexuality.

Democracy has to be understood as an ethics. The ethics of democracy is one of inclusion, of participation. It begins with the proposition that those people affected by a political decision must participate in formulating and making that decision—not simply speaking at hearings but having a domain of dialogue in which to formulate as well as to vote. Where, in representationism, people vote for representatives and those representatives then assemble and discuss politics, the ethics of pro-democracy would provide that people first assemble and discuss politics and then elect people to represent their discussions in higher bodies. Within an ethics of democracy, even the rights of property, the adventures of foreign policy, the impunity of corporate operations, and the weighing of human versus profitability interests would be up for discussion and decision.

To develop this facility organizationally or institutionally would require profound changes. A social environment of respect for all citizens, a culture of dialogue and not simply of "speech," the delegislation of sexuality, and a form of proportional representation that would permit all interests to express themselves organizationally would have to be engendered. For both states, the constitutional and the para-political, a democratic ethic of this kind would be inimical. The present elite will do everything it can, through the constitutional state, to prevent the rights of property from coming under democratic scrutiny and control. And the para-political state will do everything it can to prevent the rest (inclusion, respect, dialogue, participation). In a profound sense, the right-wing upheaval against health care reform is only a resurgence of white refusal to permit government programs that would include the interests of people of color, as did the white populist protest against welfare. In the United States, a culture of democratic participation requires an allo-cultural structure that would involve both rebellion and class struggle, but neither rebellion nor class struggle against the constitutional state alone would be sufficient.

White people, and especially white anti-racists, find themselves caught between two forms of coloniality: the corporate system, in which they are dominated, and the system of coloniality toward others, with its racialized class structure, in whose power to dominate they remain complicit. This is the legacy of the colonial ICS. Their whiteness makes their coloniality appear democratic, just, and humane to them by blinding them to the injustices in which they are forced by membership to act as accomplice.

In such a situation, the very concept of "social change" needs to be retrieved from this matrix of coloniality. The "production" of "social change" by a social movement, to the extent it does not contest and dissolve the social power of the para-political state through structures of autonomy (alternate political structures), will devolve existentially back to one side or the other of the racialized class system—to being a participant in the ICS if the movement is essentially a white movement or back into a form of subjugation to the para-political state if it is not. The process of decolonization would have to address the entire para-political paradigm, including capitalism (labor as a profitability machine, earth as a resource), the nation-state (the false representationism it calls democracy), and its legislation of sexuality, for all of which the structure of racialization constitutes the framework, the social context, the organizing principle.

Opposition to the para-political state would have to locate itself within the racialized class system; it cannot be oppositional from within the white class system, that is, from behind the ICS. Thus, the concept of the decolonization of the United States begins with opposition to the para-political state. But that implies that the hold over people, both white and of color, of the structure of racialization will have to be broken. For white people to shift their terrain of struggle to one of opposition to coloniality, the ability of the structure of racialization to wield them as its own weapons (the weaponization of white people on which the para-political state depends) will have to be neutralized and shattered. That is, the struggle against white supremacy, and the struggle against capitalism as its economic dimension, will require shifting to the racialized class system and centering that system as the domain of struggle. For people to arrive at a social space in which allo-cultural structures are sustainable against the tyranny of white supremacy and its dual state, the determinant influence of the structure of racialization will have to be perceived and eliminated.

In other words, decolonization is a struggle for liberation that is not simply a class struggle within white industrial society. Decolonization refers to the general liberation of those oppressed by coloniality and the para-political state. This does not exempt white people or automatically extricate them from their conscription by the para-political state to the criminality of its project. But it must be recognized that class struggle, even in its traditional sense, can occur only by and for a class that requires liberation; and this is not the case for the ICS in its integration and allegiance to the white society and its culture of whiteness. Indeed, the force of coloniality manifests itself both as the exploitation and derogation of people of color and the conscription of white people to an ICS for that purpose. Therefore, the struggle for that general liberation begins outside the white class system in an allo-cultural autonomy that contests the para-political state, and with the formation of alternate political structures to undermine the constitutional state.

7

The Structures of Racialization

The Three Levels of Racialization

It is the familiarity of the many racist actions, both the atrocities and the small harassments, that tells us that the machinery of racialization has conditioned our consciousness and our intentions to attribute a certain normalcy to racism. To demote the events we recognize to the background means precisely to grant the profundity of the cultural structures that condition those events and render them banal. When police shot Oscar Grant in the back, while he was lying face-down on the ground, unarmed, three officers crouched or hovering over him, the general reaction of demonstrated outrage called for the arrest and prosecution of the officer who shot him. It did not, however, call for curtailing the weaponry of the police or the impunity that negated the system of justice on which a judicial prosecution of the officer was predicated. Neither did it call for opening the police training and procedural manuals and routines to community scrutiny and modification. Two days later, it was Grant who was vilified in the press while the officer was treated with respect and fairness. Three months after that, when Lovelle Mixon shot and killed two police officers during a traffic stop, and then killed or wounded three more in the SWAT team that raided the house he ran to, he was vilified and the officers honored as heroes, even though the officer wounded by Mixon was the same one who had shot Gary King (a black teenager) in the back and killed him while he was walking away the previous year. In all three incidents, which occurred in Oakland, California, the officers were white and the civilians were black. These color terms refer to social categories, though they make vague reference to appearance. The simple counter-position of black to white in all three gets revamped as vilification versus virtue. Each incident is recast by its reracialization as a conflict between the social and the anti-social, the law and the outlaw, representing white and black, regardless of who committed the crime in question. It is the binary transformation that purifies whiteness and defames the racialized which signifies the process of racialization. But only the process; what the process signifies in turn is much bigger, much more commanding and unthinking in its vast social technologies.

The structure of racialization is a cultural structure, a structure of social categorizations of people. It has nothing to do with blood or the inheritance of appearance. It is social status that is imposed on people through political definition. Appearance is only the tag, a label to be noticed, the symbol that drives the machinery of exoneration and vilification that not only separates the social order (whiteness) from the people of color subjected to it but also normalizes that separation. Vilification and exoneration are social activities. "Race" is a structure of social activity.

There are three levels of social activity through which white people "commit" race in accord with the cultural structure of racialization. There is the individual level, the institutional level, and the cultural level. They all work together. Let us recast (in summary) the activity of race that white people commit.

On the individual level, race takes the form of a relation of dependence of white racialized identity on all the others. The components of white identity are the need for a threat (which the others provide), the assumption of a consensual white solidarity and allegiance (which the threat provides), and a desire for or acceptance of some form of violence to express that consensus against those not white. The need for a threat is produced by the purity condition for whiteness, which is indispensable to defining whiteness and race in the first place.

The threat that whites invent for themselves (which could be an unarmed man face-down on the pavement, who was rendered a threat by being shot in the back) produces the need for defensive social solidarity. Because social solidarity conceives of itself as defensive, its violence is justified in advance, against the other who is the attacker (even while walking away). White violence (whether merely an objectifying attitude, or the presumption to speak for the other, or actually shooting the other in the back) is what makes the original paranoia seem real (the imagined "gun in the waistband"). In other words, the violence (conceived as defensive) only exacerbates the original sense of threat, requiring greater social solidarity and potentiating greater violence. This cycle is the stage on which white people enact "race." It is what happens when a black man enters an elevator and the white woman already there gathers her belongings more tightly around herself, as George Yancy has described (Yancy 2008, ch. 1).

On the institutional level, racialization resides in the properness that white society feels toward its social exclusions. Segregation, police impunity, the ability of the police to criminalize people at will, the prisons, the school tracking systems, the continuance of neighborhood segregation, the high unemployment, the refusal to hire based on zip code and facial features rather than knowledge, whether part of the racist legacy of the past or engendered by the reracialization of society in the wake of the civil rights movements, are all examples. These are all established social institutionalities that receive their authority and validation from a cultural structure, not from law or political principle. We can add to this list the two-party system, which institutionally speaks for "minorities." The two-party system controls the structure of the electoral process and monopolizes the field of political thought and leadership, disallowing issues that will threaten it and using that threat to valorize its disallowance. In doing so, it commits a violence against those it speaks for. A third institutional domain is the media, which serves as the organ of dissemination for the institutional process of vilification and exoneration. These institutions can be understood as white because they enact, institutionally, the process of racialization.

In its operations, institutionality becomes white insofar as it presents a concrete situation with which white racialized identity can identify as white. Indeed, white identification with these institutionalities is what constitutes white racialized identity, as the matrix for white consensus and inclusion. In short, white racialized identity is continually reconstituted through its identification with white institutionality. There is a cyclic relation of identity, identification, and institutionality that continually regenerates itself.

Alternatives would appear in the form of demands for community autonomy, community control of policing and schools in communities of color, affirmative action and compensatory training programs, immigrant rights and civil rights organizations, Native American sovereignty, same-sex marriage, an ability on the part of the populace to abjure and veto war and militarism, and the like. These all constitute responses on the part of movement or community autonomy to institutional forms of domination. As such, they get marginalized by the constitutional state or suppressed by the para-political state.

At the cultural level, the operations of the structure of racialization take the form of the white para-political state, its periodic white vigilantism, the general support for police harassment and brutality against black and brown people, and support for U.S. interventionism. These all function to sustain and valorize the coherence and cohesion of the white cultural environment. It has a cultural logic, that of inverting criminality, locating criminality in the victim in order to decriminalize the violence that victimizes. Indeed, this inversion of criminality is an originary aspect of "race," an essential part of its original invention by the English settlers, by which they decriminalized their theft of land and their kidnapping and torture of labor. The inversion of criminality is one of the sources of the imprisonment obsession in the United States today. Whiteness is based on the social imprisonment of people of color in economic dependency and impoverishment in order to keep them in place to fulfill its own dependency on those it dominates for its very identity.

Finally, there is a messianism that is endemic to any group that superiorizes itself, precisely because it must demonstrate its superiority to others, whom it must inferiorize in order to do so. A messianism accompanies all forms of the imposition of white supremacy on others, in obedience to the fundamental compulsion of all supremacy to speak for others and tell them who they are. Ultimately, messianism is only another way of sanctifying the criminality of domination, that is, of decriminalizing it.

What all these elements of the cultural logic of racialization require is a structure of impunity to be in place and available to white people in the exercise of their white racialized identity against those through whom that identity had been defined. What makes that structure work is the invisibility of impunity to the paranoid mind simply because it is always, in everything it does, responding to an identity threat. In effect, whiteness encloses itself in three modes of self-sanctification which form the foundation for the three levels of the structure of racialization: the purity concept, the inversion of criminality, and a messianism toward those it racializes.

What this entire structure of racialization creates, with its production of white racialized identity, its self-sanctification processes, and its institutionalities, is a complex system of doubleness. U.S. society is divided into the racializers and the racialized. Because the racializers comport themselves (by definition) toward the racialized as a form of state, there is a dual-state structure (the constitutional and the para-political). This dual-state structure is defined by a double border, a white boundary of segregation and exclusionism and an official state boundary that is found on maps. And this dual border represents a dual-class structure, a white class system contained in a racialized class system, whose difference is constituted by the operations of a racializing intermediary control stratum that stands guard at the white boundary. In this dual-class structure, white workers have a dual consciousness, engendered by their participation in the control stratum: a working-class consciousness that expresses itself in class solidarity against the white capitalist class, and a white consciousness that expresses an exclusionary solidarity with white society to ensure the exploitation of people of color both as a resource for capital and as a foundation for white cultural identity.

For the racialized, the formation of community and the development of a culture of their own are necessary survival strategies. They constitute an alternate social environment in which to develop their own social and political subjectivity. Within the context of racialization, such communities are necessarily communities of resistance against the objectification that characterizes the process of racialization. They are, ineluctably, a response to the double consciousness the racialized confront in themselves. As DuBois described it, black people have a double consciousness in always seeing themselves through the eyes of others because they are always objectified, made into objects to be noticed by those who racialize and speak for them.

What would constitute an alternative for white people, against the undercurrent of violence that runs through all social processes and events in the United States, would be to simply treat others with respect as human beings. This is generally difficult for white people in the United States; it is hampered by their sense of messianism and the hegemonic mind that inherently accompanies being white in a white supremacist social framework. Instead, violence appears as a compulsion that oozes up out of white identity and seems far more natural.

What Would Constitute Anti-racism?

In the face of these structures, what would constitute a real anti-racist movement in the United States?

First of all, we would need to change how we understand "race." Socially, race is something that white people do to others. Historically, race is a product of Europeans racializing themselves as white over against those people of color they have denigrated and inferiorized by imprisoning them in colonialist structures. That is, "race" is the product of whiteness, operating through the instrument of its purity concept. The production of race through its purity concept is thus the core of the ethic of whiteness. Insofar as whiteness is a performance of membership in white society and its sense of supremacy or hegemony—performances for the benefit of other whites but staged through actions of racialization aimed at people of color—it is the ethic of whiteness that provides the scripts.

Racism as it is traditionally known can be understood as a characteristic element of those performances, that is to say, a condition of membership in whiteness. Since it can be turned on and off according to circumstances, it can be neither psychological nor ideological. It has no existence outside the realm of white performance, or the imagining of a white audience for the performance. Though enacted with respect to people of color, racism is ultimately a relation between white people. That is why arguments concerning racism's effects on its victims fall so typically on deaf (white) ears; such arguments are addressing the wrong relationship. White people apprehend how they act as natural because they see it through the eyes of other white people. To act white is to act out the elements of white racialized identity, within the ethic of white hegemony.

In general, white anti-racist people have not formed mass movements against the injustices of white supremacy. They have instead preferred to discuss the question and to use reason against racism. The traditional way of addressing racism and white skin privilege has been to try to refute the alleged benefits and expose the injustices. Tim Wise, a well-known white anti-racist speaker and activist, has done this extensively and admirably, explaining to white people how they have acted against themselves by thinking they are benefiting from their racism, especially when professing ignorance that they are racist at all.

But it is the confluence of white performativity and white solidarity that weaponizes white people and renders their violence or hostility against presumed targets an end in itself within the performance. Because the audience is white, what happens to the victim of racist hostility becomes a problem only if it is a problem for that audience. The violence, whether one's own or that of the police, or that of white populism, insofar as it is accepted by other whites, simply becomes an aspect of belonging to the white socius. In short, racism is a white project to renew white consensus, preserve white hegemony, and replenish the sanctity of white racialized identity. It is the way white people accept their own weaponization and the instrumentalization of other people by the structure of racialization.

This implies that racism is only symptomatically a problem of discrimination. Addressing the appearance of discrimination does not address the source of its continual reemergence. Instead, it is an identity problem. As such, it must be addressed through an identity paradigm rather than through experiential data, which points only to where the structures of racialization have required an identity performance. The discrimination paradigm, which is the traditional way of addressing racism and its organization of white skin privilege, says, "I do this to you because I have already decided who you are, and because you deserve it, and because I get something out of it." The identity paradigm, which is that of a cultural structure, says, "I do this to you in order to make me who I am, and in order to make me again who I have been" (L. Williams 1967). Racial discrimination, the racial prejudice that expresses it, and the personal acceptance of institutional operations that discriminate are all part of the role that people permit themselves in terms of their performativity of whiteness. The anti-racism problem cannot only be one of ending the social privilege entailed in discrimination, but must add the task of ending the entire socially generalized performance of whiteness that imprisons its performers in the enactment of discrimination for its white audience in order to reconstitute its own white identity.

What is truly horrendous about the existence of racial discrimination is the fact of its overt and extant gratuitousness. That is, it serves no social purpose. Nor does it respond to any clearly evident social or psychological problem. That is the problem; that is what has always remained unintelligible and inexplicable about it. Though it may explain itself by reference to fear or a sense of threat, the self-referentiality of that sense of threat is conveniently left out of the account. Indeed, it is that self-referentiality, the fact that white people are actually gratuitously constructing their own white racialized identity for themselves through others, which makes people of color, as well as psychologists and anti-racist whites, feel so crazy when attempting to understand white racist violence and why it has such ferocity and tenacity. But the racist violence comes first. It is primary, an elemental constituent of white racialized identity. Discrimination is one of its results. It is when discrimination and prejudice are explained as the source of the violence, the source of the hate and hostility, and of the oppression and exploitation, that the violence becomes unintelligible.

Many analysts think they see benefits in the white privileges engendered by racial discrimination. But these privileges are not payoffs. They do not result in a stable, unharassed life. Discrimination does not create privilege for whites; instead, white racialized identity creates an entire complex system of deprivation for those it has racialized—that is, for those whom white society has decided to racialize. It is always a social decision, concretized through operations of white institutions. Though it may reserve social norms for itself, white racialized identity nevertheless cannot live them since it is always living under the shadow of a threat, not because there is one but because that is the way the white socius can continue to be white. This is why derogatory terms flood the discourse of white people, especially when those to whom they refer are absent. It is in order to maintain the proper stance of aggressiveness in the eyes of other whites, as evidence that one is beset by the same threat, for which solidarity is demanded. That aggressiveness is far from a life of unharassed stability. Yet it is a chosen state for those who actively express their whiteness.

A white person cannot accept and identify with a white racialized identity and not accept the dominion or the system of deprivation that comes with it. That is not open to individual intention or personal choice. And neither is the history that whiteness brings with it. That is because the identity is given by others. Nevertheless, many white people are searching for an anti-racist whiteness. An anti-racist whiteness would involve finding a way to perform one's whiteness in an ethical manner, consistent with equality and pro-democracy. That would imply that one would accept the purity condition that is the foundation for whiteness and not have it be exclusionary (although it is by definition). One would have to dispense with the paranoia at the core of whiteness and thus abjure the white solidarity that it demands. But then, on what basis would one consider oneself white? Skin color? Ancestry? Neither functions as essential to whiteness since whiteness is hierarchical within a system of social categorization that is based on the purity concept. Skin color and ancestry are artifacts of the purity condition. To accept the purity condition in order to construct an "ethical whiteness" then cannot dispense with the hierarchy that is inherent in it.

And suppose one constructed an "ethical" (anti-racist) whiteness. Who would believe it? Erasing one's paranoia would be a hidden individual operation. To proclaim that one had canceled it would only arouse suspicion that one's paranoia was still in full flower. How would one absent oneself from solidarity with the white para-political state if to identify oneself as white is already to position oneself in its membership? If whiteness is a performance for other whites, then it is other whites, those who gave one one's whiteness in the first place, who get to say whether one is white or not by one's performance. But they are interested in preserving membership, not dispensing with it. Indeed, very often there is violence held at the ready for whites who would abjure their membership in whiteness.

To not act white would be to step outside whiteness as a cultural structure. To be recognized by other whites as not acting white, or as acting non-white, would mean to lose one's membership. Thus, because racism is a relation between whites, as a complex of victimizing performances, attempts to construct an anti-racist whiteness must also involve an abandonment of whiteness, which is what the anti-racist whiteness attempts not to do.

If racism maintains and reproduces whiteness and white society, then whiteness is inseparable from that racism. In that case, whiteness is inseparable from membership in white society. Then it is not possible to identify with one's whiteness (i.e., to "be white") and be anti-racist at the same time.

An Outline Program for the
Decolonization of the United States

Because of the dual-state character of the United States, a justice-oriented pro-democracy movement faces the task of struggling against both the coloniality of white supremacy and the cultural autocracy of the para-political state. To contest racism as an idea will have no effect on racism as a cultural practice because that practice is a product of a structure of dehumanization wrought by white paranoia, allegiance to a consensus, and a necessity for violence. In short, an anti-racist, justice-oriented, pro-democracy movement would have to address and contest the cultural structure of racialization, the constitutional state, and the para-political state, all at the same time. That is, it would have to include a struggle for some level of political power (rebellion against the state's legitimization of racial dehumanization) and the construction of community autonomy in the form of alternate political structures (to subvert the power of the para-political state). Or, to be more concrete, such a movement would have to work in three dimensions: a proactive contestation of the institutions of racialization; a movement for community control of social services, such as health, education, and policing; and the construction of alternate political structures as a network connecting those communities.

As we have seen, the main institutions preserving the structures of racialization today are the police, the prison industry, the courts, and the two-party system. An important aspect of decolonizing the police would be to open the training manuals, procedural regulations, and psychological hiring profiles to public scrutiny, subjecting them democratically to modifications through community-organized discussion. Those regulations that the community thinks contribute to police profiling or police brutality should be changed or eliminated, and police officers who think that such regulations are good or beneficial for their policing job, or who psychologically favor brutality, should be dismissed. The official police presence in a community should be made subordinate to the process of local policing by the community itself. This means canceling the ability of the police to demand instant obedience. There should be no command that the police can give that would not be discussable at the moment, on the street, with the citizenry being policed. If the police think that this hinders their ability to do their job, they should be reminded that their job is subordinate to the community, which does the major policing work.

The entire area of victimless crime laws must be eliminated, as they form the structural basis for police impunity. What would be considered a harm that a person could do to him- or herself (the thematic of victimless crime laws) would need to be democratically decided and dealt with through care and therapy, not punishment. Crime that harms people needs to be stopped, but punishment needs to be removed from being a role model for victimization, and the revenge ethic needs to be replaced by an ethic of "restorative justice" under the democratic operations of autonomous communities. It should not be forgotten that a reliance on imprisonment as punishment is an essential part of the structure of racialization in the United States.

The impunity of the prisons needs to be curtailed, and prison administration must be democratized to include the participation of the inmates themselves (there is plenty of experience in Italy of this kind of reform for us to draw on [Wright 2006]). The impunity of prosecutors to decide at what level of law to punish a person needs to be curtailed and regulated. Ultimately, most of the prisoners in the U.S. prison system need to be released. But since they have been harmed and insulted by the process of imprisonment itself, their release could only be accomplished through therapy and healing from the prison experience itself. (Think of the crime committed by parolees. What does it mean that in some regions the recidivism rate is over 75 percent?) For this to happen, there needs to be a social ethic in which government and all social institutions take as primary a sense of responsibility for the citizen, which few of them do at present.

To eliminate white racism and white supremacy, white people must abjure the purity concept. Purity concepts are the foundation for the exclusionism that in racialized terms has meant oppression, segregation, discrimination, hate, and violence. To abjure and reject the purity concept becomes the first order of business in fostering democracy. The passage of laws (civil rights or other) will not be enough. A social ethic of participation, free of the taint of any purity concept, will be needed. All institutions that militate for a social purity, whether ancestral, ethnic, genetic, or ideological, must be dismantled, as the precondition for instituting some form of democracy in the United States.

The two-party system is an anti-democratic machine. Real proportional representation will take constitutional amendments, which will not be easily forthcoming. Thus, the main pro-democratic alternatives to the two-party system will necessarily be alternate political structures at the local level, as the materialization of community autonomy.

All this is part of the basics of an anti-racism movement in the United States. The major pro-democratic transformation that has to occur is toward being a society that takes responsibility for all its citizens. Without this transformation, no anti-social behavior on the part of individuals, neither the autocracy of the police nor the cries of the members of the para-political state that they are supporting welfare cheats or drug addicts or meritless employees, neither the criminality of white supremacy nor the crime to which the oppressed often turn to survive, will ever be curtailed. This means that the very basics of social life, such as a job and a home, must be seen as human rights. In a society in which everything (food, clothes, shelter, health, knowledge and learning, entertainment, and so on) has been commodified, because that is the way capitalism operates, the first need for anyone is an income to purchase the commodities needed. An income is a matter of life and death in a wholly commodified society. The first commodity that must be provided in order for a person to maintain an income is a place to live. Nothing about the structure of racialization will be curtailed or eliminated, nor will the criminality and impunity by which it expresses itself, if that one ethical question, the institutional responsibility for the life and well-being of the citizen, is not included in social thinking.

Impunity versus Dialogue

Impunity resides at the very core of the structures of racialization. For white racism to be eliminated, white impunity needs to be criminalized as unethical, autocratic, and therefore anti-democratic. Yet the need to prohibit it points directly at the irrationality and practical impossibility of dealing with it through a revenge ethic, that is, through a judicial system that deploys a revenge ethic as the essence of punishment. If impunity is to be prohibited, its criminalization cannot imply the kind of punishment (e.g., imprisonment) that white supremacist institutionality necessitates. The revenge ethic by which the prison industry and police brutality are organized, as the quintessential expression of the hegemonic mind and its presumption of a social purity, must be replaced. An entirely different ethic for dealing with impunity as a crime can only be developed on a community basis, in which people actually talk to each other, carrying on a multi-dimensional dialogue in which the autonomy of each is respected.

In accord with the principle of autonomy, the act of speaking for other people remains one of the most unethical. To speak for other people is to violate the dialogic relation for which participant autonomy is the foundation. The principle of freedom contained in this is that one's own freedom to think and say what one needs is predicated on guaranteeing the ability of the other to do so. People can say what they need to, and others respond under the assumption of equality and mutual respect. The principle of responsibility for the citizen's well-being has a reflection at the level of dialogue in each person's responsibility to listen and to respond in a way that takes responsibility for having heard what the other has said (which does not imply necessarily agreeing with it, but does imply granting it standing in the dialogue and taking it as part of the field of one's responses). That responsibility to the other in a dialogue holds for all participants, of course, and a person who tends to hog the airspace (or the "mike," as they say) is abrogating that responsibility to the other.

When and if someone involved in the dialogue fails in the mutual respect required, falling perhaps into a form of intellectual or ideological violence, then the dialogue is broken and no democratic outcome of the discussion is possible until it is reconstituted.

Democracy as an Alternate Political Structure

Given that white racialized society is anti-democratic, structures of democracy that can fulfill the principle of democracy—namely, one in which the people affected by a policy participate in deciding what the policy will be—still have to be developed. These do not have to be uniform throughout the society. In fact, given that these alternate structures must evolve out of the real needs of people, and be developed democratically by them, they need primarily to accord with the specifics of the communities that create them. How they are coordinated and networked will be a function of how they develop and what their actual character is.

For the purposes of deracializing U.S. society, a movement will be needed that takes as its task the development of an alternate identity for white (formerly white) people. This movement would have to be anti-supremacist, anti-messianic, anti-militarist, and anti-purity. Instead, it would have to prioritize the messiness of democratic procedure and principle and a general refusal of hegemony in the name of dialogue. It will not succeed if it is composed just of white people. White people need the critiques, advice, and guidance of non-white people to find their way out of the labyrinth of the coloniality that made them white. They need the critique and guidance of the non-hegemonic to begin to see what the hegemonic mind by which they live their whiteness is made of.

Forms of individualism have been part of the problem. The knowledge of how to construct alternate political structures will have to be learned through an abandonment of the traditional obsession with individualism—in principle, because it will rely on an overthrow of alienation toward others. In the realm of employment, for instance, this would involve cooperatives; for education, community participation in curriculum formation; for health care, free access for all persons, regardless of their health needs.

The primary form of political expression of whiteness is populism (as opposed to dialogue, analysis, and understanding). It is white populism that constitutes the white para-political state. Populism is a form of organization that associates members with a leadership that makes decisions for them and calls them to activity when needed. Leadership may propose what should be done and allow members to speak to the proposal and vote on it, but leadership then tells people what to do. Dialogic assemblies in which members spend time analyzing and discussing what they face or need to do are foreign to a populist organization. It is that alienness that most clearly demonstrates the contradiction between pro-democracy and populism.

Solidarity is populism's central ideological principle, sometimes to the point of ignoring or silencing what the solidarity is for. The raising of political or cultural issues from which controversy might ensue that could disrupt a populist solidarity will usually be repressed by a populist leadership. The solidarity to support government interventionism is of that sort; to question it is to incur charges of betrayal. Even labor unions operate as populist organizations. The leadership, charged with negotiating with employers or an industry, tells the members what is needed from them and, after some members have spoken to this, enforces it on the union. Advocacy of political issues is generally prevented in union meetings because it could threaten to create divisions in the membership. This is a paradigm that prevented many white anti-slavery workers before the Civil War from raising the issue of slavery in their organizations. The idea of operating according to a class consciousness, and forming the core of an alternate social structure that is working class in its awareness of itself, is foreign to the way unions operate in the United States. For the unions of the United States, solidarity is the totality of their ideology, often simply expressed as the binary of organizational allegiance and betrayal. Working-class consciousness (and the anti-racist, deracialized solidarity that would emerge not from a populism but from a community of dialogue) would see and understand many more avenues and possibilities of struggle for the well-being of working people as a class than is contained in those limited to contract negotiations and strikes.

Community Autonomy

White society has shown historically that the suppression of social and cultural autonomy in racialized communities has been one of its primary concerns. This has been constant throughout U.S. history, from the slave codes to the indictment of Regina McKnight and the murder of Oscar Grant. The forced labor, the sterilization projects, the police murders, as expressions of the hegemonic thinking of white supremacy, all have a dimension of weakening the possibility of people's autonomy.

Autonomy for communities of color would be a first step toward a decolonization of U.S. society, which is what is meant by eliminating the structures of racialization. Such autonomy would not be a form of "national" independence because autonomous communities would still belong to and reside in this society. It would not be secessionist or separatist. It would still be composed of people who are citizens. But it would be a liberation of social and political practices in and for those communities.

What autonomy means is local democracy, the ability of people affected by political decisions to participate in articulating, forming, and making those decisions. Severing connections with the white institutions that foster the coloniality of race and racism would be one of the decisions that people of color have to be able to make, in whatever way they see fit, under community autonomy. That is the first step toward undoing the imposition of centuries of racialization on them. Community control of schools and of policing would be a second area of decolonization that local democracy would offer. The necessary funding would come under the category of governmental responsibility for its citizens. Responsibility does not mean control. Coloniality means control. A government that takes responsibility for its citizens is one that has abjured the structures of coloniality.

The funding necessary for local community institutions, under the principle of decolonization, must be provided on a non-corporate basis, with no strings attached. To find the money, of course, the government need only cease building unneeded, redundant, and hyper-militarist weapons systems and end its programs of corporate welfare—that is, stop bailing out corporations when they become too big to succeed or remain healthy. A movement for community autonomy would thus have to be anti-militarist, anti-interventionist, and opposed to corporate impunity as well as to government responsibility for corporations to the detriment of its responsibility for its citizens. In addition, to advocate community autonomy would place at the center of one's political thought the principle of sovereignty, which would imply giving precedence to the principle of national sovereignty (of other nations) in foreign policy. Ending racism and ending interventionism are two sides of the same coin.

The most serious problem that a movement for community autonomy would face would be how to defend itself against the violence of white supremacy and its two states, the constitutional and the para-political, which would oppose autonomy out of their dependency on people of color for their identity, their impunity, and their oppression of people. Using whatever excuse they could—national unity, national security, cultural heritage, political process, and the like—they would attempt to destroy local autonomy out of desperation. Their need is to keep the racialized imprisoned under their hegemony. The racializers will even seek to trade funding of autonomous projects for subservience, but that would mean using funding to undermine the foundation of autonomy. Thus, strong rebellious and power-oriented movements of both people of color and white people will be necessary to accomplish and protect community autonomy. In general, then, local autonomy means a strong yet decentralized form of anti-coloniality—the decolonization of all the people of the United States, both white and of color.

A Proposed Step toward an Alternate Decolonized Consciousness

Perhaps, as an alternative to trying to construct an anti-racist whiteness, a first step toward decolonizing the United States, and the white mind, and weakening its cultural structures of racialization can be made by adopting an inverse form of DuBoisian double consciousness.

DuBois theorized the notion of a double consciousness as the condition under which black people found themselves. For him, it meant always seeing oneself through the eyes of others. A black person was both excluded from being American by being black and striving to transcend the white-imposed mark of being black in order to be American. Each black person is judged in advance by those other eyes, and always already rendered guilty in both the white gaze and one's own interiorization of it. Yet one remains guilty of nothing more than having been seen, of having been noticed because rendered noticeable by the other's racialization of oneself. That is, a black person is noticed by whites because of something whites do to themselves, through which the black person is then seen, and oppressed by being seen and socially categorized by the whites' act of noticing.

A reverse double consciousness for whites, as a step toward a decolonizing anti-racism, would be to see themselves as they are seen by the oppressed, by those they racialize. The dominant tend to see themselves as the norm, as simply human. Thus, a double consciousness would entail seeing themselves not as the norm but rather as the oppressors that they are in the eyes of those they oppress and racialize. It would be to see their hegemony, their dominance, their pretense to privilege through the eyes of those who suffer from it. This is not a question of guilt, but rather of seeing who one is, and who one is made to be, by one's position, one's role, and one's complicity in the machinery of whiteness.

Three things would happen. First, for a person to see himself as he or she is seen by another would be to grant that other person a subjectivity, an autonomy of consciousness that is denied to that other by racism and white supremacy. One would have to see oneself as judged by that other, not as an individual but as a part of a social machine. Part of the purpose of the vilification of the victims of racist violence is to de-authorize the racialized from rendering such judgments. Second, since white identity is based on the ability of whiteness to objectify those it racializes for itself, to see oneself as seen by those racialized would dispel both the other's objectification by one's white identity and one's own ability to use them for white identity construction. One's white identity, which depends on that objectification, would unravel. And third, one would become an object (in one's own mind) because one had become an object for those others. But one would become an object whose nature, in its capacity or potentiality to dominate, would be seen as other, as objectified, by oneself. One could see the dehumanization one had imposed on others in oneself. One could then see the modes by which one dominates or oppresses simply by being white, because seen as such by those whom whites have racialized.

It might be a place to start.

Notes

INTRODUCTION

1. The incident occurred on December 2, 2006. See Curry 2007. The student, Robert Bailey, had been jumped and beaten by some white students the day before.

2. Rachel Corrie was a member of the International Solidarity Movement, which attempted to interpose itself between the illegal Israeli occupation of Gaza and the Palestinian inhabitants of that land. She was wearing a bright orange fluorescent jacket and using a bullhorn when hit by the bulldozer. See "American Peace Activist" 2003.

3. The civil rights movements were an attempt to put an end to the racial hierarchy constructed by white supremacy and to establish a society based on equality, one in which race would no longer be a factor. The term "colorblind" was coined to signify this goal. But after the civil rights acts were written, it was found that something had been left out (Skrentny 1996, 30). A person subjected to a degraded or distorted education could not compete with a person with a fully developed education, even at the high school level. So the movements took the next step and demanded that the disparity in background and preparation be rectified (affirmative action). For the movements, it was simply a question of white society taking responsibility for the situation it had created for people of color. The goal of affirmative action was to bring the percentage of black people on jobs and in institutions up to what was roughly their proportion of the local population. What brought the government to accede were the urban uprisings that began in 1963: the government instituted affirmative action programs not out of a sense of justice but for crisis management (Skrentny 1996, 67–110). But the programs were not given a chance to work, though many training programs and educational opportunities were opened up. By the time the Bakke case (*Regents of the University of California vs. Bakke* [1978]) was decided, a vast resistance to affirmative action had grown in local government, unions, populist movements, and court decisions. Where originally the federal government sought to protect black people from racism, now it was attacked for

its programs, accused of taking black people under its wing and allowing them to live off its largesse.

4. For example, Naomi Zack, in Cuomo and Hall 1999, 77–78; Greg Moses, in Yancy 2005; Joe Kincheloe and Shirley Steinberg, in Kincheloe et al. 1998.

5. "Second Chances: Juveniles Serving Life without Parole in Michigan," a report by the ACLU of Michigan about juvenile sentences of life without parole, available at http://www.aclumich.org/sites/default/files/file/Publications/Juv Lifers V8.pdf.

6. Barnes 1967, 9. In these terms, one chooses oneself; one chooses one kind of self rather than another (10). One exists in the manner of an "event" (12).

7. Let us name a few. Amadou Diallo was shot by four New York City policemen in the middle of the night on February 4, 1999, as he was entering his apartment building. Sean Bell was shot on November 11, 2006, by three plainclothes detectives in Brooklyn as he sat in his car after his wedding. Oscar Grant was shot in the back on January 1, 2009, as he lay on his stomach in a BART station in Oakland. Tyisha Miller was shot on December 28, 1998, by three Los Angeles police officers in the middle of the night as she slept in her car. Gary King was shot in the back by an Oakland policeman in the middle of the afternoon in September 2007. All the killers (police officers) were exonerated. Though massive protests caused the four officers who murdered Diallo to be tried (not for murder but for violation of human rights), the day after they were acquitted, Malcolm Ferguson, a black man who had been active in organizing the protests, was shot and killed by the police, and the officer who did it was exonerated. The *San Francisco Chronicle* researched its own records in 2009 and found that, over the preceding fifteen years, out of 350 incidents in which a police officer had killed a person, only six were prosecuted, and in none of those six was the victim a person of color. Bulwa 2009.

8. Palast 2002, ch. 1; Perkins n.d.

9. The incident occurred on April 15, 1986. It was called "Operation El Dorado Canyon," and the government claimed that it was in retaliation (as if gang-related) for the firebombing of La Belle Discotheque in Berlin on April 5, 1986, in which a U.S. soldier and a Turkish civilian were killed and some 200 others injured. The perpetrator was never discovered. Over the course of twelve minutes, fourteen U.S. fighter bombers dropped 60 tons of munitions on Libya. See http://en.wikipedia.org/wiki/Bombing_of _Libya.

10. Wright 1945, 30–31, 83–86; P. Williams 1991, 119.

11. I give an analysis of these cultural transformations, as supplementary to Allen's primary focus on economic transformations, in my book *The Rule of Racialization* (2003b, ch. 1).

12. Different historians have pointed to different moments when the modern concept of race came into existence. Barbara Fields (1982), for instance, locates that moment in the nineteenth century. David Goldberg (2002), on the other hand, finds it emerging during the fifteenth century in Europe. I tend to agree with T. Allen (1996, 1997) that race was invented at the beginning of the eighteenth century in Virginia. See Martinot 2003b, 64–72.

13. To speak of the origin of race means to return to that original colonialist white/ black binary, from which it germinated. Though Native Americans were the first non-European people the Virginia settlers encountered, their inability to enslave the indigenous led the colonists to exclude Native Americans entirely from the colony. The

origin of whiteness and race located itself internal to the colony, in the direct relationships that the colony established with the Africans. Later, when others were brought into the purview of white colonization or white society (e.g., the Mexicans, the Chinese), that black/white binary would provide the template for their racialization by whites. Tomás Almaguer (1994) gives a fascinating description of the variations in the processes of racialization by which white settlers in California constructed their white racialized identity in their different encounters with other peoples: namely, the indigenous, the Mexicans, and the Chinese.

14. The term "race" was used in medieval Europe to signify social status, for instance, between those families that had collaborated with the Roman occupation of northern Europe and those that had not. The social concept of "limpieza de sangre" (purity of blood) played the same role in fifteenth-century Spain, signifying those who had maintained a certain separation from the Moorish occupation of Iberia. See Barzun 1966.

15. This is not intended to take away from the judgments of those people of color for whom whiteness is already an ethical question, insofar as they live in its shadow and confront it at every turn. I am simply attempting to redraw the picture from other parameters, using those axioms that white supremacists themselves take for granted, in order to reveal the inner mechanism of whiteness.

16. If whites are the only ones who have an interest in maintaining the hierarchy of race, then there can be only one form of racism, that is, white racism. Only whites have the hierarchical position to recategorize, denigrate, and deprecate people hierarchically lower in society. Though terms of denigration may be used between subordinate groups, it only reflects the hierarchy to which those groups have been subordinated by whites. Since black or brown people as groups do not dominate whites as a group, the use of racial derogations by people of color is for the purpose not of maintaining hierarchy but of neutralizing it.

17. See C. Harris 1993; Lipsitz 2006.

18. A note on my capitalization of the racialized term "black": At the center of my argument is the notion that Europeans invented themselves as white first, through a process of socio-political exclusionism and colonization that defined others as "other" using color terms for the purpose of that exclusionism and hierarchy (an invention subsequently institutionalized through the codification of "race"). That is, in the development of the modern concept of "race," whiteness as a cultural identity came first, after which races were invented as categorical divisions of the human species. When I refer to the categories of that colonizing system, and the color terms that emerge from that colonizing process, I leave the color terms in lower case. Thus, I refer to people as white, black, brown, without capital letters. I capitalize "Black" when it refers to some social entity that has arisen at the autonomous hands of black people, in response to their racialization. Thus, I refer to a Black community, a Black culture, a Black voice, insofar as these emerge from the socio-cultural substrate of racialization as varying forms of resistance, communal self-affirmation, and the construction of an alternative social and cultural identity to that which had been invented for black people by whites. In general, I capitalize in referring to those aspects of Black or Latino or Native American life that reflect the ineluctable emergence of something of their own, as an aspect of autonomy, sovereignty, and social identity. I do not capitalize white because in all respects it depends on white people's racialization of others, as a form of exclusion,

oppression, and derogation of those others, and thus emerges not as something of their own culturally but only as a manifestation of their construction of a form of dominance and hegemony.

19. Carmichael and Hamilton (1967); Stuckey 1987; and Hacker (1992) address this issue from a number of different perspectives.

20. Cf. John Griffin (1961). When Joshua Solomon, a white University of Maryland student, decided in 1994 to repeat John Griffin's experiment in living black, he chemically darkened his skin and went to Gainesville, Florida. He lasted three days. When he returned, he said he could not stand the hate. The subtitle of his article in the *Washington Post* is "My Own Journey in the Heart of Race-Conscious America." In 1994, race consciousness among whites was alive and well. Joshua Solomon, "Skin Deep: Reliving 'Black Like Me,'" *Washington Post*, October 30, 1994, C-1.

CHAPTER 1

1. The use of the welfare system against black women is a recent phenomenon. When the welfare system was first instituted during the New Deal, it was segregated, and acceptable as long as it excluded blacks (D. Roberts 1997, 243). When black people were finally admitted to eligibility, after the civil rights movements, the system became something to dismantle and abandon. Roberts mentions cases of white women on welfare in Louisiana who voted for David Duke, knowing he favored dismantling welfare, in order to remove black people from it (D. Roberts 1997, 244).

2. Once a woman entered the justice system through detected drug use, she was given the choice by the courts either to use Norplant or to be incarcerated (this was true at the time Roberts was writing; Norplant was taken off the market in 2002) (D. Roberts 1997, 176, 181).

3. See my analysis of the linguistic transformations that signified the evolution toward the eventual invention of "race" in the Virginia colony, in Martinot 2003b, 65–66.

4. The narrative of propriety still exists for white "southern womanhood" (at least as male mythology) well into the present era (Dollard 1949, 136). Oliver Cox points out that the "honor and sanctity of white womanhood" is but another cover for an absolute white refusal of peer status or equality for black people through black men (Cox 1970, 387).

5. The major elements of this account are condensed from my book *The Rule of Racialization* (2003b, ch. 1), in which I rely extensively on T. Allen 1996, DuBois 1935, and Zinn 1980. I diverge from Allen's and Zinn's accounts of the colonial period insofar as I do not restrict my account of whiteness to class relations as they do, but extend it to a cultural structure that supervenes class relations.

6. It is interesting that Goldberg (2002) conceives of the role the racial state plays in direct analogy to this corporate structure, though he does not mention it. One of the critical statements of his book is that the political is not reducible to the economic. Although he makes this statement with respect to race (110), it is also true of the corporate structure in its layered administrative and bureaucratic character. He maps out four roles for the state. (1) It defines populations into racially identifiable groups (through law, policy, and bureaucratic practice). (2) It regulates social, political, economic, legal, and cultural relations between those groups racially defined (that is, between whites and others). (3) It governs those populations identified as racial groups. (4) It oversees economic life and manages the racialized groups economically (in particular, the racialized are treated as a resource).

7. It is also worth noting here that when the first Africans appeared on a Dutch slave ship at the port of Jamestown in 1619, they were purchased by the Colonial Council and distributed to various plantations. The number of Africans remained insignificant until the 1660s (Boskin 1979, 14). In 1650, there were only 300 Africans within a total bond-labor population of many thousands.

8. In the Caribbean, the price of newly transported Africans was so low that it was more profitable to work them to death than provide sufficient sustenance for extended survival. Laborers were seen as expendable. Because the Virginians came to view African labor as wealth, subsistence care was provided. Thus, they were integrated into the political economy of the colony more intensively than in the Caribbean, but at the same time they were excluded from the colony socially in a way that free Africans were not in the Caribbean. The process of social categorization that differentiated the English and Africans beyond mere juridical definition or descriptive (phenotypic) differences became part of the basis on which the English developed a sense of being white. In this way, the corporate structure played a central role in the development of the modern concept of race.

9. See T. Allen 1997, 250–252; Stampp 1956, 214–215; Genovese 1976, 5, 135, 619; and Martinot 2003b, 67, 79–80.

10. "Black criminal conduct" labels anything that threatens white supremacy. This includes such things as autonomous organizational activity and mass gatherings. Black social events must jump through the proper police hoops to assure the state that the people involved will not be questioning white hegemony (D. Roberts 1997, 186).

11. Ultimately, what has to be understood about state control of sexuality is that it is a form of thought control—indeed, it is the primary form of thought control. The control of sexuality is a control over whom one can be intimate with, which then amounts to control over whom one can count as one's friends. Not that all friendship involves intimacy, but the possibility of intimacy or the choice to extend friendship to intimacy is an essential dimension of friendship. The control of friendship constitutes thought control because it delimits and constrains the domain of one's social discourse. The primary form of thinking about the world occurs in one's dialogues with people. That is why any social constraint of the free play of dialogue, whether through consumerism or censorship or entertainment or social alienation, is a constraint of thought.

12. See, for instance, Massey and Denton 1993. One might refer to the Boston busing riots of 1974 and the Deerfield (Illinois) events (1959–1961). Though real estate values are used as an excuse to bar black families from a neighborhood, what the Deerfield events clearly show is not a simplistic notion of "racism" but the totalitarian white need to maintain purity. See, for instance, Rosen and Rosen 1962.

13. Similarly, the Cold War campaign (its sense of threat entailing a pastiche of ideological export and military assault) was attractive because its confusions and contradictions only increased the sense of threat as a desired state. Those who examined the real history of these years were generally ignored. See W. A. Williams (1962).

14. A white supremacist might say to this, you are turning against yourself and your race. To which I would answer, you and your society gave me my whiteness. I did not choose it. And what I am presenting here for all whites is the possibility that if this is what whiteness means, perhaps the ethical thing to do would be to give it back.

15. For an elegant description of how this works out in a specific encounter, see Yancy 2008, ch. 1.

CHAPTER 2

1. Significant moments in which the subjugated have found their own mode of existence include the gladiators led by Spartacus after their rebellion against Rome, the black farm and labor cooperatives that former slaves formed after the Civil War, and the current Zapatista movement in Chiapas, in southern Mexico.

2. Bennett 1969; DuBois 1935; E. Foner 1988a.

3. Davis 2003. See also Davis 1998; Schlosser 1998, 51–77; and the Web page of the Center on Juvenile and Criminal Justice (http://www.cjcj.org/facts.php).

4. There have even been books on the topic, titled *Driving while Black*, one by Kenneth Meeks and one (*Driving while Black: Coverup*) by Kelvin Davis.

5. There has been a gradual relaxation of the need for warrants—for instance, the use of defective warrants (*U.S. vs. Leon*)—by the courts and the legislature, which enhances this police power (M. Parenti 1995, 48).

6. William Fisher (2007) tells the story of the arbitrary and gratuitous police raids on impoverished Black communities in Florida during the 1950s, resulting in the beating and killing of black people for the miniscule bounty the police received.

7. The requirement for obedience often takes lethal form. Teenagers have been shot in the back and killed in Oakland, California, when they have turned and walked away from an officer who was harassing them (e.g., Gary King, shot in the back by an Oakland police officer in September 2007). See http://www.counterpunch.org/maher09242007.html. But the demand for obeisance to humiliation goes back to slavery. Saidiya Hartman writes of the enforcement of "contentment performance" in her book *Scenes of Subjection* (1997). The torture of black bond-laborers by whipping was the usual form the demand for obedience took, to the point of requiring a performance of contentment and gratitude at being tortured. Former slaves from the Port Royal area of South Carolina recounted how a failure to smile and show gratitude doubled the punishment. In one of the accounts, reported by Austa French, a landowner asks his bond-laborers if they want to be whipped; they not only say yes but crowd in to be first, knowing two things: that the whipping gets worse the more this man does it, and that to say no would make the whipping all the more severe (French 1969, 68). Torture is the fundamental expression of impunity.

8. A recent example of the process of felonization occurred in Tulia, Texas, in 2000. Tom Coleman was hired by the police department to do an undercover drug investigation. After eighteen months, he surfaced and provided evidence for forty-six indictments of cocaine sales. Thirty-nine of the forty-six defendants were black, practically the entire black teen generation of that small town. The first defendants fought for their innocence. The juries convicted on Coleman's testimony alone, against evidence that the defendants were not where he said they were. The first convictions resulted in outrageous sentences of from sixty to ninety years. The rest accepted a plea bargain to a lesser felony. For those convicted, no defense by public defenders was offered, and discrepancies in Coleman's stories were ignored by the all-white juries. He was eventually investigated by a battery of lawyers who took an interest in the case, was convicted of perjury, and his victims released—after some four years in prison. He was not, however, sentenced to anything more severe than probation. That is, he was not punished for having harmed the eighteen persons who spent four years in prison. He succeeded in reconstituting the solidarity of the white community of Tulia through his persecutions of its black citizens. See *Tulia,*

Texas: The Price Americans Pay for the War on Drugs, a 2007 documentary film by Cassandra Herrman and Kelly Whalen, which showed on PBS channels in March 2009.

9. In a 1987 death penalty appeal, lawyers presented reams of sociological data showing racism to be a factor in who got convicted, what their sentences were, and who got the death penalty. The ratio of black or brown to white was eight to one (*McKleskey vs. Kemp* (481 US 279 [1987]). The attorneys moved to vacate the death sentence in light of the clear presence of racial discrimination. The judge agreed with the statistical conclusion but denied the motion, saying that racism had to be proved for this specific case, while statistical data was derived only from other cases (Dieter 1998). Thus, a provable totalitarian dynamic can hide behind individuation within a judicial process that itself reduces individuals to generalizations through profiling.

10. See http://www.sentencingproject.org/template/page.cfm?id=133.

11. This question has been especially carefully researched by Fellner and Mauer (1998) and by Mauer and Young (1995).

12. Interestingly, Goldberg (2002, 207) comprehends the closing of the Cold War as the "ultimate victory of states of whiteness," the state of "whitened colorblinding." He misses the structural connection between the Cold War and the war on drugs.

13. Toby Muse, "Jump in Coca Cultivation in Colombia Shocks UN," *San Francisco Chronicle,* June 19, 2008, p. A-9. See also Carolyn Lockhead, "Strategy Shifts from Illegals to Cash, Weapons," *San Francisco Chronicle,* March 18, 2009, p. A-1.

14. Moments of exposure of direct police involvement in drug trafficking are extant: Serpico, the disappearance of the drugs seized in the "French Connection" case, and the story of Adam Hakim (Drori 1992).

15. Drugs are also used as a political weapon. Community self-education projects have often fallen prey to this. The police have used drugs to close down black bookstores hosting reading and discussion groups on black history and social thought, for instance. Typically, an undercover agent would enter, leave a bag of heroin behind some books, and the police would raid a few minutes later, find the bag, impound the store, and imprison the proprietor. See Powell n.d.

16. One saw this new structure of racialization in effect in the last presidential election. In California, where Obama defeated McCain by two to one, a proposition that would have lightened the sentences and parole period for non-violent drug offenders, most of whom would presumably be black or brown, was defeated by the same margin. In other words, while Californians take the word of the political establishment that Obama, though black, is the best man for the job, their attitude toward the criminalized population of racialized people continues unaffected by that fact. Obama has been accepted into the white world, which is still involved in giving itself cohesion through its racialization (segregation and criminalization) of people of color, who continue to be seen as the necessary threat.

17. This white supremacist modus operandi was evident in 2008 in Jena, Louisiana. When massive protest demonstrations brought people to Jena from the entire nation to register their opposition to the indictments, the KKK and the National Movement (two white supremacist organizations) visited white people who also thought the indictments unjust and counseled them to absent themselves from the issue and to express a fear of black violence.

18. The largest was the ICE raid on the Agriprocessors meatpacking plant in Pottsville, Iowa, involving 900 agents. On May 12, 2008, 390 persons were arrested in one

morning and 306 were held for prosecution. The town lost one-third of its population that day. Hundreds of families were torn apart, said a nun who worked as a relief worker for the children. On October 7, 2008, ICE raided a Columbia Farms poultry plant in Greenville, S.C., arresting 300 persons. On May 2, 2008, ICE raided a taqueria chain, El Balazo, in San Francisco, arresting 60 employees. On August 25, 2008, ICE raided Howard Industries, an electrical equipment manufacturer, arresting 481 persons and taking them to a privately run detention center in Jena, Louisiana. According to Bacon (n.d.), the raid was carried out to hamstring an International Brotherhood of Electrical Workers organizing campaign in the plant and the area.

CHAPTER 3

1. David Walker's *Appeal* was made in 1829. Hubert Harrison was a contemporary of Alain Locke, writing in the 1930s. See also Smith 1949; Montagu 1964; Myrdal 1962; and Locke 1989.

2. Anna Stubblefield is a constructivist who argues that race as constructed is real and should be taken into account as an important moral principle. She begins with the history of the invention of race and whiteness in the English colonies, and sustains throughout her discussion the notion that whites and white identity are what have an interest in maintaining race and racism and thus constitute the core of the problem. If the role of racism is to maintain a hierarchy with respect to race, then it belongs to those who have an interest in doing so. All racism, by implication, is then white racism. Others, beset by that hierarchy, primarily have an interest in resisting it. She calls on white people to take responsibility for what whiteness and white supremacy have done to others in the course of their colonialist criminalities and their distribution to white society of their unmerited and ill-gotten gains. See Stubblefield 2005.

3. Among these constructivists, we could cite Cox (1970), Outlaw (1996), T. Allen (1996, 1997), Martinot (2003b), and Duster (2003).

4. This is the central argument throughout Martinot 2003b. See also Saxton 1991 and Morrison 1992, which address the question from alternate perspectives.

5. Non-parity and (negative) purity emerge as adjuncts to coloniality. They antedate Linnaeus, Buffon, Gobineau, Kant, and Jim Crow, as well as the various racializations of Native Americans, Latinos, Asians, and so on undertaken in the name of race. And both live on in a domestic coloniality founded on the continual redefinition of others as other. Neither negative purity nor non-parity has any source in its object (people of different colors). They only have to do with a specific (white) knower.

6. The Spanish invented the notion of "limpieza de sangre" (purity of blood) in the interest of political purpose during their wars to ethnically cleanse Iberia of Arab influence and hegemony. For Spanish colonialism, purity came before race and was added to the sense of entitlement and supremacy inherent in its Christianity. Making no restrictions on mixed marriages, the Spanish constructed a hierarchy on both ethnic and economic grounds. Whiteness as a racial category (the modern concept of race) was invented in the English colonies. (See the Introduction, note 14.)

7. As George Yancy says, speaking of the middle passage and its devastations, "power produces; it produces reality." That is, what it produces are the objects of its knowledge (2004b, 114). What power produces as fact and truth, becomes objective. Race and racism, as objective entities and as the products of 500 years of colonialism,

are manifestations of power. Constructed by the power of coloniality, they become objective as central organizing principles of the present forms of the coloniality of power. See Grosfoguel 2006.

8. On the generation of the white racialized identity through the other, see Yancy 2004a. See also Martinot 2003b, ch. 4.

9. If Obama is president, it is because the Democratic Party, and the corporate economy that supports and directs it, chose him. He will play the role of president as best he can on the basis of his background and experience, but the campaign advisers behind him and the administrative appointees under him are mostly white career politicians and think-tank members. He is very high up in the white power structure, where he is isolated both as a political figure and as a black man. Politically, he is enmeshed in complex structures and networks, while existentially, he is very alone.

CHAPTER 4

1. Zoltan Grossman tabulates more than 110 instances of U.S. military intervention in the world (see http://www.neravt.com/left/invade.htm). See also Grimmett 1999.

2. In an interview on July 24 and 25, 1990, April Glaspie, U.S. ambassador to Iraq, stated that when she spoke to Saddam Hussein a few weeks earlier, she informed him that the United States had no "defense or security commitments" with Kuwait and would not interfere in "Arab-Arab" affairs (Sifry and Cerf 1991, 122–133).

3. See Sifry and Cerf 1991 and Scott 2003. When the United States invaded Iraq in 2003, after twelve years of embargo, Iraq's social infrastructure was still in shambles and the country was a threat to nobody. Indeed, 1.5 million Iraqis, a third of them children, had died before the U.S. invasion from conditions directly linked to the embargo.

4. Dana Milbank and Justin Blum, "Document Says Oil Chiefs Met with Cheney Task Force," Washington Post, November 16, 2005; Public Record Staff, "The Secret Deal for Iraq's Oil," August 16, 2008, available at http://pubrecord.org/nation/403/the-secret-deal-for-iraqs-oil/.

5. See the FBI Web page at http://www.fbi.gov/wanted/topten/fugitives/laden.htm.

6. A tape of the public execution of a woman was smuggled out of Afghanistan. The Revolutionary Association of Women of Afghanistan, the largest women's organization in that country, pleaded against using such images to invade; it would only be worse in the aftermath (http://www.rawa.org/us_flyer.htm). Cf. Brodsky 2003.

7. On Bill Maher, see Binelli 2006. Nancy Oden, a peace activist and Green Party organizer, was kept off a plane by federal agents on November 1, 2001, in Maine. Katie Sierra, a fifteen-year-old West Virginia high school student, was suspended from school for wearing a T-shirt that said, "After I saw all the Afghani children on TV killed by our bombs, I felt so much safer." Barbara Wein, an instructor at the U.S. Institute for Peace in Georgetown, was fired in November 2001 for making public statements against the war in Afghanistan. These events, among many others, occurred in a growing post-9/11 anti-Arab environment. Two Palestinian women (Alia Atawneh and Hiam Yassine) were fired a week after 9/11 from a department store in San Jose, California, because they were Palestinian. All told, fifty-some people, of many ethnicities, were fired in the San Francisco Bay Area because of 9/11 in the following months. A tenured professor (Sami Al-Arian) at the University of South Florida in Tampa was suspended with intent to

terminate on September 28, 2001, and was then charged with terrorism for having made pro-Palestinian remarks in the mid-1990s.

8. The problem of terrorism becomes a mere footnote to the extent that the attack itself fulfilled the definition of terrorism accepted by both the United States and the United Nations. According to the United Nations, terrorism is "criminal acts intended or calculated to provoke a state of terror in the general public, a group of persons or particular persons for political purposes [that] are in any circumstance unjustifiable, whatever the considerations of a political, philosophical, ideological, racial, ethnic, religious or other nature that may be invoked to justify them" (General Assembly Res. 51/210, "Measures to Eliminate International Terrorism," 1999). Nothing fulfills this definition like an unprovoked military assault on a nation. Terrorism is defined in the U.S. Code of Federal Regulations as "the unlawful use of force and violence against persons or property to intimidate or coerce a government, the civilian population, or any segment thereof, in furtherance of political or social objectives" (28 C.F.R. Section 0.85). An essential aspect of both definitions is the notion of political purpose. For there to be political purpose for an act, and for an act to be terrorism, someone has to take credit for it.

9. Stan Goff, a retired Special Forces instructor, provides an analysis of the military preparations needed for the assault (see http://www.narconews.com/goff1.html).

10. The charter of the Organization of American States, Articles 18, 20, and 27. The invasion also violated the UN Charter, Article 2(4), and the Geneva Conventions (1949), Article 3, as well as Articles 51, 52, and 57 of Protocol I of those Conventions, to all of which the United States is a signatory. See Maechling 1990; see also Inter-American Commission on Human Rights 1993. Noriega was indicted under Title 18 and 21 of the U.S. Code, but not under international law. The United States called for his extradition and, failing that, imposed an economic embargo on Panama, after which it invaded. See Chomsky 1991, ch. 5.

11. The intervention in Yugoslavia was complex. Aside from the international campaign to dismantle the Yugoslav federation, there was the NATO creation of the Kosovo Liberation Army (KLA); the Rambouillet ultimatum, which would have dissolved Yugoslav sovereignty; and the U.S./NATO violation of international law. See, for instance, Thomas 2000. The KLA was a paramilitary group organized, armed, and financed under NATO auspices to invade Kosovo and provoke a civil war there by attacking Serbian people and police, beginning in late 1996 (Wood 1999). At the time, negotiations between the Kosovars (Rugova's Kosovo Democratic Union) and the Serbs were progressing toward settlement of their differences. The KLA derailed that process, opening the door to NATO intervention (Keith 1999; Stone 2005). See Progressive Response/ Foreign Policy in Focus 1999 and Chatelot 1999 on false atrocities used to rationalize NATO intervention. See also Wayne 1999; and Frank Viviano, "Kosovo Crisis Serves as Model of Wars to Come," San Francisco Chronicle, April 7, 1999. The Rambouillet proposal would have given NATO free reign to station troops within Serbia itself. Yugoslavia's representatives simply walked out on it (Nambiar 1999). Intervention was the goal. When Nelson Mandela proposed to bring a team from Africa to mediate the many-sided conflicts in Kosovo, he was waved aside by NATO.

12. Demonization does not mean that the person demonized is a paragon of virtue. Some political leaders are less corrupt than others, but corruption and dimensions of autocracy come with the political territory, for the most part. What "demonization" of a person signifies is an attribution of evil, which involves biasing one's interpretations of

all the person's words and actions as being bad or wrong, and obliterating any claim to legitimacy or validity of his or her position (such as being constitutionally elected, as all the political leaders targeted by the attack sequence have been, although, by hapless fortune, under their own local constitutions and not that of the United States). The true domain of demonization is good and evil rather than innocence or guilt.

13. Even in the Philippines in 1899 the United States saw its occupation as "defensive." See Chomsky 1985, 87.

14. During the Vietnam War, for instance, the facts only served to generate a sociopolitical debate on the morality of the war, as if carpet bombing rural populations or poisoning an entire ecosystem with Agent Orange could be dealt with as "moral" issues. In 1991, the facts about the bombing of Iraq were censored by the Pentagon. They have since become available, yet knowledge of the resulting social devastation and mass starvation has sparked no national discussion. Even though the facts are known, little concern for right or justice ensues. In effect, the problem was not that "facts" about the injustice of an intervention were ignored; those facts instead participated in its actual justification. Though half a million Iraqi children died of disease and starvation because of the embargo, Secretary of State Madeleine Albright publicly stated that this was acceptable ("60 Minutes," CBS, May 12, 1996). The facts concerning U.S. violations of the sovereignty of other nations seem only to reinforce one's "American" sense of sovereignty, in which case the charge that the government had violated the principles of sovereignty through intervention becomes incomprehensible a priori.

15. The history of the intervention in El Salvador is instructive, but it is too long and complex a story to do it justice in a few words. A two-party system was imposed on a nation with a different tradition, which succeeded in keeping the death squad leadership in power for the next 20 years. See Chomsky 1985,101–127; Menéndez Rodríguez 1983; and America's Watch 1991.

16. For example, in New York, the black vote was considered to have been the deciding factor in the contest between Hamilton's Federalists and Jefferson's Republicans. But since black and white voted alongside each other, it was only the white mind that could single out the "black vote" as an entity different from any other vote. Otherwise, outside that paranoid construction, the concept of a "black vote" had no organizational meaning. After 1821, when the (Jeffersonian) Republicans succeeded in restricting the vote in New York to "white male citizens" (Litwack 1961, 82) and the few free African-American men with sufficient property, black people were still considered the determining factor on anti-slavery issues (Litwack 1961, 90). See also Martinot 2003b, ch. 1.

17. Zilversmit 1967, 183. This is really the origin of the similarity between the two parties which, as the corporate economy developed, became an agreement on how to serve capital—which Chomsky calls a one-party system with two factions (Chomsky 1991, 373).

18. Although the Democratic Party has sought since the 1960s to adopt as a constituency the people of the various movements of the sixties (e.g., "minorities," women, labor, and environmentalists), it does so not to represent them but to embed them in the structure of white politics. Thus, it failed as a party to vote against the wars in Afghanistan and Iraq or against repeal of affirmative action, or even to take a stand in California against the anti–affirmative action Proposition 209, which was passed during the first Clinton administration.

19. Historically, a principled or ideologically oriented candidacy has been unwinnable in the United States, with perhaps three exceptions—Jack London, Vito Marcantonio, and the Farmer-Labor Alliance. When Dennis Kucinich was proclaimed unelectable by his own party in the presidential race of 2004, it was because he could not squelch his need to be principled in his political thinking, something that had characterized his entire political career.

CHAPTER 5

1. Turner 1911, 149–154. See also Litwack 1961, 66–70. Litwack lists Indiana, Ohio, Connecticut, and Illinois as having prominently passed "anti-immigration" statutes. In Illinois, the enactment stated its purpose to "exclude further ingress of negroes, and to remove those already among us as speedily as possible" (71).

2. In particular, Article 4, Section 2. Wiecek 1977.

3. In pursuit of this white nationalism, many northern whites supported slavery in the South even as it was being abolished in the North (and had already been effectively abolished in Massachusetts and Pennsylvania). Slavery, for them, served the misanthropic goals of, first, keeping labor in place and working (in reality, captive) in the nation's chief source of capital wealth and, second, keeping black people from mingling in white society.

4. With the election of Jefferson to the presidency in 1800, the party that he led, which evolved into the Democratic Party, became a strong representative of southern slaveholders' interests in the northern states. It helped redirect the abolition process into gradualism and pressed for a general segregationism whose severity and malevolence toward black people were intended to dissuade slaves from running away. See McManus 1973, 186; Litwack 1961, 73.

5. The title of the documentary was taken from one of W.E.B. DuBois's writings about Johnson and the attacks on his character as he won and defended his championship.

6. Fanon 1968, ch. 1. The government's violation of Black citizenship was especially extended to Johnson. In the wake of his demonstrated undefeatability, the state fabricated charges under the Mann Act (which prohibited transporting women across state lines for immoral purposes), arguing that because a couple of his lovers were white, his very intimacy with them was "illicit." The fact that the one former lover who agreed to testify against him had traveled with him before the Mann Act was passed, making the charges ex post facto, did not bother the government. Johnson was convicted in 1913 and sentenced to a year in prison.

7. The general hostility toward Johnson is not something restricted simply to the dark period of Jim Crow, with its para-political structures of anti-black violence. It recurs even in the present. The attacks on Lani Guinier by a mob made up of press and politicians, by people who had never read her works but were critical of what was said in them, and which resulted finally in the withdrawal of her appointment to the Civil Rights Commission in June 1993 (she had been appointed in April), is an example. She had a carefully worked-out theory of how to reform elections and voting that would make them more equitable and democratic. All the mob could scream from newsprint and television screens was that "she's against our system." No one in a responsible position dared interpret "our system" to mean "white impunity against any independently thinking black

person." The recent re-indictment of eight former Black Panthers in January 2007 (the "San Francisco Eight") for cases 30 years old which, even in the 1970s, rested only on confessions extracted by torture evinces a similar obsessive refusal by the government to relinquish its self-defined sense of having been attacked or offended. The refusal of the state of Pennsylvania to grant Mumia Abu-Jamal a new and fair trial despite a confession by the person who committed the murder for which Mumia was framed in the 1980s is another case. To do so would not only reveal the frame-up but also release a journalist who was targeted by the police because he had reported police brutality in his journalism (see Lindorff 2003).

8. Jones 1960, 89, 149. On the prison industry, see Davis 1998; C. Parenti 1999; and Schlosser 1998, 51–77. See also the Web page of the Center on Juvenile and Criminal Justice. The United States has more than 2 million people incarcerated, the largest among all nations both per capita and in actual numbers, with an incarceration rate more than seven times the world average.

9. Others have dealt with how different groups have escaped from the prejudicial indictments of the immigrant. Noel Ignatiev has written *How the Irish Became White* (1995), and Karen Brodkin has written *How the Jews Became White Folks and What That Says about Race in America* (1998). The goal of racialization is not just the derogation of others but the hegemonic consolidation of the racializers, the creation and re-creation of whiteness and white racialized identity. It is entry into this process that constitutes "becoming white." See Morrison 1992.

10. Douglass 1996; DuBois 1903, chs. 7 and 8. The white racialized border I am addressing should not be confused with DuBois's notion of the double consciousness. DuBois is speaking of the psycho-cultural effects on black people of living in a hostile social environment, whereas the racialized border delineates the social domain in which white people express and enact that hostility.

11. The political economy of Latino immigration is a complex phenomenon having to do with the structural impoverishment of Latin America by foreign (mostly U.S.) investment and the exploitation of Latin American labor and resources by multinational corporations, recently ideologized as "neo-liberalism." During the first phase, foreign investment in Third World countries extracted raw materials with cheap labor, removing both product and earnings to the metropole and exporting manufactured goods whose marketing would complete the process of financial extraction from that country. In the second, neo-liberal phase, all land and public assets are privatized and multinational corporations dominate the economic process, destroying local (often non-market) economic structures and social welfare institutions that the people had relied on during the previous phase to survive. Faced with a doubly devastated economy, people migrate to the center to which their home wealth had been removed in a conscious or unconscious process of retrieval. See Jalée 1968; Gerassi 1965; Arévalo 1961; Stiglitz 2003.

12. U.S. Border Control 2004.

13. "North Carolina: Pickles" 1998; Balderrama and Molina 2005. It is significant that a great number of the migratory agricultural laborers on the East Coast are black.

14. For an interesting view of these Latino communities and networks from the inside, see Pérez 1991.

15. Lydersen 2007. Also see Lydersen 2002. A hint of the effect of profiling and racialized arrests and sentencing can be obtained by comparing the ratio of the African-American population by region to that of whites, and relating it to the ratio of African-

American prisoners to white prisoners. That is, the ratio of black to white prisoners is divided by the ratio of black to white residents to produce an index. For the United States as a whole, this index is 5.57 (for 2005). For California, it is 6.5. That means that the national incarceration rate for African-Americans is 5.57 times that for whites (while crime rates for both populations are about the same). And that is just relating African-Americans to whites. Adding Latinos and Native Americans would change this index in different directions, depending on the region. For prison statistics for the United States, see the Sentencing Project, at http://www.sentencingproject.org/StatsbyState.aspx.

16. For more on this concept, see Foucault's deconstructions of power and knowledge in his many writings on that subject (Foucault 1980) and Bourdieu's notion of the "habitus" in *The Theory of Practice* (1977). Most important, see Jean-Paul Sartre's concept of "seriality" as he develops it in his *Critique of Dialectical Reason* (1976), especially in his application of it to coloniality and racism.

CHAPTER 6

1. Ward Churchill had made reference to U.S. financial domination of third world nations through debt, which has caused economic dislocation that is severe enough to produce mass starvation, disease, and cultural collapse (amounting to genocide in many areas). The bureaucrats who manage the global financing apparatus sit in tidy little offices in banks and brokerages. Their collective administration of this genocide, Churchill argued, places them in an analogous position to Eichmann, who likewise administered genocide from his office. Churchill made this analogy about those who worked in the financial offices in the World Trade Center (though he did not say this about all who perished in the collapse of those towers, as he is falsely accused of doing). For his original essay, see http://www.politicalgateway.com/news/read.html?id=2739. Also see http://wardchurchill.net, the URL for much of the discussion concerning his case.

2. Fanon has become recognized as a foremost theoretician of anti-colonialist struggle, and especially of the decolonization of the mind of the colonized. His thinking, especially in *The Wretched of the Earth* (1968), spread widely throughout the third world, as well as racialized communities in the United States (Black, Chicano, Native American, Puerto Rican, Asian, and others), many of which saw themselves as "subcolonies" (in George Jackson's [1970] phrase) in solidarity with national liberation movements. It .spread to the Vietnam anti-war movement, which had recognized the U.S. military adventure there as a form of colonialism.

3. The coloniality of U.S. society has, of course, two sides. To be categorized as black or brown is to be colonized in body by the para-political state and in mind by being spoken for by the structures of racialization (to think that the constitutional state is democratic, for instance). White people are colonized in mind by racialization to see themselves as a norm, a standard that flaunts itself through its alienation of others. They are instructed to adopt whiteness as an identity and identification and to forget the brutal, criminal history of white supremacy.

4. Jackson 1970. Certain job categories are set aside for people of color (e.g., agricultural labor, janitorial, hotel and restaurant service). As a category of political economy, Jackson's concept of a "subcolony" would also hold for women.

5. Though Fanon did not articulate the racism he himself experienced as a form of state (metaphoric or otherwise), he felt its para-political nature through his own black-

ness, through the constant (though never uniform) otherness that buried him alive under the presumptive, unthinking words of the white people he encountered. And despite his own retrieval of a history and a subjectivity through the Negritude movement and through the writings of Aimé Césaire, he knew that other reality persisted, demanding resignation, assuming unreason, and strategizing entrapment. He restated the premise of the para-political state thus: "All those white men in a group, guns in their hands, cannot be wrong. I am guilty" (Fanon 1967, 139).

6. One historical example is given by a statement of Senator Benjamin W. Leigh of Virginia in 1836 in an argument against abolition. He pointed to the several white mob riots that had occurred in cities such as Cincinnati and Philadelphia and asked what those riots might have done had there been general emancipation. No question was raised about possibly charging the white mobs with criminal behavior or bringing their instigators to justice. Rather than be marked as illegal, the white mobs were understood by Leigh to be simply demonstrating the Anglo-Saxon propensity to dominate and "enslave other races" (Horsman 1981, 209). It was a covert way of claiming that black people should properly be enslaved so that good "civilized" white people (the para-political state) would be spared the necessity and indelicacy of mob barbarity.

7. At the core of the issue of violence is not its existence but rather the question of how it is defined and who does the defining. Bill Haywood pointed out that for working people to strike, to stop work and put their hands in their pockets, is considered the quintessential act of violence by the capitalist class. Johnson's violence was his autonomy, his refusal of obedience and obeisance to para-political culture, his refusal to acquiesce.

8. Fanon provides a view of the other side of this refusal. He is famous for having proposed that anti-colonialist violence was, for the colonized, a mode of breaking free of the chains of subjection and beginning to create a new autonomous subjectivity (1968, ch. 1). This violence was not to be considered therapy for what colonialism had done psychologically through its oppressions. Instead, it made autonomous agency possible for the colonized by breaking the internalized constraints of those oppressions and the individual's accommodations to those constraints.

9. See *The Color of Fear*, directed and produced by Lee Mun Wah (1994). It is a documentary of a workshop on race, involving individuals from different races. Its focus is a spontaneous demonstration of the inability of white people to hear what black people are saying because they have already spoken for them.

10. This was an issue that Fanon fairly shouted at Sartre when Sartre slipped into the rhetorical closet of the dialectician (Fanon 1967, 133–138). Despite his anti-colonialism, Sartre had not freed himself from the Eurocentric myth of reciprocity with respect to racialization and para-political enslavement. He too easily slipped into the integument of the Hegelian master/slave dialectic, which Fanon discards as extraneous to racial oppression. Sartre was not deaf to Fanon, however; he heard him, and expressed the fact that he had heard him in *Critique of Dialectical Reason* (1976).

11. For Native Americans, the question of sovereignty is already at the center; their problem has been reconstructing an allo-cultural existence that would both ground itself on the language of tradition and speak the narratives of their present condition as Native peoples. In a profound sense, what the Zapatistas have taught, as an indigenous movement, is an alternate decolonizing epistemology for transforming the political space. Fanon traverses this domain in his articles on the African revolution (e.g., *L'An Cinq de*

la Révolution Algérienne [1962]), as does Amílcar Cabral (1969). The Zapatista refusal to grant legitimacy to the Mexican state's refusal to grant political autonomy to indigenous culture deconstructs the nation-state's self-defined pretense to sovereignty and shifts real legitimacy to the autonomy of indigenous communities.

12. Litwack 1961; McManus 1973; Martinot 2003b, 90–96.

13. Only rarely has this definitional error been challenged (DuBois did so, as did the IWW). Generally, white labor unionism and white leftism have thought only to ask white workers to stop being exclusionary. But most early working-class organizers refused to redefine slavery as "prison labor" or call on white workers to make common cause with slaves as workers. Many abolitionists sought solidarity between white workers and the bond-laborers but were generally rejected by white workers. It suggests why today the massive incarceration of black and brown people succeeds in producing disdain and further discriminatory attitudes among most whites, rather than class solidarity.

14. Hill 1988 discusses the presence of racism in the United Mine Workers Union at the turn of the century and tells a number of stories that aptly exemplify this syndrome.

15. With the exception of two or three industrial unions, labor unions remained segregated until after World War II. They thus generally participated in the ICS until well after the civil rights movements. To the extent the unions maintain a racialized division of job categories, they are part of the ICS and thus part of the ruling class in the racialized class system. To the extent they model themselves on a corporate form of organization (an executive committee, a stratification of personnel such as officers, business agents, shop stewards, and so on), restrict their membership to "speech" at meetings, and use a contract system that constitutes their "property" relation to management, they function above the working class within the white class system.

16. Many of the revolutionaries who led third world anti-colonial struggles after World War II sought to invent an independence out of dependence (the colonizer's tradition), rather than invent a tradition out of the allo-cultural structures embedded in their past. It is in examining this experience that Fanon, for instance, realized that true liberation could occur only through a total refusal of the Eurocentric paradigm that was materialized in the power matrix of capitalism, the nation-state, and the legislation of sexuality. Amílcar Cabral (1969) was another who recognized this truth.

References

Adelson, Alan, and Kate Taverna, dirs. 1989. *The Lodz Ghetto: A Documentary.* Holocaust/ Independent Film.

Airola, Jim. N.d. "Use of Remittance Income in Mexico." Working Paper, Defense Resources Management Institute Working Papers Series. Available at http://www.nps .navy.mil/drmi/WorkingPapers/DRMI%20Working%20Paper%2006-01.pdf.

Alcoff, Linda Martin. 2006. *Visible Identities: Race, Gender, and the Self.* New York: Oxford University Press.

Allen, Austin. 2006. *The Origins of the Dred Scott Case.* Athens: University of Georgia Press.

Allen, Theodore. 1969. *Can White Radicals Be Radicalized?* Detroit: Radical Education Project.

———. 1996. *The Invention of the White Race.* Vol. 1. New York: Verso.

———. 1997. *The Invention of the White Race.* Vol. 2. New York: Verso.

Almaguer, Tomás. 1994. *Racial Fault Lines.* Berkeley: University of California Press.

Alpert, Jonathan. 1970. "The Origin of Slavery in the United States—the Maryland Precedent." *American Journal of Legal History* 14:189–221.

"American Peace Activist Killed by Army Bulldozer in Rafah." 2003. *Haaretz,* March 18.

America's Watch. 1991. *El Salvador's Decade of Terror.* New Haven, Conn.: Yale University Press.

Amuedo-Dorantes, Catalina, Cynthia Banzak, and Susan Pozo. N.d. "On Remitting Patterns of Immigrants." Federal Reserve Bank of Atlanta. Available at http://www.frb atlanta.org/filelegacydocs/BANZAK%20article-final.pdf.

Arendt, Hannah. 1958. *The Origins of Totalitarianism.* New York: Meridian Books.

Arévalo, Juan José. 1961. *The Shark and the Sardines.* Trans. June Cobb and Raul Osegueda. New York: L. Stuart.

Bacon, David. 2003. "Saddam's Labor Laws Live On." *The Progressive* (December).

————. 2008. *Illegal People: How Globalization Creates Migration and Criminalizes Immigrants.* Boston: Beacon Press.

————. N.d. "The Politics Driving Mississippi's ICE Raid." Available at http://www.alternet.org/immigration/97279.

Balderrama, R. J., and Hilario Molina. 2005. "Networks of Exploitation: The View from North Carolina Farm Labor Camps." Paper presented at the annual meeting of the American Sociological Association, Philadelphia, August 12.

Balko, Radley. 2006. *Overkill: The Rise of Paramilitary Police Raids in America.* Cato Institute, July 17. Available at http://www.cato.org/pubs/wtpaper/balko_whitepaper.pdf.

Barnes, Hazel. 1967. *An Existentialist Ethics.* Chicago: University of Chicago Press.

Barzun, Jacques. 1966. *The French Race: Theories of Its Origins.* Port Washington, N.Y.: Kennikat Press.

Beals, Carleton. 1963. *Latin America: World in Revolution.* New York: Abelard-Schuman.

Beinin, Joel. 1991. *Origins of the Gulf War.* Westfield, N.J.: Open Magazine Pamphlet Series.

Bell, Linda, and David Blumenfeld, eds. 1995. *Overcoming Racism and Sexism.* Lanham, Md.: Rowman and Littlefield.

Bennett, Lerone. 1969. *Black Power USA: The Human Side of Reconstruction.* Baltimore: Penguin.

Bernasconi, Robert, ed. 2001. *Race.* Malden, Mass.: Blackwell.

Binelli, Mark. 2006. "A Man for Our Time." *Rolling Stone,* August 24.

Blum, Lawrence. 2002. *I'm Not a Racist, But . . . : The Moral Quandary of Race.* Ithaca, N.Y.: Cornell University Press.

Boas, Franz. 1916. "The Origins of Totemism." *American Anthropologist* 18 (2): 319–326.

Boskin, Joseph. 1979. *Into Slavery: Racial Decisions in the Virginia Colony.* Washington, D.C.: University Press of America.

Bourdieu, Pierre. 1977. *Outline of a Theory of Practice.* Trans. Richard Nice. New York: Cambridge University Press.

Breen, T. H. 1976. "A Changing Labor Force and Race Relations in Virginia, 1660–1710." In *Shaping Southern Society,* ed. T. H. Breen, pp. 116–134. New York: Oxford University Press.

Britt, Lawrence. 2003. "Fascism Anyone?" *Free Inquiry* (Spring): 20.

Brodkin, Karen. 1998. *How the Jews Became White Folks and What That Says about Race in America.* New Brunswick, N.J.: Rutgers University Press.

Brodsky, Anne. 2003. *With All Our Strength: The Revolutionary Association of the Women of Afghanistan.* New York: Routledge.

Bulwa, Demian. 2009. "Ex-officer in Rare Company: Police Charged with Murder," *San Francisco Chronicle,* February 15.

Burns, Ken, dir. 2005. *Unforgivable Blackness: The Rise and Fall of Jack Johnson.* Florentine Films.

Cabral, Amílcar. 1969. *The Struggle in Guinea.* Cambridge, Mass.: Africa Research Group.

Carmichael, Stokely, and Charles V. Hamilton. 1967. *Black Power: The Politics of Liberation in America.* New York: Random House.

Carr, Leslie G. 1997. *"Color-Blind" Racism.* Thousand Oaks, Calif.: Sage Publications.

Cash, Wilbur Joseph. 1941. *The Mind of the South.* New York: Knopf.

Cassidy, Peter. 1997. "Operation Ghetto Storm: The Rise of Paramilitary Policing." *Covert Action Quarterly* 62:20–25.

Castillo, Celerino. 1994. *Powderburns: Cocaine, Contras and the Drug War.* Buffalo, N.Y.: Sundial Press.

Chatelot, Christophe. 1999. "Les Morts de Racak ont-ils été tuent vraiment froidement?" *Le Monde,* January 21.

Chomsky, Noam. 1985. *Turning the Tide: U.S. Intervention in Central America and the Struggle for Peace.* Boston: South End Press.

———. 1991. *Deterring Democracy.* New York: Verso.

Chossudovsky, Michel. 1999. "Kosovo 'Freedom Fighters' Financed by Organized Crime." Available at chossudovsky@sprint.ca.

Churchill, Ward. 2002. *The COINTELPRO Papers: Documents from the FBI's Secret Wars against Dissent in the United States.* Cambridge, Mass.: South End Press.

Clark, Ramsey. 1992. *The Fire This Time: U.S. War Crimes in the Gulf.* New York: Thunder's Mouth Press.

Commons, John R., Ulrich B. Phillips, Eugene A. Gilmore, Helen L. Sumner, and John B. Andrews, eds. 1910. *Documentary History of American Industrial Society.* 11 vols. Cleveland: A. H. Clark.

Cox, Oliver. 1970. *Caste, Class, and Race.* New York: Monthly Review Press.

Crenshaw, Kimberlé, ed. 1995. *Critical Race Theory: The Key Writings That Formed the Movement.* New York: New Press.

Crozier, Michel, Samuel Huntington, and Joji Watanuki. 1975. *The Crisis in Democracy.* New York: New York University Press.

Cunningham, Noble E., Jr. 1957. *The Jeffersonian Republicans: The Formation of Party Organization, 1789–1801.* Chapel Hill: University of North Carolina Press.

Cuomo, Chris, and Kim Hall, eds. 1999. *Whiteness: Feminist Philosophical Reflections.* Lanham, Md.: Rowman and Littlefield.

Curry, George. 2007. "Jena 6: Too Early to Celebrate," September 17. Available at http://www.georgecurry.com/columns/jena-6-too-early-to-celebrate.

D'Amato, Anthony. 1990. "The Invasion of Panama Was a Lawful Response to Tyranny." *American Journal of International Law* 84:516–524.

Davis, Angela. 1998. "Masked Racism: Reflections on the Prison Industrial Complex." *ColorLines Magazine* 1, no. 2 (Fall): 11–17.

———. 2003. *Are Prisons Obsolete?* New York: Seven Stories Press.

Dieter, Richard. 1998. "The Death Penalty in Black and White." Death Penalty Information Center, June. Available at http://www.deathpenalty info.org/.

Dollard, John. 1949. *Caste and Class in a Southern Town.* New York: Doubleday Anchor.

Douglass, Frederick. 1996. *Life and Times of Frederick Douglass.* Ware, U.K.: Wordsworth American Classics.

Drori, Thalia, dir. 1992. *Adam Abdul Hakim: One Who Survived.* Thalia Drori Productions.

DuBois, W.E.B. 1903. *The Souls of Black Folk.* New York: Vintage Books, 1990.

———. 1915. "The Souls of White Folk." In *Dusk of Dawn.* New York: Oxford University Press, 2007.

———. 1928. *Dark Princess.* New York: Oxford University Press, 2007.

————. 1935. *Black Reconstruction*. New York: Atheneum, 1975.

————. 1940. *Dusk of Dawn*. New York: Harcourt Brace.

Duster, Troy. 2003. *Backdoor to Eugenics*. New York: Routledge.

·Esteva, Gustavo. 1998. *Grassroots Postmodernism: Remaking the Soil of Cultures*. New York: Zed Books.

Fanon, Frantz. 1962. *L'An Cinq de la Révolution Algérienne*. Paris: Maspero.

————. 1967. *Black Skin, White Masks*. New York: Grove Press.

————. 1968. *The Wretched of the Earth*. New York: Evergreen Press.

Federici, Sylvia. 2004. *Caliban and the Witch*. New York: Autonomedia.

Fellner, Jamie, and Marc Mauer. 1998. "Losing the Vote: The Impact of Felony Disenfranchisement Laws in the US." Washington, D.C.: Sentencing Project. Available at http://www.sentencingproject.org.

Fields, Barbara. 1982. "Ideology and Race in American History." In *Region, Race, and Reconstruction*, ed. J. Morgan Kouser and James McPherson, pp. 143–177. Oxford: Oxford University Press.

Fisher, William. 2007. "Jim Crow Remembered." *Truthout*, February 12. Available at http://www.truthout.org/docs_2006/021207J.shtml.

Fitts, Catherine Austin. 2001. "How the Money Works in the Illicit Drug Trade, Part II: The Narco Money Map." Available at http://www.narconews.com/narcodollars2.html.

Foner, Eric. 1988a. *Reconstruction: America's Unfinished Revolution*. New York: Harper and Row.

————. 1988b. *Reconstruction, 1863–1877*. New York: Harper and Row.

Foner, Philip. 1976. *Organized Labor and the Black Worker*. New York: International.

Foucault, Michel. 1980. *Power/Knowledge: Selected Interviews and Other Writings, 1972–1977*. Ed. Colin Gordon. New York: Pantheon.

Frankenberg, Ruth. 1993. *White Women, Race Matters*. Minneapolis: University of Minnesota Press.

Franklin, Benjamin. 1755. *Observations Concerning the Increase in Mankind*. Boston: S. Kneeland.

French, Austa. 1969. *Slavery in South Carolina*. New York: Negro Universities Press.

Frye, Marilyn. 1995. "White Woman Feminist." In *Overcoming Racism and Sexism*, ed. Linda Bell and David Blumenfield, pp. 113–134. Lanham, Md.: Rowman and Littlefield.

Fukurai, Hiroshi. 1998. *Further Affirmative Action Strategies for Racial and Ethnic Equality in the Jury System: The Case Study of the Eugene "Bear" Lincoln Trial and the Native American Jury*. Santa Cruz, Calif.: Chicano/Latino Research Center.

Garroute, Eva Marie. 2003. *Real Indians: Identity and the Survival of Native Americans*. Berkeley: University of California Press.

Genovese, Eugene. 1976. *Roll, Jordan, Roll*. New York: Vintage Books.

Gerassi, John. 1965. *The Great Fear in Latin America*. New York: Collier Books.

Geyer, Alan, and Barbara Green. 1992. *Lines in the Sand: Justice and the Gulf War*. Louisville, Ky.: John Knox Press.

Giroux, Henry. 1998. "Youth, Memory Work, and the Racial Politics of Whiteness." In *White Reign*, ed. Joe Kincheloe, Shirley Steinberg, Nelson Rodriguez, and Ronald Chennault, pp. 123–136. New York: St. Martin's Press.

Godbeer, Richard. 1999. "Eroticizing the Middle Ground: Anglo-Indian Sexual Relations." In *Sex, Love, Race*, ed. Martha Hodes, pp. 91–111. New York: New York University Press.

Goldberg, David. 2002. *The Racial State*. Malden, Mass.: Blackwell.

Goldhagen, Daniel Jonah. 1996. *Hitler's Willing Executioners*. New York: Knopf.

Goodwyn, Lawrence. 1976. *Democratic Promise: The Populist Moment in America*. New York: Oxford University Press.

Gordon, Avery. 2006. "U.S. Supermax Lockdown: Prison Looks Like Waging a Security War." *LeMonde Diplomatique* (November 1): 1–7.

Gordon, Lewis Ricardo. 1995. *Bad Faith and Antiblack Racism*. Atlantic Highlands, N.J.: Humanities Press.

Gourevitch, Alex. 2003. "Exporting Censorship to Iraq." *American Prospect* 14, no. 9 (October 1).

Griffin, John Howard. 1961. *Black Like Me*. Boston: Houghton Mifflin.

Grimmett, Richard. 1999. *Instances of Use of United States Armed Forces Abroad, 1798–1999*. Congressional Research Service Report, May 17. Washington, D.C.

Grosfoguel, Ramón. 2006. "World-Systems Analysis in the Context of Transmodernity, Border Thinking, and Global Coloniality." *Review of Fernand Braudel Center* 29 (2): 167–188.

Guinier, Lani. 1994. *The Tyranny of the Majority*. New York: Free Press.

Hacker, Andrew. 1992. *Two Nations: Black and White, Separate, Hostile, Unequal*. New York: Scribner's.

Hale, Grace. 1998. *Making Whiteness*. New York: Pantheon Books.

Handlin, Oscar. 1951. *The Uprooted: The Epic Story of the Great Migrations That Made the American People*. New York: Grosset and Dunlap.

Harris, Cheryl. 1993. "Whiteness as Property." *Harvard Law Review* 106:1709–1791.

Harris, Leonard, ed. 1999. *Racism*. Amherst, N.Y.: Humanity Books.

Harrison, Hubert. 2001. *A Hubert Harrison Reader*. Ed. Jeffrey Perry. Middletown, Conn.: Wesleyan University Press.

Hartman, Saidiya. 1997. *Scenes of Subjection: Terror, Slavery, and Self-Making in 19th Century America*. New York: Oxford University Press.

Haywood. William D. 1958. *Bill Haywood's Book*. New York: International Publishers.

Hazley, Donna. 2001. "Women's Prison Population Growing." *National NOW Times* (Summer). Available at http://www.now.org/nnt/summer-2001/prisons.html.

Hening, William W., ed. 1809. *Statutes at Large: A Collection of All the Laws of Virginia*. 18 vols. Richmond, Va.: Samuel Pleasants, Jr.

Hill, Herbert. 1988. "Myth-Making as Labor History: Herbert Gutman and the United Mine Workers of America." *Politics, Culture, and Society* 2, no. 2 (Winter): 132–200.

Hofstadter, Richard. 1966. *The Paranoid Style of American Politics*. New York: Knopf.

Holwerda, Danielle. 2006. *Prison Reform and the California Correctional Peace Officers Association*. Available at http://www.law.stanford.edu/program/centers/scjc/working papers/DHolwerda_06.pdf.

hooks, bell. 1992. "Representing Whiteness in the Black Imagination." In *Cultural Studies*, ed. Lawrence Grossberg, Cary Nelson, and Paula Treichler, pp. 338–346. New York: Routledge.

Horsman, Reginald. 1981. *Race and Manifest Destiny*. Cambridge, Mass.: Harvard University Press.

Ignatiev, Noel. 1995. *How the Irish Became White*. New York: Routledge.

Inter-American Commission on Human Rights. 1993. Report No. 31/93, Case 10.573, United States, October 14.

Isaacs, Julian, and Kobena Mercer. 1996. "De Margin and De Center." In *Stuart Hall*, ed. David Morley and Kuan-Hsing Chen, pp. 450–464. New York: Routledge.

Jackson, George. 1970. *Soledad Brother: The Prison Letters of George Jackson*. New York: Bantam.

Jalée, Pierre. 1968. *The Pillage of the Third World*. New York: Monthly Review Press.

James, Joy. 1996. *Resisting State Violence*. Minneapolis: University of Minnesota Press.

Jefferson, Thomas. 1964. *Notes on the State of Virginia*. New York: Harper and Row.

Jones, Maldwyn. 1960. *American Immigration*. Chicago: University of Chicago Press.

Jordan, Winthrop. 1977. *White over Black: American Attitudes toward the Negro, 1550–1812*. New York: Norton.

Keith, Rollie. 1999. "The Failure of Diplomacy." *The Democrat* (journal of the New Democratic Party of British Columbia), May. Available at http://www.bc.ndp.ca/welcome-frame.htm.

Kelley, Robin. 2002. *Freedom Dreams: The Black Radical Imagination*. Boston: Beacon Press.

Kincheloe, Joe, and Shirley Steinberg. 1998. "Addressing the Crisis of Whiteness." In *White Reign*, ed. Joe Kincheloe, Shirley Steinberg, Nelson Rodriguez, and Ronald Chennault, pp. 3–29. New York: St. Martin's Press.

Kincheloe, Joe, Shirley Steinberg, Nelson Rodriguez, and Ronald Chennault, eds. 1998. *White Reign*. New York: St. Martin's Press.

Klare, Michael. 1991. "The Pentagon's New Paradigm." In *Gulf War Reader*, ed. Micah Sifry and Christopher Cerf, pp. 446–476. New York: Times Books.

Kraditor, Aileen. 1989. *Means and Ends in American Abolitionism*. Chicago: Ivan Dee.

Kraus, Henry. 1985. *The Many and the Few: A Chronicle of the Dynamic Auto Workers*. Urbana: University of Illinois Press.

Laurie, Bruce. 1980. *Working People of Philadelphia, 1800–1850*. Philadelphia: Temple University Press.

Lee Mun Wah, dir. and prod. 1994. *The Color of Fear*. Berkeley: Stir-Fry Productions.

Leonard, Gerald. 2002. *The Invention of Party Politics*. Chapel Hill: University of North Carolina Press.

Lévi-Strauss, Claude. 1963. *Totemism*. Trans. Rodney Needham. Boston: Beacon Press.

Lindorff, David. 2003. *Killing Time: An Inside Account of the Case of Mumia Abu-Jamal*. Monroe, Maine: Common Courage Press.

Lipsitz, George. 2006. *The Possessive Investment in Whiteness*. Philadelphia: Temple University Press.

Litwack, Leon. 1961. *North of Slavery*. Chicago: University of Chicago Press.

Locke, Alain. 1989. "The Concept of Race as Applied to Social Culture." In *The Philosophy of Alain Locke: Harlem Renaissance and Beyond*, ed. Leonard Harris, pp. 187–199. Philadelphia: Temple University Press.

Logan, Rayford W. 1965. *The Betrayal of the Negro*. New York: Collier Books.

Lopez, Ian Haney. 2006. *White by Law*. New York: New York University Press.

Lydersen, Kari. 2002. *Out of the Sea and into the Fire: Latin American–US Immigration in the Global Age*. New York: Common Courage Press.

———. 2007. "Behind Bars: Jailing Children of Immigrants." *These Times*, February 22.

Maechling, Charles, Jr. 1990. "Washington's Illegal Invasion." *Foreign Policy* (Summer): 113–131.

Martinot, Steve. 2003a. "The Militarization of the Police." *Social Identities* 9, no. 2 (June): 205–224.

———. 2003b. *The Rule of Racialization*. Philadelphia: Temple University Press.

———. 2005. "Pro-democracy and the Ethics of Refusal." *Socialism and Democracy* 19, no. 2 (July): 106–115.

Massey, Douglas, and Nancy Denton. 1993. *American Apartheid*. Cambridge, Mass.: Harvard University Press.

Mauer, Marc, and Huling Young. 1995. "Black Americans and the Criminal Justice System." Washington, D.C.: Sentencing Project. Available at http://www.sentencingproject.org.

McCoy, Alfred W. 1991. *The Politics of Heroin: CIA Complicity in the Global Drug Trade*. Brooklyn, N.Y.: Lawrence Hill Books.

McIntosh, Peggy. 1997. "White Privilege: Unpacking the Hidden Knapsack." Excerpted from "White Privilege and Male Privilege: A Personal Account of Coming to Correspondences through Work in Women's Studies." In *Critical Whiteness Studies: Looking Behind the Mirror*, ed. Richard Delgado and Jean Stefancic, pp. 291–305. Philadelphia: Temple University Press. Also available at http://www.case.edu/president/aaction/UnpackingTheKnapsack.pdf.

McLaren, Peter. 1998. "Whiteness Is . . . the Struggle for Postcolonial Hybridity." In *White Reign*, ed. Joe Kincheloe, Shirley Steinberg, Nelson Rodriguez, and Ronald Chennault, pp. 63–76. New York: St. Martin's Press.

McManus, Edgar. 1973. *Black Bondage in the North*. Syracuse, N.Y.: Syracuse University Press.

Meierhoefer, B. S. 1992. "The General Effect of Mandatory Minimum Prison Terms." Washington, D.C.: Federal Judicial Center.

Menéndez Rodríguez, Mario, ed. 1983. *Voices from El Salvador*. San Francisco: Solidarity Publishers.

Messerschmidt, James W. 1983. *The Trial of Leonard Peltier*. Boston: South End Press.

Mills, Charles. 1997. *The Racial Contract*. Ithaca, N.Y.: Cornell University Press.

Mills, Kay. 1993. *This Little Light of Mine: The Story of Fannie Lou Hamer*. New York: Dutton.

Mokhiber, Russell, and Robert Weissman. 1999. *Corporate Predators: The Hunt for Mega-profits and the Attack on Democracy*. Monroe, Maine: Common Courage Press.

———. 2003. "12 Reasons to Oppose War in Iraq." *Dissident Voice*, February 21.

Montagu, Ashley. 1964. *Man's Most Dangerous Myth: The Fallacy of Race*. Cleveland: World.

Morrison, Toni. 1992. *Playing in the Dark: Whiteness and the Literary Imagination*. Cambridge, Mass.: Harvard University Press.

Moses, Greg. 2005. "Unmasking through Naming: Toward an Ethic and Africology of Whiteness." In *White on White/Black on Black*, ed. George Yancy, pp. 49–69. Lanham, Md.: Rowman and Littlefield.

Mosley, Albert. 1999. "Negritude, Nationalism, and Nativism: Racists or Racialists?" In *Racism*, ed. Leonard Harris, pp. 74–86. Amherst, N.Y.: Humanity Books.

Myrdal, Gunnar. 1962. *An American Dilemma: The Negro Problem and Modern Democracy.* New York: Harper and Row.

Nambiar, Satish. 1999. "The Fatal Flaws Underlying NATO's Intervention in Yugoslavia." *United Services Institution of India Documents.* New Delhi, April 6.

"North Carolina: Pickles." 1998. *Rural Migration News* (July).

Omi, Michael, and Howard Winant. 1994. *Racial Formation in the United States.* New York: Routledge.

Outlaw, Lucius. 1996. *On Race and Philosophy.* New York: Routledge.

Palast, Greg. 2002. *The Best Democracy Money Can Buy.* London: Pluto Press.

Parenti, Christian. 1999. *Lockdown America: Police and Prisons in the Age of Crisis.* New York: Verso.

Parenti, Michael. 1995. *Imperialism 101.* San Francisco: City Lights.

Patterson, Monica Beatriz Demello. 1998. "America's Racial Unconscious: The Invisibility of Whiteness." In *White Reign,* ed. Joe Kincheloe, Shirley Steinberg, Nelson Rodriguez, and Ronald Chennault, pp. 103–122. New York: St. Martin's Press.

Pavlik, Keith. 1999. "NATO's Sponsorship of the Kosovo Liberation Army, KLA." New York: International Action Center Commission of Inquiry.

Pérez, Ramón. 1991. "Tianguis." In *Diary of an Undocumented Immigrant,* trans. Dick J. Reavis. Houston: Arte Publico Press.

Perkins, Stephanie. N.d. "Twice Disenfranchised: The NAACP's Commentary on the 2000 Presidential Election and News Coverage." International Communications Association. Available at http://www.allacademic.com/meta/p113067_index.html.

Physicians for Human Rights. 1991. *Operation "Just Cause": The Human Cost of Military Action in Panama.* Boston: Physicians for Human Rights.

Piven, Frances Fox, and Richard Cloward. 1977. *Poor People's Movements: Why They Succeed, How They Fail.* New York: Pantheon Books.

Powell, Elwin. N.d. "Martin Sostre: Bookseller Turned Black Revolutionary (1967)." *The Buffalonian.* Available at http://www.buffalonian.com/history/articles/1951-now/1960santiwar/powellbuff1965sostre.html.

Progressive Response/Foreign Policy in Focus. 1999. "Plotting the War against Serbia: An Insider's Story." Press Bureau of PDS. *Democratic Socialist Party* 2, no. 10 (March). German original available at http://balkania.tripod.com/resources/military/insider_story.html.

Public Record Staff. 2008. *The Secret Deal for Iraq's Oil.* August 16. Available at http://pubrecord.org/nation/403/the-secret-deal-for-iraqs-oil/.

Rabb, Christopher. 2006. "The Crime of Breathing while Black." *The Nation,* December 7.

Rains, Frances. 1998. "Is the Benign Really Harmless? Deconstructing Some 'Benign' Manifestations of Operationalized White Privilege." In *White Reign,* ed. Joe Kincheloe, Shirley Steinberg, Nelson Rodriguez, and Ronald Chennault, pp. 77–102. New York: St. Martin's Press.

Roberts, Dorothy. 1997. *Killing the Black Body.* New York: Pantheon Books.

Roberts, Paul Craig. 2007. "A Pandemic of Police Brutality." *Counterpunch*, September 26. Available at http://www.counterpunch.org/roberts09252007.html.

Robinson, Donald L. 1971. *Slavery in the Structure of American Politics, 1765–1820*. New York: Harcourt Brace Jovanovich.

Rodriguez, Nelson. 1998. "Emptying the Content of Whiteness." In *White Reign*, ed. Joe Kincheloe, Shirley Steinberg, Nelson Rodriguez, and Ronald Chennault, pp. 31–62. New York: St. Martin's Press.

Roediger, David. 1991. *The Wages of Whiteness*. New York: Verso.

Rosen, Harry, and David Rosen. 1962. *But Not Next Door*. New York: Avon.

Rymer, Russ. 1998. *American Beach*. New York: Harper Collins.

Sabol, William, Todd Minton, and Paige Harrison. 2007. "Prison and Jail Inmates, Midyear 2006." In *Bureau of Justice Statistics*. Washington, D.C.: U.S. Department of Justice.

Saks, Eva. 1988. "Representing Miscegenation Law." *Raritan* 8 (2): 39–69.

Sartre, Jean-Paul. 1976. *Critique of Dialectical Reason*. Trans. Alan Sheridan. Atlantic Highlands, N.J.: Humanities Press.

Saxton, Alexander. 1971. *The Indispensable Enemy: A Study of the Anti-Chinese Movement in California*. Berkeley: University of California Press.

Schlosser, Eric. 1998. "Prison Industrial Complex." *Atlantic Monthly* (December): 51–77.

Scott, Peter Dale. 2003. *Drugs, Oil, and War: The United States in Afghanistan, Colombia, and Indochina*. Lanham, Md.: Rowman and Littlefield.

Scott, Peter Dale, and Jonathan Marshall. 1991. *Cocaine Politics: Drugs, Armies, and the CIA in Central America*. Berkeley: University of California Press.

Sharkey, Joe. 1991. *Deadly Greed: The Riveting True Story of the Stuart Murder Case*. New York: Simon and Schuster.

Sifry, Micah, and Christopher Cerf, eds. 1991. *The Gulf War Reader: History, Documents, Opinions*. New York: Times Books.

Skrentny, David John. 1996. *The Ironies of Affirmative Action*. Chicago: University of Chicago Press.

Smith, Lilian. 1949. *Killers of the Dream*. New York: Norton.

Sohn-Rethel, Alfred. 1987. *The Economy and Class Structure of German Fascism*. London: Free Association.

Spillers, Hortense. 1987. "Mama's Baby, Papa's Maybe: An American Grammar Book." *Diacritics* 17, no. 2 (Summer): 65–81.

Stampp, Kenneth. 1956. *The Peculiar Institution: Slavery in the Ante-bellum South*. New York: Vintage Books.

Stiglitz, Joseph. 2003. *Globalization and Its Discontents*. New York: Norton.

St. John de Crevecoeur, Hector. 1981. *Letters from an American Farmer*. New York: Penguin Books.

Stone, Brendan. 2005. *The U.S.-NATO Military Intervention in Kosovo: Triggering Ethnic Conflict as a Pretext for Intervention*. Available at http://www.globalresearch.ca/index.php?context=va&aid=1666.

Street, Paul. 2003. *Racist Felony Disenfranchisement*. ZNet, December 16, 2003. Available at http://www.zmag.org/znet/viewArticle/9358.

Stubblefield, Anna. 2005. *Ethics along the Color Line*. Ithaca, N.Y.: Cornell University Press.

Stuckey, Sterling. 1987. *Slave Culture: Nationalist Theory and the Foundations of Black America.* New York: Oxford University Press.

Talvi, Silja J. A. 2003. "Criminalizing Motherhood." *The Nation,* December 3.

Taylor, Keeanga-Yamahtta. 2006. "Racism and the Criminal Injustice System." *International Socialist Review* (Summer): 33–36.

Thandeka. 1999. *Learning to Be White: Money, Race, and God in America.* New York: Continuum.

Thomas, Raju G. C. 1999. "NATO, the U.N., and International Law." *Mediterranean Quarterly* 10 (3): 25–50.

Tise, Larry. 1987. *Proslavery.* Athens: University of Georgia Press.

Turner, Edward R. 1911. *The Negro in Pennsylvania.* Washington, D.C.: American Historical Society.

U.S. Border Control. 2004. "Are Guest-Worker Plans Doomed?" October 24. Available at http://www.usbc.org/info/2004/oct/guestworker.htm.

Van den Berghe, Pierre. 1967. *Race and Racism.* New York: Wiley and Sons.

Walker, David. 1829. *Walker's Appeal, in Four Articles, Together with a Preamble, to the Coloured Citizens of the World.* Chapel Hill: University of North Carolina Press, 2001.

Wayne, Anthony. 1999. "The Hidden Origins of the KLA." *Lawgiver.org,* April 11. Available at http://ecclesia.org/Lawgiver/weekly5.asp.

Webb, Gary. 1998. *Dark Alliance: The CIA, the Contras, and the Crack Cocaine Explosion.* New York: Seven Stories Press.

Wells, Ida. 1969. *On Lynching: Southern Horrors.* New York: Arno Press.

West, Cornel. 1993. *Race Matters.* Boston: Beacon Press.

Whitley, John (publisher of the Toronto-based *New World Order Intelligence Update*). 1999. Interview, *Jeff Rense Program,* Toronto, Canada, March 31.

Wideman, John Edgar. 1984. *Brothers and Keepers.* New York: Penguin.

Wiecek, William. 1977. *The Sources of Antislavery Constitutionalism in America, 1760–1848.* Ithaca, N.Y.: Cornell University Press.

Williams, Patricia. 1991. *The Alchemy of Race and Rights.* Cambridge, Mass.: Harvard University Press.

Williams, Robert. 1962. *Negroes with Guns.* New York: Marzani Munsell.

Williams, William Appleman. 1962. *The Tragedy of American Diplomacy.* New York: Dell.

Wilson, Lynne. 1997. "Selling SWAT." *Covert Action Quarterly* 62 (1997): 22.

Wilson, William Julius. 1980. *The Declining Significance of Race: Blacks and Changing American Institutions.* Chicago: University of Chicago Press.

———. 1997. *When Work Disappears: The World of the New Urban Poor.* New York: Vintage Books.

Winant, Howard. 1997. "Behind Blue Eyes: Whiteness and Contemporary US Racial Politics." In *Off White: Race, Power, and Society,* ed. Michelle Fine, Lois Weiss, Linda Powell, and Lee Mun Wah, pp. 40–53. New York: Routledge.

Wood, Ellen Meiksins. 1999. "Kosovo and the New Imperialism." *Monthly Review* 51 (2): 46–53.

Wright, Richard. 1945. *Black Boy.* New York: Harper and Row.

Wright, Steve. 2006. *Storming Heaven: Class Composition and Struggle in Italian Autonomist Marxism.* London: Pluto Press.

X, Malcolm. 1965. *Autobiography of Malcolm X.* New York: Ballantine Books.

Yancy, George. 2004a. "W.E.B. Du Bois on Whiteness and the Pathology of Black Double Consciousness." *APA Newsletter* 4 (1): 10–22.

———. 2004b. *What White Looks Like: African-American Philosophers on the Whiteness Question*. New York: Routledge.

———. 2008. *Black Bodies, White Gazes*. Lanham, Md.: Rowman and Littlefield.

———, ed. 2005. *White on White/Black on Black*. Lanham, Md.: Rowman and Littlefield.

Zack, Naomi. 1993. *Race and Mixed Race*. Philadelphia: Temple University Press.

———. 1999. "White Ideas." In *Whiteness: Feminist Philosophical Reflections,* ed. Chris Cuomo and Kim Hall, 77–84. Lanham, Md.: Rowman and Littlefield.

Zilversmit, Arthur. 1967. *The First Emancipation: Abolition of Slavery in the North*. Chicago: University of Chicago Press.

Zinn, Howard. 1980. *The People's History of the United States*. New York: Harper and Row.

Index

abolition of slavery, 20, 51, 68, 79, 119, 122, 141, 198n4, 201n6
abolitionism, 79, 80, 119, 120; opposed by white populism, 80
abolitionist movement, 79, 120
Abu-Jamal, Mumia, 149, 198–199n7
affirmative action, 3, 69, 73, 76, 121, 173, 187; defeat of, 44, 80, 102; equal opportunity agencies, 80; white opposition to, 70, 137, 152, 161
Afghanistan, 111, 195n7
Africa, 91
African-Americans, 26, 52, 54, 120, 200n15; and autonomy, 14, 103, 149, 154; disenfranchised in state constitutions, 120; and disenfranchisement, 7, 21, 68, 69, 74, 106, 119, 121–124, 129, 131, 136; free and disenfranchised, 120; incarceration index and, 199n15; and kinship in blackness, 91; petitioning Congress, 20; and resistance, 14, 24, 28, 58, 132; social situation of emancipated, 62, 119, 131, 201n6; and struggle against slave system, 20, 120. *See also* black disenfranchisement
African anti-colonialism, 91
African unity, 91
Africanism, white metaphysics of, 24
Africanist consciousness, 91, 92
allegiance, 46, 49, 56, 62, 68–69, 115, 137, 151–152, 172

Allen, Theodore, 91, 161; and concept of white skin privilege, 27, 56; *The Invention of the White Race*, 16, 17
"allo-cultural," definition of, 156
allo-cultural anti-coloniality, 158
allo-cultural autonomy, 157, 159
allo-cultural community, 160, 168
allo-cultural structure, 159, 169, 170
allo-cultural subjectivity, 156–160
Almaguer, Tomás, 145
alternate political structures, 155, 157, 158, 159, 169, 170, 179, 180, 182
American Indian Movement (AIM), 70, 150, 156, 157, 160
anti-abortion movement, 70
anti-black racism, 20, 119, 122, 131, 132, 134, 136, 138, 166, 198n7. *See also* white racism
anti-colonialism, 91, 167; and anti-racism, 184
anti-colonialist movements, 103, 201n8
anti-colonialist race (Africanity), 91, 92
anti-coloniality, 103, 168, 185; and allo-cultural structures, 202n16; fundamental principle of, 103; and liberation from para-political state, 170
anti-communist campaign, 1950s, 61
anti-discrimination laws, 80
anti-immigrant movements, 142, 166; campaign of 1830, 61; commonalities among, 140; against fugitive slaves, 130–131;

STEVE MARTINOT is Instructor Emeritus at the Center for Interdisciplinary Programs at San Francisco State University. He is the author of *The Rule of Racialization: Class, Identity, Governance* and *Forms in the Abyss: A Philosophical Bridge between Sartre and Derrida* (both Temple). He is also the editor of two previous books and the translator of *Racism,* by Albert Memmi. He has written extensively on the structures of racism and white supremacy in the United States, as well as on corporate culture and economics, and he leads seminars on these subjects in the Bay Area.